Prague

U KAPRA

www.baedeker.com

Verlag Karl Baedeker

SIGHTSEEING HIGHLIGHTS ✶ ✶

There is a long list of sights worth seeing in Prague. Old Town Square, Prague Castle and Charles Bridge should not be missed on any account. To make sure you don't find you've overlooked something when your visit comes to an end, the main highlights are listed here.

✶✶ Charles Bridge
Charles Bridge links the city districts of Malá Strana and Staré Msto; its magnificent avenue of Baroque statues is very impressive. Very popular with entertainers and those out on a stroll. ▶ **page 131**

✶✶ Josefov
Today the former Jewish quarter is a museum, and the synagogues tell their own story. ▶ **page 151**

✶✶ Karlštejn Castle
Bohemia's most famous medieval castle was built 40km/25m southwest of Prague as a safe place to preserve the Bohemian crown jewels. Don't miss the Chapel of the Holy Cross with panels by Master Theoderic. ▶ **page 165**

✶✶ Loreta
The cult of the Virgin Mary led to the creation of the Casa Santa; sculptures and reliefs narrate the life of the Madonna. ▶ **page 179**

Charles Bridge
would not be half so attractive without its Baroque figures of saints

Josefov
Graves recall the dead

✱✱ Old Town Square
Next to Prague Castle, the most important historic location in Prague. ► **page 202**

✱✱ Old Town Hall
The main attraction is the 16th-century Astronomical Clock, and the 69m/226ft-high tower of the town hall offers the best view of Old Town Square. ► **page 204**

✱✱ Prague Castle
Over centuries, most rulers left their mark in the form of diverse building projects.
► **page 215**

✱✱ Royal Palace
A further castle highlight. The defenestrations from the official chambers went down in history. The sight of Vladislav Hall is enthralling – and not only for art historians. ► **page 226**

✱✱ St Nicholas
Here on Little Quarter Square you can feel the full effect of consummate high Baroque, and enjoy the best view of the Malá Strana rooftops. ► **page 174**

✱✱ St Vitus Cathedral
Peter Parler was a young man when he created his masterpiece, and he immortalized himself in it. ► **page 220**

✱✱ Strahov Monastery
The 25 frescos in the library's Theological Hall symbolize the struggle for wisdom in the context of scholarship and literature. The Philosophical Hall features an enormous ceiling fresco by Franz Anton Maulbertsch. ► **page 242**

✱✱ Vyšehrad
The memorial cemetery is the resting-place of the country's greatest composers and the best painters of their time.
► **page 254**

Strahov Monastery
Idyllically located on a hill above Malá Strana

Loreta
The Annunciation chiselled in stone

BAEDEKER'S BEST TIPS

Here is a selection of the most interesting Baedeker tips. See and enjoy the metropolis on the Vltava at its best!

⚠ A royal route
You can still follow the route once taken by Bohemian kings and emperors on their coronation procession. It runs from Vyšehrad via Old Town Square to Prague Castle. ▶ **page 116**

⚠ Sightseeing
Get a glimpse of all the city's main sights on the no. 22 tram – it will take you past them in 20 minutes. ▶ **page 118**

⚠ The Three Ostriches
One of the best culinary addresses in the Vltava metropolis: Armenian Deodatus Damajan opened Prague's first coffee-house here in 1714. Try the house dumplings! ▶ **page 134**

⚠ Rock for Ave Maria
The church of Emmaus Monastery has been very simply restored. Inside, there are concrete walls and unplastered masonry. An interesting location for the rock concerts that now take place here from time to time. ▶ **page 144**

Grand Hotel Evropa
Memories of the past

Earthenware pots
from Prague's Cubist era

⚠ Fascinating Golem
Golem, the most famous of Prague's mythical figures, is the subject of many legends. He was created out of clay by Rabbi Löw, and has received literary treatment at the hands of Meyrink and Kisch. ▶ **page 161**

⚠ Canoe, ahoy!
Prague's canoeists can be admired from Kampa Island, practising their skills in dramatic rapids. ▶ **page 163**

Coming to terms with the past

The Museum of Communism invites visitors to review the country's recent history. Shopping in the Communist era, with tins piled high, and a secret police interrogation room recall the past.

► page 192

Coffee with Václav Havel

Out of season, Prague's Bohemians gather in Café Slavia opposite the National Theatre. Czech models, Oscar laureate Miloš Forman and ex-president Václav Havel are Slavia enthusiasts.

► page 198

Kafka's Prague

No other writer has such close ties with the city; discover traces of him all over Prague.   ► page 211

Shakespeare

Prize-winning marionette performances of *Hamlet* and *Romeo and Juliet* are staged with Prague Castle as historic backdrop.

► page 219

Memories of childhood

Prague Castle's Toy Museum attracts both young and old.   ► page 235

Go back in time ...

to the era of the Přemyslid rulers, in Vyšehrad's fortress, seat of Princess Libuše.   ► page 257

Heavens full of violins

Belligerent Albrecht of Wallenstein loved music too. The Sala terrena protected the chamber orchestra. There are still concerts here, with the dream setting of Prague Castle in the background.   ► page 258

Hotel Evropa

The hotel was founded at the turn of the 19th/20th century. For those with no nostalgic yearnings, the Art Nouveau café is enjoyable nonetheless.   ► page 260

Fresh dumplings
Better here than anywhere

Wallenstein Palace
Concerts in a dream setting

Art Nouveau everywhere
► page 45

BACKGROUND

12 En Route for Europe
16 Fakten
17 Population · Politics · Economy
22 City History
23 Prehistory
25 The Luxembourg Rulers
27 Habsburg Dynasty
30 Republic of Czechoslovakia
34 Arts and Culture
35 Art History
46 *Special: Open the Windows to Europe*
48 Famous People

Charles IV on Old Town Bridge Tower
► page 49

PRACTICALITIES

58 Accommodation
66 Arrival · Before the Journey
69 Electricity
69 Emergency
69 Entertainment
71 Etiquette and Customs
72 Festivals, Holidays and Events
74 Food and Drink
76 *Special: Czech Passions*
85 Health
85 Information
87 Language
91 Literature & Film
93 Media
93 Money
94 Museums and Exhibitions
97 Post and Communications
97 Prices and Discounts
98 Shopping
100 Sport and Outdoors
101 Theatre · Concerts
105 Time
105 Tours and Guides
106 Transport
108 Travellers with Disabilities
109 When to Go

House signs
► page 200

*Gothic perfected:
the Royal Palace*
► page 226

TOURS

114 Getting Around in Prague
115 Tour 1: Malá Strana (Lesser Quarter)
117 Tour 2: Staré Město (Old Town)
119 Tour 3: Nové Město (New Town)
120 Excursions

SIGHTS FROM A TO Z

124 Belvedere
125 Bethlehem Chapel
126 Bevnov Monastery

127 Celetná
140 *Special: Slants and Diagonals, or Cubism Bohemian-Style*
131 Charles Bridge
134 Charles Square
137 Charles University
138 Church of Our Lady Victorious
139 Church of the Assumption of the Virgin Mary and Charlemagne
140 City Gallery Prague
140 Convent of St Agnes
143 Dancing House · Ginger & Fred

The changing of the guard at Prague Castle
► page 216

Old Town Square
▶ **page 202**

144 Emmaus Monastery
145 Estates Theatre
146 Grand Priory Square
148 Hradčany Square
151 Josefov
156 *Special: Golem, Graves and Scholars: The Prague Ghetto*
162 Jungmann Square
163 Kampa
164 Karlova
165 Karlštejn Castle
167 Klementinum
169 Knights of the Cross Square
171 Letná Gardens
172 Lesser Quarter Square
177 Lobkowicz Palace
178 Loretánská ulička
179 Loreta Square
183 Mánes Exhibition Hall

Art Nouveau by Mucha and others
▶ **page 46**

183 Mariánské Square
185 Municipal House
186 Museum of Decorative Arts
187 Na příkopě
188 *Special: Amadeus, Yentl and Jackie Chan*
193 National Gallery
193 National Museum
195 National Technical Museum
195 National Theatre
196 *3 D: National Theatre*
199 Nerudova
200 *Special: Medieval Signs*
202 Old Town Square
211 Palace Gardens
212 Petřín
214 Poděbrady Palace
215 Prague Castle

St Wenceslas in St Vitus Cathedral
► **page 37**

222 *3 D: St Vitus Cathedral*
230 *3 D: Royal Palace*
236 Prague City Museum
236 Rotunda of the Holy Cross
237 Rudolfinum · Dům umělců
238 St Longinus Rotunda
238 Smetana Museum
239 Smíchov
240 Sternberg Palace
242 Strahov Monastery
246 Stromovka
248 Troja Chateau
249 Týn Courtyard
250 Tyrš House
250 Veletrní Palace
252 Villa Amerika
252 Villa Bertramka
254 Vyšehrad
258 Wallenstein Palace
260 Wenceslas Square
262 White Mountain
263 Žižkov

266 Index
272 Photo credits
273 List of maps and illustrations
273 Publisher's information

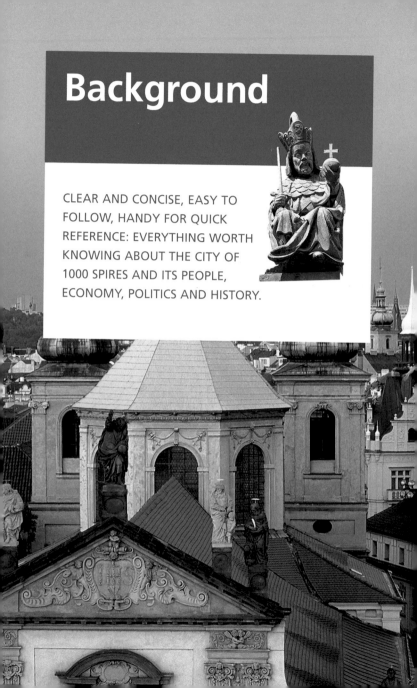

Background

CLEAR AND CONCISE, EASY TO FOLLOW, HANDY FOR QUICK REFERENCE: EVERYTHING WORTH KNOWING ABOUT THE CITY OF 1000 SPIRES AND ITS PEOPLE, ECONOMY, POLITICS AND HISTORY.

EN ROUTE FOR EUROPE

Prague is moving into the new era at breathtaking speed. Once upon a time the city on the river Vltava was pictured as a romantic idyll in black-and-white, but this has since changed to dynamic Technicolor. It has been a long journey, via coronations, wars, soaring triumphs and saints falling from pedestals.

The story began with Hradčany, and its centrepiece, Prague Castle (Pražský hrad). St Vitus Cathedral, alongside the presidential palace, towers above the whole area. This Gothic masterpiece was commissioned by Charles IV and executed by the Swabian architect Peter Parler. It seems that the rulers in the castle wished to be remembered by means of their architectural achievements, sometimes extensive; those visiting the castle today thus take a trip through all eras and styles.

The Royal Palace was the scene of the »Prague defenestration«: two imperial governors were thrown out of the window by the Bohemian Estates in 1618 – and were fortunate enough to land on a dung-heap. This sparked off the Thirty Years' War, which made General Albrecht of Wallenstein one of the wealthiest men of the time. Below Hradčany he built the city's first Baroque palace. Not far from this spot, Charles Bridge (Karlův most) links Malá Strana (the Lesser or Little Quarter) to Staré Město (the Old Town).

Modern times
After the black-and-white idyll, a new departure for modern times. Prague takes its cue from the west.

Here, too, there are historic landmarks: on their way to the city centre, royal coronation processions used to pass the bridge saints, John Nepomuk and Wenceslas, carved in stone.

Once over the bridge, there is a choice between the Josefov (the Jewish quarter) with its many synagogues, where Golem once turned to dust, and Old Town Square (Staroměstské náměstí), where a statue commemorates the reformer Jan Hus, burnt at the stake for his convictions. His death precipitated violent conflict between Catholics loyal to the king and the Hussites, which led ultimately to the bloody Hussite Wars. A site important in more recent history is Wenceslas Square (Václavské náměstí), where Russian tanks put an end to the »Prague Spring« in 1968; here, in turn, in 1989 the »Velvet Revolution« ended Communist domination.

City on the water
*The Vltava flows through the middle of Prague.
18 bridges span the river to link the city's districts.*

A rousing history
*Old Town Square façades, of
Romanesque or Gothic origin, tell the story.*

Leap forward in time
*Prague likes to see itself as the most western city in
the east. EU eastward expansion has enabled it to
strengthen the connection.*

Timeless?
Horse and carriage wait on Old Town Square for patrons wanting to experience Prague the old-fashioned way.

Centre of power
Once upon a time the Bohemian emperors and kings' coronation processions traversed Charles Bridge on their way to Prague Castle.

Sentries
The parade uniforms of Prague Castle's guards attract the tourists' gaze, and demonstrate discipline and strength.

And now? As author Milan Kundera puts it, the Czech Republic's membership of the EU confirms »that the Czech people have been a western people since the 11th century, and their culture is a western culture«. As long ago as 1348, Charles IV founded Charles University (the Karolinum) in Prague, the first university in central Europe. The city on the Vltava was intended to become the »Rome of the North«. At the beginning of the 17th century, Rudolf II summoned the most important intellectuals and artists of his day. Scholars such as Tycho Brahe and Johannes Kepler taught at the university. Master builders created wonderful Renaissance, Baroque, Art Nouveau and Cubist buildings. At the end of the 19th century Otto Wagner's pupil, Jan Kotěra, sounded the clarion call: »Open the windows to Europe!«. It was not until later that the Iron Curtain drew Prague into an eastern sphere of influence.

Prague was not destroyed in World War II; UNESCO has declared the entire city centre a heritage site, where historic buildings must be preserved.

Prague Has Arrived

There have been new developments in culinary matters, too. At midday and in the evenings, the aroma of dumplings and roast pork now mingles with the scent of fresh herbs: Italian, French and Asian cuisine have gained a foothold. Josefov has the most interesting new restaurants, where Western or Far Eastern dishes are given a Czech flavour in retro-design settings. Bistros, cocktail bars and cross-cultural cuisine are to be found alongside high-class designer outlets. Prague has become elegant.

Prague's house-signs
Houses in Prague's Old Town have not only numbers, but also house-signs such as »The Three Little Violins«

Time has run out, however, for one former national hero: the Good Soldier Švejk, once the nation's talisman. It turned out that the affection for him was based on a misconception. Contrary to the widespread view of him as an entertaining comic, for Czechs he now represents something deadly serious, endurable only by means of biting sarcasm. The old strategies for survival are no longer valid. Since the introduction of globalized franchise rules, passive resistance has become counter-productive. So it's time to bid Švejk farewell – and no-one will shed a tear.

Facts

In the 14th century Prague was the capital of the German Empire and one of the largest cities in Europe. The upward trend is again visible. The division of Czechoslovakia and the Czech Republic's entry into the European Union make Prague a popular destination for city breaks.

Population · Politics · Economy

Continuous Population Growth

In the 14th century, when Emperor Charles IV first made Prague the **Development** capital of the German Empire, the city on the Vltava had approx. 40,000 inhabitants. This meant that it was one of the largest cities in Europe, alongside Rome, Constantinople and Paris. Under Charles' successors Bohemia became less important for the empire, and towards the end of the 17th century, after the losses of the Thirty Years' War, the population was still approx. 40,000. From that time on, however, it rose. In 1786 Prague had 73,000 inhabitants; by 1890 the number had risen to 193,000. The rise is attributable above all to industrialization. Thousands flocked from the Bohemian villages to Prague to seek their fortune. Entirely new city districts sprang up, such as Karlín and Žižkov. In 1920 legislation was approved for the incorporation of further suburbs: the population of the expanded city rose to 677,000. At the beginning of the 1960s the million mark was reached. Further incorporation in the 1970s gave Prague the population it has today, of 1.2 million. This remained largely unaffected by the political changes of 1989.

The Bohemian rulers summoned German settlers early on, in order **Ethnic** to guarantee rapid economic development. From the time of Charles **composition** IV the Germans resided mostly in Staré Město, the Czechs mostly in Nové Město (New Town). When the Counter-Reformation forced the rebellious Hussites to their knees after the Thirty Years' War, the political significance of the Germans in Prague continued to grow. Not until the middle of the 19th century did they lose their majority on the city council. At the beginning of the 20th century, Prague's total population of 400,000 included 30,000 Germans, of whom 25,000 were Jews. After the founding of Czechoslovakia in 1918 many Germans left the city; others were driven out in 1945, after World War II. Only 4000 of Prague's Jews survived the holocaust.

At the beginning of the 21st century the Czechs have Prague almost to themselves. The largest minority is that of the Romany gipsies, whose numbers are estimated at 45,000–50,000. The Jewish community has some 1500 members. A distinctive feature of Prague is the strong US community: around 20,000 young Americans came to the city after 1989, drawn by the »Velvet Revolution« and »poet-president« Václav Havel; several thousand have stayed on, and have joined in the exhilarating canoeists process of rejuvenating this city.

← Baroque houses on the south side of Old Town Square: they have evocative names, such as »House of the Storks« and »House of the Blue Fox«.

State and Society

Parliament, senate, president Unlike Czechoslovakia, the Czech Republic is not a federal state. It is made up of the two historic regions of Bohemia and Moravia. Parliament has two chambers: the lower house, the Chamber of Deputies – in Czech »Sněmova« – has 200 members elected for four years by proportional vote, with a minimum threshold of 5%, while the Senate, or upper house, has 81 senators elected by majority vote for six years; every two years, one third of the seats come up for election. Both chambers, and of course the government, can initiate legislation. The president is elected for five years, by the two chambers of Parliament rather than by the people.

Political parties The driving force of the »Velvet Revolution« was the »Civic Forum«, which emerged in the stirring November days of 1989. The leader, and indeed the symbolic figurehead, was dramatist Václav Havel, who became the first president after the collapse of the Communist system. This »revolutionary league« soon divided into several splinter groups. The ODS (Democratic Citizens' Party) secured a new, broad basis of support. Its leader, economist Václav Klaus, was regarded as the father of privatization. He was prime minister from 1993–1997, but following a corruption scandal was forced to resign by his former comrade and subsequent critic Václav Havel. In 1998 the Socialists (CSSD) took over. Theirs was not a newly formed party, but one which had been in existence since 1878, and which was prohibited by the Communists in 1948. Milos Zeman was their first premier, followed by Vladimir Spidla, who resigned in 2004. With Stanislav Gross as the new head of government, the Socialists formed a coalition with the Christian Democrats (KDU-CSL) and the Free Democratic Union (US-DEU), and stayed in power. Václav Klaus, former head of the ODS, became president, with his party in opposition. The Communists (KSCM) have approximately 15% of the electorate behind them. The influence of the nationalist Republicans has disappeared.

> **? DID YOU KNOW …?**
>
> ■ how the Czech communists transformed the old red party star? They made it into two red cherries with green stalk and leaves. Red-and-green functions as a symbol for the new collective.

Czech Republic and the EU The division of Czechoslovakia on 1 January 1993 went smoothly, and brought the Czech Republic more advantages than disadvantages. It freed the economically stronger republic from the need to make balancing payments to Slovakia, and sped up its approach to becoming a member of the European Union. On 1 May 2004 the Czech Republic joined the EU, as the union expanded to include ten new member countries from Eastern Europe. Initially the republic wanted to introduce the euro in 2007, then in 2010. Now 2013 is regarded as a possible date. However, the country does not yet meet the Maastricht criteria; and at home, too, the introduction of the euro is still a controversial topic. The strongest party at the present time, the ODS, opposes it. Prague has set itself an ambitious goal: to become the information technology capital of the EU. 70 million euros of EU funds have already flowed into Charles IV's »golden city« in order to create Europe's largest store of internet information. In future, those wishing to source a product, book or event will be instantly provided with all available data on screen. Europe at a single click, thanks to Prague.

Economy

Czech economic policy was considered to be exemplary for the whole of Eastern Europe during the first half of the 1990s. Unemployment was just 3.5%, exports showed a surplus, and the national budget showed a profit. Moreover, in Prague, where more than 10% of production is concentrated, there were not enough people to fill all the jobs. The numerous foreign businesses that had set up in the Czech Republic after 1989 competed with one another for highly qualified young employees. Yet by 1997 the republic's problems were apparent: the large state concerns had been turned into share companies, but the state, or the banks it controlled, continued to maintain large holdings. In order not to endanger his re-election, prime minister Václav Klaus prevented these

Wenceslas Square, the consumer centre: shops and restaurants invite visitors to dig into their pockets.

companies from going into liquidation. Wages rose more sharply than productivity, so the price advantage of Czech products abroad was lost. By the late 1990s unemployment had risen to 10%. A slow-down occurred only when the Social Democrats renewed the privatization process, after winning the parliamentary elections in 1998. Today the average monthly earnings are around CZK25,280/£670/US$1,200.

Since the fall of the Communist system tourism has become the **Tourism** most successful branch of the Czech economy. There were approxi-

Facts and Figures Prague

Prague

© Baedeker

Administration
► Prague's lord mayor, the »Primator«, is elected for 5 years by the 70 city delegates; he heads an 11-member council (Rada).
► 57 districts and 22 administrative areas. Today Old Town (Staré Město), New Town (Nové Město), Lesser Quarter (Malá Strana), Hradčany and Josefov constitute the district Praha 1

Economy
► 4.1 million tourists with average 3-night stay
► Pro-capita income equivalent to £670/$1234
► Unemployment rate 3.4%; Czech Republic 6.3%
► Employment figures: industry 38%, construction 12%, public services 39.5%, tourism 8%, agriculture 2.5%
► Main business partner: Germany (70% of turnover)

Area
► 496 sqkm/192sqm , approx. one-fifth designated UNESCO world heritage site

Geographical location
► Latitude 50°05', longitude 14°27'

Language
► Czech

Population
► 1.2 million
► 80% Czech, 10% Slovakian and Moravian, 5% Romany; Russian, Ukrainian and American minorities

In comparison
► Czech Republic, 10.3 million inhabitants
► London, 8.2 million
► Budapest 1.9 million

Religious affiliation
► 58.3% no denomination, 26% Roman Catholic, 1% Hussite, 0.05% members of the Jewish community, 14.65% other

PRAŽSKY HRÁD A HRADČANY
(Prague Castle and Hradčany)

JOSEFOV

MALÁ STRANA
(Lesser Quarter)

STARÉ MĚSTO
(Old Town)

NOVÉ MĚSTO
(New Town)

Moldau (Vltava)

mately 12.7 million visitors in 2006; these came not only from the traditional source countries such as Germany, the UK and Italy, but also from Russia, China and others. More than 4 million tourists visited the capital in 2006; there were more Russians in Prague than ever before, but a 14% drop in the number of British visitors, a certain proportion of whom – possibly those interested in the availability of cheap alcohol – were attracted instead to the Baltic states. Numerous new hotels, however, confirm that Prague's tourist industry is thriving. Films with a high quota of American stars have done a useful PR job for the city: thanks to its powerful presence in cinema and music videos, the medieval capital has won acclaim as a youthful metropolis.

City History

Why is the phrase »Rome of the North« so often mentioned in connection with Prague? How did the Second Prague Defenestration spark off the Thirty Years' War, and why do people speak of the »Prague Spring« of 1968? The »Velvet Revolution« of 1989 led ultimately to the end of Communist domination. What will be Prague's role in the EU as Czech capital?

Prehistory

c800	Prague founded by Princess Libuše
921	St Wenceslas (Václav) becomes ruler
973	Boleslav II founds the diocese of Prague and the first monastery
1198	Pemyslid prince Otakar becomes king
1230	Prague receives municipal charter
1306	End of Přemyslid dynasty rule

Earliest settlements

Human settlers probably inhabited the area covered by today's city of Prague from the early Stone Age (Palaeolithic era); the earliest known traces of settlement date from several hundred-thousand years before the common era. In 4000 BC a few tribes advanced from Bohemia, the heartland of European settlement, over the Moldavian heights towards the region that became Prague. During the next 3000 years the area alongside the Vltava ford below Hradčany was settled by merchants; it was the intersection point of the Amber Road and the Salt Road.

At the beginning of the most recent Ice Age, from 400 BC (La Tène culture), the **Celtic Boii** (from whom the region of Bohemia takes its name) overran Bohemia and gradually subjugated the earlier population; there is a large Celtic oppidum on Závist mountain (10km/6mi south of Prague).

Roman era

During the Roman era, in the year 10 BC, the Boii were subjugated by the Marcomanni, whose chieftains were probably Germanic. In the course of the period of migration, in the 6th century, **West Slavs** occupied the terrain of the current Czech capital. Settlements arose on what is now the castle hill (Hradčany), and in Malá Strana.

Foundation Myth

Libuše

Legend has it that Prague, which in AD 800 comprised several small fortified settlements, was founded by Princess **Libuše**, who had the gift of prophecy. As she had foreseen in her vision of a city which would one day be famous the world over, the princess's retinue found the spot where Prague would be founded on the banks of the Vltava: a spot at which a man was chiselling the threshold (»práh«) of his house. When, after several years, the people tired of female leadership, Libuše sent her companions to the river Biela. There, close to Stadiz – as the princess had said they would – they met a

← *The »Velvet Revolution« of November 1989 deserves its name. It led to the non-violent overthrow of Communism.*

young ploughman named **Přemysl Oráč**, who became Libuše's husband and the first Přemyslid prince.

Přemyslid Rule

Building of Prague Castle Duke **Boivoj**, the first historically attested representative of the **Pemyslid dynasty**, subjugated the Czech tribes. Prague Castle (Pražský hrad) was built at this time. In 874 Bořivoj was baptized by Methodius, who brought Christianity to the Slavs. After Bořivoj's death, his widow **Ludmila**, who had also been baptized, was murdered in the course of family feuds. She is regarded as the country's first martyr, and is venerated as a patron saint of Bohemia.

The duke **St Wenceslas (Václav)**, a grandson of Ludmila, came to power in 921. A Christian ruler, he established close contact with the Saxon court of King Heinrich I. In 935 he was murdered by his brother Boleslav I, the Cruel, in Stará Boleslav. After his canonization he was venerated as a patron saint of Bohemia, and became the symbol of unity and independence for his country, which often suffered under arbitrary foreign power.

Boleslav II Under Boleslav II, the Pious, the **diocese of Prague** was established in 973, and the first monastery (of St George) was founded. Bohemian rule extended as far as the borders with Kiev territory. Jewish and German merchants settled in Prague, as did those from France and Italy. In 993 St Adalbert, bishop of Prague, founded the **Benedictine monastery of Bevnov (Klášter Bevnov)**.

In 1085 Duke Vratislav II became the first king of Bohemia (Vratislav I) and moved his royal seat from Hradčany to Vyšehrad.

Vladislav II Duke Vladislav II was declared **King of Bohemia** in 1158. Construction of the **first stone bridge over the Vltava** (Judith Bridge; later replaced by Charles Bridge) secured Prague's pre-eminence as trading metropolis for a long period.

In 1178 Duke Soběslav II decreed that German merchants should operate according to German law, be exempt from military service, and enjoy tax privileges, measures intended to keep the colonists in Prague.

In 1198 the emperor crowned Duke **Přemysl Otakar I** King of Bohemia. This gave the rulers *de facto* right to royal status, and from 1212 (Sicilian Golden Bull) this was confirmed *de jure* as a hereditary right. From 1289 to 1806 the Bohemian king also bore the title of Elector of the Holy Roman Empire. The town of Prague was fortified in 1230 and received its **municipal charter** in the same year. In 1257 King Přemysl Otakar II founded **Malá Strana (the Lesser Quarter)** for German colonists; it was administered according to Magdeburg law. In the years that followed Otokar was able to extend his kingdom to Austria and large parts of northern Italy, but his attempts to become emperor were in vain.

The first **Prague groschen** were minted c1300. The groschen went on to become the most important coin in Eastern Europe.
The **murder of King Wenceslas III** in 1306 brought to an end the Přemyslid dynasty, which had lasted for more than 400 years. With the king's demise, the direct Přemyslid line died out.

The Luxembourg Rulers

1344	Building of St Vitus Cathedral
1346	Charles IV becomes King of Bohemia, Prague becomes the »Rome of the North«
1348	Founding of Charles University (Karolinum)
1355	Charles IV becomes emperor of the Holy Roman Empire
1419	First Prague defenestration
1420	Battle of Vitkov Mountain
1458	Under George of Podebrady, Prague loses its pre-eminence as economic centre

Archdiocese of Prague

After a period of confusion, during which the Habsburgs were able to stake their first claim to the Bohemian throne through the brief reign of Rudolf I (died 1307), the German king Heinrich VII, of the house of Luxembourg, was able in 1310 to arrange for the marriage of his son John to the Přemyslid heiress Elisabeth, and thus to secure the Bohemian crown for the Luxembourgs, with support from France and the church.

Charles IV

Charles IV governed Bohemia. In 1344 the building of St Vitus Cathedral began on castle hill – the cathedral of the newly created archdiocese of Prague.
In 1346 Charles IV became King of Bohemia, and in 1347 official German king (from 1346 king in opposition). Brought up in France, well educated, cultured and nurturing a pious interest in religious relics, this ruler made Bohemia the heartland of the German empire, and brought Bohemia, Moravia and Silesia together under the Bohemian crown. As metropolis of the Holy Roman Empire, Prague became the **»Rome of the North«**. The city attracted scholars and artists from all over Europe. In rapid succession, scarcely pausing for a moment, Charles IV commissioned the Gothic masterpieces which have made medieval Prague famous. His leading master builder was **Peter Parler**, summoned to Prague from Germany at the age of 22. Charles commissioned the Church of Our Lady of the Snows (Marie Sněžné), on which building began in 1347, and the castle of Karlštejn (1348–1357).

In 1618 two imperial governors were thrown out of the window of Prague Castle.

In 1348 **Charles University (the Karolinum)** was founded as the first university in central Europe. Nové Město was designed on a large scale, with imposing squares (Wenceslas Square, Charles Square), wide streets, harmonious churches and monasteries, and extensive fortifications which include the Gothic enclosure around Vyšehrad. This meant that for several centuries it was possible to accommodate the growing population, above all people working in crafts and trades, without further expansion; in terms of area as well as population Prague was the largest city in central Europe. In 1355 Charles IV became emperor of the Holy Roman Empire, and two years later he commissioned the building of the **Charles Bridge** and the **Old Town Bridge Tower**.

Political and religious tensions   During the regency of Wenceslas IV which followed the death of Charles IV (1378), grave social and religious tensions developed, as well as controversy regarding succession to the throne. In 1400 Wenceslas was deposed as German king, but continued to be King of Bohemia. Master Jan Hus persuaded Wenceslas to curtail the rights of Germans in favour of Czechs at the universities in 1409; some 2000 German students and many teachers left the country, and founded several universities, including the University of Leipzig.

Hussite Wars

Jan Hus burnt at the stake   The aims of the reformer **Jan Hus** and many who shared his views were initially moderate – they wanted only to return to the original source of Christianity and do away with corruption in the church. Yet this developed into a religious, social and national movement which made increasingly radical demands, and became even more volatile when Hus refused to recant at the Council of Constance and was publicly burnt at the stake. His death in 1415 triggered an anti-ecclesiastical uprising in Bohemia.

On 30 July 1419 a crowd led by **Jan Želivský** stormed the town hall in Nové Město, freed the Hussites who had been imprisoned there, and threw two Catholic councillors out of the window. This **first Prague defenestration** signalled the beginning of the Hussite Wars, which lasted until 1436. Wenceslas IV died that year.

In 1420 Pope Martin V issued a bull which proclaimed a crusade against the heretics in Bohemia. On 14 July the Hussite army under **Jan Žižka** vanquished King Sigismund's much larger crusader army at the Battle of Vitkov Mountain (►Žižkov), enabling the Hussites to prevent the capture of Prague. Thereafter the Hussites even went on the offensive under Procopius the Great, and launched retaliatory campaigns against Bavaria, Brandenburg, Saxony and Austria. The Hussites lost the war, but were successful in some of their demands (among them, dispossession of the church's secular property).

◄ Hussite victory at Vitkov Mountain

After a short interregnum under Albrecht of Habsburg and a 13-year vacancy of the throne, a Bohemian nobleman with Hussite leanings – **George of Podebrady** – became first regent and then, from 1458, King of Bohemia (until 1471). Under his rule building activities in Prague continued (Týn Church). The dispossession of church property had made the nobility rich, and the nobles gained in influence at the expense of the cities; Prague's position as centre of the economy declined as towns close to the frontier grew more important. The significance of the university also declined increasingly.

Declining significance

In 1490 the lands of the Bohemian crown were united with Poland and Hungary. King **Vladislav Jagiello** (Vladislav II) moved the royal seat from Prague to Budapest. During this time Prague's significance decreased hugely. Feuding between the aristocracy and the city intelligentsia inhibited further development.

Habsburg Dynasty

1526	Prague falls to the Habsburgs
1556	Ferdinand I becomes German emperor
1618	Second Prague defenestration leads to Thirty Years' War
1621	The 27 leaders of the nobles' revolt are executed
1641	Prague forfeits its cultural and economic significance
1784	Hradčany, Malá Strana, Staré Město and Nové Město are united in a single administrative unit

Battle of Mohács After the death of Vladislav II's son Ludvík in 1526, at the Battle of Mohács fought against the Turks, Ludvík's Habsburg brother-in-law-**Ferdinand I** was chosen as king. Wide-ranging rights were granted to the country, and especially to the city of Prague (the restoration of the archdiocese, and of Prague as royal residence). In 1547 these rights were set to be curtailed, and there was an **uprising of towns and Estates** led by Prague against the king. After the revolt had been put down, the capital and many other Bohemian towns were severely punished by loss of privileges, authority and income.

Counter-Reformation From 1549 an influx of Germans of Lutheran persuasion streng-thened the opposition to the Counter-Reformation taking place under the Catholic Habsburgs. **Ferdinand I** became German emperor in 1556. He summoned the Jesuits to Prague; they busied themselves with new buildings, and educated a new generation of strictly Catholic noblemen and burghers. These measures, and repeated attempts on the part of the king to restrict the religious freedom guaranteed in 1436, were the basis for continued **conflict between the Bohemian Estates and the house of Habsburg**, which also overshadowed the reign of Maximilian II (1564–1576).

In Prague Castle, Maximilian's son **Rudolf II** lived for his art collections and for his scientific and astronomical studies; to assist him he had brought the scholars **Tycho Brahe** and **Johannes Kepler** to Prague. He had to call on his brother Matthias and the Bohemian Estates for help in resisting an attack by his nephew, the archduke Leopold. In return for the nobility's help he confirmed to them the guarantee of religious freedom in the »royal charter« of 1609. In 1611 Rudolf II abdicated; his brother Matthias became king.

Second Prague Defenestration

Start of the Thirty Years' War Renewed controversy over freedom of religion and the rights restored to towns and Estates led to the second Prague defenestration of 23 May 1618, effectively the signal for a revolt of radical Protestant noblemen against the Catholic Habsburgs, and the start of the Thirty Years' War. The Bohemian Estates proclaimed the deposition of Habsburg monarch Ferdinand II in 1619, and chose the Palatinate Elector Friedrich V as king. Ferdinand II vanquished the Palatine Friedrich, the »Winter King« (1619–1620), on 8 November 1620 at the **Battle of the White Mountain** and re-established his hereditary rights.

Execution of the rebels The **execution** on 21 June 1621 of the leaders of the nobles' revolt – 27 Bohemian representatives of the uprising against the Habsburgs –

took place in **Old Town Square**. The Protestant aristocracy and wealthy citizens were disempowered or banished, and the non-Catholic clergy driven out.

In 1624 Ferdinand moved the Bohemian chancellery to Vienna. In the »revised constitution order« of 10 May 1627, Bohemia's heritability was anchored in the Austrian house of Habsburg. Catholicism was the only permitted religion. **Prague loses its cultural supremacy**

In the Battle of the White Mountain, 1620, the Bohemian army was crushingly defeated.

The monarch was given prime legislative rights, and was enabled to make appointments to high office and to reverse parliamentary decisions. This constitution for Bohemia and Moravia destroyed the power of the Estates irrevocably; it forced the majority of the educated class to leave the country and deprived Prague of its intellectual and cultural pre-eminence.

In 1631 Wallenstein repelled the Swedes, who had advanced as far as Prague during the course of the Thirty Years' War. Shortly after the Swedes had occupied Malá Strana in 1648 came news of the **end of the war**. The **Thirty Years' War** was a catastrophe for Bohemia. The country lost almost half its population, and continued to be subjected to oppressive taxation during subsequent Habsburg wars. This resulted in the irretrievable loss of Prague's cultural and economic significance.

During the Austrian wars of succession, 1740–1748, Prague was occupied by Bavarians, Saxons, French and Prussians. In 1757, during the Seven Years' War, Frederick the Great of Prussia defeated the Austrians outside Prague, but did not raise the siege of the city after his own defeat at Kolín. In 1781 Joseph II introduced **reforms** with his patent for the abolition of serfdom, revival of religious freedom and introduction of the German elementary school in Bohemia. Use of the German language was further encouraged. In 1784 the four previously independent city districts of Hradčany, Malá Strana, Staré Město and Nové Město were joined into a single **administrative unit**. The Jewish district Josefov was added in 1850. **Austrian Wars of Succession**

In 1845 the railway link between Prague and Vienna was opened. The Czech national revolution, centred on Prague, failed. František Palacký declined to take part in the national gathering in Frankfurt in 1848. In the same year there was a meeting of the **Slav congress**. Tensions between Germans and Czechs intensified.

Lessening of German influence Since the late 18th century a new Czech movement had been gradually gaining momentum, with impassioned adherents particularly in intellectual and artistic circles. This led to repression of the German language, after violent parliamentary debates. In 1861 the Germans lost their majority in Prague city council for the first time. The 1866 **Treaty of Prague** brought an end to the war between Prussia and Austria over control of Germany.

In 1886 the Germans left parliament, but continued to dominate the economy. The industrial exhibition of 1891 took place in Prague. Through **industrialization**, especially in areas of German settlement, Bohemia became a key industrial centre for the Austro-Hungarian Empire. In 1913 national tensions made it impossible for parliament to function. During World War I Bohemia was administered under emergency legislation.

Republic of Czechoslovakia

1918	Founding of the Republic of Czechoslovakia
1960	»Socialist« prefix
1969	»Prague Spring«, entry of Warsaw Pact troops in August
1989	»Velvet Revolution« ends Communist domination, Václav Havel elected president
1992	Division into Czech Republic and Slovakia
2004	Czech Republic joins EU

Founding of SR The Republic of Czechoslovakia (ČSR) was founded as the Slav successor state to the Austro-Hungarian monarchy (28 October 1918). Its founding president was **Tomáš Garrigue Masaryk**. Constant tensions between the national groups (Czechs, Slovaks, Germans, Magyars, Poles) put the multiracial state at risk. The municipal area of Prague was considerably extended by incorporation of outer suburbs, and in 1922 it was divided into 19 districts.

As a consequence of the **Munich Agreement** of 1938 – in which Czechs had no voice – the borderlands of Bohemia and Moravia (Sudetenland) settled by Germans became part of the National Socialist (Nazi) German Reich. In 1939 the remaining Czech territory was incorporated into Hitler's »Greater Germany« as the »Protectorate of Bohemia and Moravia«.

On 26 May 1942 the deputy Reich Protector, **Reinhard Heydrich**, was fatally wounded in an assassination attack. The Nazis retaliated brutally with the total destruction of the village of **Lidice**, and with an era of terror against any kind of Czech resistance (Heydrich's assassins' hiding-place and reprisals, ►p.136).

According to the **»Košice programme«** of 22 March 1945 announced by Social Democrat Zdeněk Fierlinger, the Czech state borders of 1937 were to be restored, and the country was to be ruled on a socialist popular front model. The uprising of the people of Prague on 5 May in the same year spread throughout the whole country; the expulsion of Sudeten Germans began. On 25 May **Edvard Beneš** returned to Prague from exile in London; he was state president until his retirement on 7 June 1948. The Communist Party (KPČ) came to power in 1948: Czechoslovakia became a »people's republic«. In 1949 Prague was re-divided into 16 districts. In 1960 came the **founding of the Czechoslovakian Socialist Republic (SSR)** and a further re-division of the city, this time into ten districts.

Socialist state

»Prague Spring«

During the »Prague Spring« of 1968 the Czech Communist Party under First Secretary **Alexander Dubček**, who had been elected in January, tried to move towards reform, aiming for »socialism with a human face«. The programme for liberalization and democratization was widely supported by the people. On 21 August the USSR and four other Warsaw Pact states finally put a violent end to the Prague Spring by **sending in troops**. The Soviet Union asserted its right to keep troops stationed in Czechoslovakia for an unlimited period. In 1968 the municipal area of Prague was extended to include 21 outlying districts.

In 1968 Warsaw Pact troops occupied Prague.

On 16 January 1969 the 20-year-old philosophy student **Jan Palach** poured petrol over himself and burnt himself to death on Wenceslas Square in protest against the arrival of Warsaw Pact troops. Six weeks later the 18-year-old schoolboy Jan Zajíc took his own life in the same manner on Wenceslas Square. A **new constitution** determined the federation of the Czech state (ČSR) and the Slovakian (SSR), with their own state parliaments and governments in Prague and Bratislava (Pressburg), and a joint parliament attached to the seat of the federal government in Prague.

Czechoslovak-German treaty On 8 December 1973 a treaty was signed regarding mutual relations between the ČSSR and the Federal Republic of Germany. Among other things, it declared the Munich Agreement of 1938 null and void, agreed renunciation of force on both sides, and established diplomatic relations.

Prague was enlarged considerably through the incorporation of rural areas. Prague's first underground railway (Metro) opened in 1974.

Charter 77

Demonstration for freedom and civil rights In 1977 a civil rights group under the leadership of former foreign minister **Jiím Hajek**, dramatist **Václav Havel** and philosopher **Jan Patoka** published »Charter 77«, which included demands for freedom of opinion and religious conviction as granted in the constitution.

On 21 August 1988, the 20th anniversary of the occupation by Warsaw Pact troops, thousands of demonstrators protested against the occupation and in favour of freedom, civil rights and the rehabilitation of supporters of the Prague Spring who had suffered political discrimination. On 28 October, in Wenceslas Square, police put a brutal end to demonstrations critical of the regime; these demonstrations commemorated the founding of the first Czechoslovakian republic in 1918. Prior to the day of national celebration there had been large-scale harassment of respected members of the civil rights movement.

In **1989** several demonstrations marking the 20th anniversary of the self-immolation of Jan Palach in Wenceslas Square were terminated by massive police deployment; protest rallies by the civic rights movement »Charter 77« were prohibited (January). The might of the state reacted to people's growing discontent with even harsher repression, culminating in the callous intervention of state security forces in a university students' procession commemorating the death in 1939 of student Jan Opletal. This finally triggered the »**Velvet Revolution**«, which in the end, without the use of force, led to the overthrow of the Communist domination which had lasted more than 40 years.

The first milestones on the way to a new democracy in Czechoslovakia were the appointment of a new »government of national understanding« (10 December) and the election of Václav Havel as president of the republic (29 December).

Political Change

New federal republic The ČSSR was re-named ČSFR (Czechoslovakian Federative Republic, 29 March 1990); at the insistence of the Slovaks the name was soon changed to »Czech and Slovak Federative Republic«.

In free parliamentary elections (8 June 1990), the civil rights movements came out on top in both Czech and Slovak Republics; they formed the nucleus of the new »government of national sacrifice«

(27 June 1990). **Václav Havel** was again elected head of state (5 July 1990). In the subsequent parliamentary elections of 1992, the Democratic Citizens' Party (ODS) in the Czech Republic and the Movement for a Democratic Slovakia (HZDS) in the Slovak Republic gained the most votes. Václav Havel was not able to win the presidential election at this point.

Division into Two Independent States

On 27 August 1992 the Czech prime minister and his Slovak counterpart agreed that the Czechoslovakian Federation be divided into two independent states from 1 January 1993. The division law was passed by the federal government in Prague on 25 November, though not without a struggle.

Václav Havel becomes first president of the Czech Republic

On 7 November 1992 **Alexander Dubek** (born 1921), leader and icon of hope for the Prague Spring suppressed by force in 1968, died of injuries received in a road accident.

With effect from 1 January 1993 the two successor states, the Czech Republic and Slovak Republic (Slovakia), replaced the ČSFR. On 26 January 1993 the Czech Václav Havel was elected as the first president of the Czech Republic; he was re-elected five years later.

In 1999 the Czech Republic became a **member of NATO**, as did Hungary and Poland. In August the river Vltava flooded parts of the town, including the Metro, with a record height of 4m/15ft; fortunately, Staré Město (the Old Town) was not affected.

In June 2003 Václav Havel's presidency finally ended irrevocably after three periods in office. The elections for a new president were at times farcical. There was even talk of Karel Gott, the »golden voice of Prague«, otherwise known as »the Sinatra of the East«, standing as a potential candidate. After a tough struggle, **Václav Klaus** was

? DID YOU KNOW ...?

■ how much Václav Havel earns as ex-president? The equivalent of 1,500/£1,000/US$2,100 per month, plus the same amount in expenses for his office. His official car and chauffeur are also paid for by the state. The fee for Havel's lectures: between 50,000/£34,750/US$71,200 and 100,000/£69,500/US$142,400. Havel is in great demand in America.

finally able to organize a small majority. Political irony indeed: Klaus, the former guru of privatization, who during his time as prime minister had become Havel's chief enemy and had been forced to resign by Havel after a corruption affair, now inherited the post of president. This was the final chapter in the story of Havel's bitter defeat.

In May 2004 **the Czech Republic joined the EU**, as one of ten new member states from the east.

Arts and Culture

Why did Bohemia become renowned for arts and culture under Charles IV? What is meant by Parler Gothic? What was the significance of the Bavarian Dientzenhofer family? Why was Art Nouveau so important in Prague? And how did it lead to Cubist architecture? Why does Frank O. Gehry's building »dance«?

Art History

The earliest remains of stone-built Christian churches in the present-day Czech Republic date back to the days of the missionaries to the Slavs, Cyril (Constantine) and Methodius, and are located in what was then the Great Moravian Empire. A pre-9th-century fortified settlement with five sacral buildings was situated in southern Moravian Mikulčice. In the Old Town of Uherského Hradiště Staré (the »Veligrad« of Great Moravia), three 9th-century churches have been identified.

Earliest
sacral buildings
in the Great
Moravian Empire

The Přemyslid duke Bořivoj (c850–895), who had been baptized at the Great Moravian court, brought Christianity to Bohemia, and during the first half of the 9th century he founded St Clement's Church on the river Vltava, to the north of what is now Prague. After the ducal seat had been moved to Prague, the Church of Our Lady was built (894). The foundation walls of this small round building are in the castle gallery.

Romanesque Architecture

Under Vratislav (c905–921) **St George's Basilica** was founded in Hradčany in 912. Notwithstanding the alterations of 1142–1150 (to the towers, east and west choir, and crypt), it still remains the best-preserved Romanesque building in Prague. An important building in the history of sacred structures, the **St Vitus Rotunda**, was erected under St Wenceslas in 926–930. The round Ottonian design, with four apses in place of the Wenceslas Chapel in the modern St Vitus Cathedral, served as the pattern for several single-aisled round churches (»Bohemian rotundas«) characteristic of Bohemia, such as the Staré Město **Chapel of the Holy Cross** (c1100), **St Martin's Chapel in Vyšehrad** (mid-11th century) and the **Longinus Chapel** (12th century) in Nové Město.

The St Vitus Rotunda was replaced in about 1060 by St Vitus Basilica, which has two choirs, a west transept and two crypts, similar to St Emmeram in Regensburg. At around this time Prague Castle (Pražský hrad) had a Romanesque ducal palace; the remains (9th–12th century) have been preserved beneath Vladislav Hall. In the second half of the 11th century there was already a Romanesque stone castle in Vyšehrad with several sacral buildings (remains of the St Lawrence Basilica).

In the monasteries founded from the late 10th century (973, castle monastery of St George; 993, Břevnov; 1148, Strahov) arts and crafts flourished, and in their scriptoria valuable manuscripts were produced, the most famous being the **Codex Vyšehradiensis** of 1086.

← *The city on the Vltava has seen many schools of art come and go. Art Nouveau has left unmistakeable traces.*

Gothic Art and Architecture

The Cistercians and Mendicant Friars were the first to bring the Gothic style to Bohemia, in the second quarter of the 13th century. The new manner of building was extended to non-ecclesiastical buildings such as the Old-New Synagogue (Staronová synagóga) in Josefov (1273), and the Gothic palace in Prague Castle (c1250–1400). The aspiring burghers used the new style for buildings designed for pomp and ceremony, such as the town hall (from 1338) in Staré Město.

Late Gothic

Under Charles IV (1346–1378), a ruler open to arts and to the world, the Bohemian lands were put on the map of central European art and architecture; the transition to Late Gothic was made. Initially French influence was strong; changes to Prague's Royal Palace were modelled on the French palace on the Île de la Cité in Paris, where Charles had grown up. For the new building of St Vitus Cathedral (foundation stone laid 21 November 1344), Charles first summoned **Matthias of Arras** from papal Avignon, whose design followed the characteristic pattern of French cathedrals (choir with radiating ambulatory chapels). However, after Matthias' death (1352) **Peter Parler** (1330–1399) took over the building project with his sons, and introduced entirely new, original aspects (emphasis on the south side with Wenceslas Chapel, transept portal and tower). His constant flow of ingenious ideas gave Prague architecture a dynamism all its own, and the influence of »**Parler Gothic**« on architecture and sculpture was extensive, reaching as far as Italy and Spain. The Parler workshop created further cathedrals in Kolín and Kutná Hora. The Old Town Bridge Tower in Prague, not completed until the beginning of the 15th century, was also constructed from Parler's drawings.

Court art

The court art of Charles IV's era anticipated important features of the Renaissance: the first ribbed vaulting and effigies (triforium busts in St Vitus Cathedral), and the first free-standing equestrian statue (St George at Prague Castle), by the brothers Martin and Georg Klausenburg.

Prague »Malerzeche«

A distinctive and independent school of painting, evident in all genres, grew out of a synthesis of foreign (especially Italian) and specifically Bohemian characteristics. The leading artists of this fraternity, the so-called **Prague »Malerzeche«** were the **Master of Hohenfurt**, active in Prague c1350, **Master Theoderic** (documented 1359–1380) and the **Master of Wittingau** (documented 1380–1390), who mainly created altar panel paintings (▶ Sights from A to Z, St Agnes Monastery, Karlštejn Castle).

Also characteristic are the Bohemian »pictures of grace«, half-figure portraits of the Madonna with child by anonymous masters, which show Byzantine influence. The most important wall-paintings, usually difficult to assign to individual artists, are found in Emmaus

Monastery in Prague, founded in 1357, and at Karlštejn Castle (1348–1357), where the Strasbourg master Nikolaus Wurmser (documented 1357–1360), and probably also Tommaso da Modena (c1325–1379), were active. Outstanding illuminated manuscripts were produced, frequently commissioned by the Silesian humanist John of Neumarkt, under whom a standard written form of German began to establish itself as the language of the Prague chancellery. After the death of Charles IV (1378) and Peter Parler (1399) the arts declined. Contrasting with the rather realistic approach of the Prague »Malerzeche«, there now arose the »International« and **»Soft« styles**, a subtly refined manner of painting found mainly in pictures of the Madonna c1400 (► Sights from A to Z, St Agnes Monastery).

Charles IV's activities as **planner and patron** are evident in Prague to this day (founding of Nové Město, Charles Bridge, Na Karlově Church). However, he was not able to complete all his ambitious projects. The eruption of the Hussite revolution (1419, first Prague defenestration) put an abrupt end to the unparalleled flowering of the city, and some buildings remained unfinished, either for ever (Church of Our Lady of the Snows (Marie Sněžné)), or for a long time (St Vitus Cathedral, Týn Church).

The master of Litoměřice painted the polychrome pictures in St Wenceslas Chapel, St Vitus Cathedral.

15th century – architecture

After the Hussite Wars, the character of Bohemian art – now almost entirely Czech – remained conservative and eclectic until the end of the 15th century. The most important Czech architect of the time was Matthias Rejsek, who was responsible for the Powder Gate (Prašná brána) in 1474. The most important artist invited to Prague under King Vladislav II (1471–1516) was Benedikt Ried. His designs were used for Vladislav Hall in Prague Castle's Royal Palace, one of the most magnificent secular interiors of the time (1493–1502), and for the nave of St Barbara's Church in Kutná Hora (1512–1547), with arguably the most beautiful late Gothic ribbed vaulting to be found anywhere.

Sculpture and painting

The sculpture and painting of the period, like many of the buildings, belong by and large to the Renaissance; they reflect almost all the important schools and trends of the Dürer epoch.

The most remarkable of the Czech artists is the master of the Litoměřice altar (► Sights from A to Z, St Agnes Monastery), who participated in the painting of the upper part of Wenceslas Chapel in St Vitus Cathedral in around 1509; he himself painted the most important scenes from the Wenceslas legend.

House »At the Minute« with sgraffito ornamentation

Renaissance

Italian Renaissance art was probably established earlier in Prague   **Architecture**
than anywhere else in central Europe, except Hungary. As early as
1538–1555 the **Belvedere** colonnade in Prague Castle's royal garden
was constructed from plans by Paolo della Stella. This was commissioned by Ferdinand I (1526–1564) for his wife Anna, and is one of
the purest examples of Renaissance architecture north of the Alps.
Archduke Ferdinand also provided the idea for the bizarre Star Summer Palace, **Letohrádek hvzda**, constructed by Italians in the years
1555–1558 on a star-shaped ground plan. After the mid-16th century
Bohemia's leading architect was the imperial court master builder
Bonifaz Wohlmut from Überlingen on Lake Constance (organ loft in
St Vitus Cathedral, 1557–1561; Ball-Game Hall in Prague Castle gar-
den, 1568; ribbed vaulting in castle Assembly Hall, 1559–1563; stellar
vault dome in the Church of Our Lady and Charlemagne, Nové
Město, 1575). The new style developed specific Prague features.
After the great fire of 1541, which destroyed large parts of Prague
Castle and Malá Strana, several aristocratic residences were built,
such as **Martinický Palace** (late 16th century) and **Schwarzenberský
Palace** on Hradčany Square, both in the Bohemian Renaissance style
that adorned the façades with lavish sgraffito ornamentation. Such
sgraffiti also decorate many civic buildings of the Renaissance, such
as the houses of »The Three Ostriches« (1585) near Charles Bridge
and the »At the Minute« (late 16th century) next to the town hall in
Staré Město. Here the façade ornamentation shows scenes from
antiquity and the Bible, and allegories of the virtues.

Under the Habsburg ruler Rudolf II (1576–1611), a keen art collec-   **Mannerism**
tor, Prague once more became an imperial seat and a centre for Mannerist works. The emperor drew artists of the most diverse of origins
to his court: the sculptors and bronze-casters Benedikt Wurzelbauer
and Adriaen de Vries (whose work anticipated many Baroque features), and the painters Hans of Aachen, Bartholomäus Spranger, Jan
Brueghel (»Velvet Brueghel«), Guiseppe Arcimboldo, Roelandt Savery, Joseph Heintz, Hans Rottenhammer and Aegidius Sadeler. Sadeler left a prospect of Prague, 1606, consisting of nine engravings
which present a good overview of the architecture of the time.
Yet Mannerist art served the interests of the court alone, and did not
resonate widely in Bohemia. The Czech engraver Wenzel Hollar
(1607–1677) and still-life painter Gottfried Flegel (1563–1638) both
made a name for themselves, abroad as well as at home, as representatives of a Bohemian art of the period rooted more strongly in their
native country.
St Roch Chapel in Strahov shows that Gothic influences were retained right down to the late Renaissance. It exhibits an exciting synthesis of Gothic features such as pointed arches and buttresses with
Renaissance motifs.

Baroque

Italian influences

The Counter-Reformation finally triumphed through the Catholic victory at the Battle of the White Mountain (Bílá hora) in 1620, and brought Baroque architecture to Prague, largely from Italy in the early stages. For approx. half a century Italian craftsmen dominated almost all construction work. They were organized into fraternities, and most of them came from the Como region. For their own community they built the »Italian Chapel« as early as 1590–1600, the first Baroque central-plan building in Prague.

Palace and castle construction ▶

In the 17th century the emphasis initially was on the building of palaces and castles. The most important patrons among the Prague magnates were Albrecht of Wallenstein, for whose enormous Valdštejnský Palace (1623–1630) an entire district of the city had to be demolished, and Humprecht Count of Černín (Černínský Palace, 1669–1692). Church building was at first strongly influenced by the Jesuits' church in Rome »Il Gesù«; this was the model for the alterations in 1611–1616 to what had been the Protestant Church of St Maria de Victoria (Kostel Panny Marie Vítězné). The most prolific experts in this Jesuit style were Carlo Lurago (Church of St Ignatius or Kostel sv Ignáce, 1665–1678) and Giovanni Domenico Orsi de Orsini (Jesuits' house, Church of St Nicholas (Chrám sv Mikuláše) in Malá Strana, 1673). However, some church buildings continued earlier Czech traditions (galleries, wall pillars), such as St Salvator's Church (Kostel sv Salvátora) in Knights of the Cross Square (Křižovnické náměstí).

Painting and sculpture ▶

In the fields of sculpture and painting, by contrast, Czech artists, or migrants from nearby countries, continued to dominate the scene. The most important sculptors from the mid-17th century were **Johann Georg Bendl** (c1630–1680; statues on the façade of St Salvator's Church and Vintners' Column in Knights of the Cross Square, St Wenceslas in the old deanery at Prague Castle); and **Hieronymus Kohl** (1632–1709; statues on the façade of the Church of St Thomas (Kostel sv Tomáše) in Malá Strana, fountain in the second courtyard of Prague Castle). The most prominent painters were Karel Škréta (1610–1674), born into an aristocratic Bohemian family, who emigrated for religious reasons and returned as a convert; and Michael Leopold Willmann (1630–1706), a pupil of Rembrandt (works in the Bohemian art collection from the time of Rudolf II to the Baroque era, in St George's Monastery).

Late Baroque

Late Baroque reached its peak in Prague during the first half of the 18th century, the most productive era for the arts since the time of Charles IV. The Frenchman **Jean Baptiste Mathey** (c1630–1695), who had trained in Rome, was the first to make the link with European developments: in church architecture, with the central plan of the Knights of the Cross Church (also, the Church of St Francis of Assisi, 1679–1688); in secular building with Troja Chateau

The figures on Charles Bridge, seen in peace at dawn, are by Prague's foremost Baroque sculptors.

(1679–1685). This brought Italian hegemony to an end. Soon Prague's own artists were able to take the lead, after assimilating the formative influence of Austrian and Bavarian architecture of the time. The Viennese court architect Johann Bernhard Fischer von Erlach worked on Clam-Gallas Palace from 1707, and left several pupils in Prague.

Christoph Dientzenhofer (1655–1722) came from a family of Bavarian architects who were active in many locations. He settled in Prague, and with his brilliant son Kilian Ignaz Dientzenhofer (1689–1751) created **Dientzenhofer Baroque**, a synthesis of the traditional Bavarian wall-pillar system and the baldachin principle of Guarino Guarini; this was the pre-requisite for the last, supreme phase of central European ecclesiastical building. Works begun in rather conventional manner by the father were often perfected architecturally and stylistically by his more gifted son. This was the case in Břevnov Monastery, in the Church of the Nativity of Our Lord (behind the Loreta), and especially in the Church of St Nicholas (Kostel sv Mikuláš) in Malá Strana, one of the most important late Baroque church edifices anywhere in central Europe with regard to historical development and urban architecture.

Christoph Dientzenhofer had planned the dome according to the Bavarian wall-pillar system. His son gave it the space-creating conch motif, and with the asymmetrical exterior dome-scape he deftly

The National Theatre displays historic neo-Renaissance architecture; it reflects Czech cultural self-assurance.

added a crucial ingredient to Prague's silhouette. The overall view of Prague and the wider Baroque cultural landscape of Bohemia would be unthinkable without Kilian Ignaz Dientzenhofer's contribution. Further important buildings of his are: Villa Amerika, the Church of St Nicholas in Staré Město, the Church of St John Nepomuk on the Rock (Kostel sv Jana Nepomuckého na Skalce) and the Ursuline nunnery in Kutná Hora; furthermore, he carried out the remodelling of the Church of St Thomas in Malá Strana. He also designed the plans for Goltz-Kinský Palace and Sylva-Taroucca Palace, both of which show early Rococo features.

Giovanni Santini-Aichl (1667–1723) designed Morzinský Palace and Thun-Hohenštejnský Palace; in sacral building he subscribed to a historicizing Baroque Gothic style (Church of Our Lady at Sedlec, Kutná Hora), as did Octaviano Broggio (1668–1742). Other architects of the period included **František Maximilian Kaňka** (1674–1766), whose designs included the terraces of the Vrtba Garden (Vrtbovská zahrada) and various parts of the Klementinum; and **Giovanni Battista Alliprandi** (1665–1720).

Sculpture ▶ One of the most important of the many sculptors active in Prague around 1700 was **Matthias Wenzel Jäckel** (1655–1738), whose works included statues for Charles Bridge and the former Church of the Knights of the Cross (also, the Church of St Francis of Assisi, on

Křižovnické náměstí). **Ferdinand Maximilian Brokoff** (1688–1731) was another sculptor responsible for several groups of figures on Charles Bridge. Matthias Bernhard Braun (1684–1738) brought the influence of Bernini to Bohemia, and his works represent the high point of Bohemian Baroque sculpture. Some of his figures, too, are found on Charles Bridge, others in the Vrtba Garden (Vrtbovská zahrada) and by the portal of Thun-Hohenštejnský Palace.

Rococo

There is some representation of the Rococo style in Prague; yet in Bohemia, as in Austria, it never became an independent variant, as it did, for instance, in Bavaria, Franconia and Potsdam.
Empress Maria Theresa's chief court architect, Nicolo Pacassi, was in charge of the 1753–1775 extension of Prague Castle; Johann Joseph Wirch was responsible for the extension of the archbishop's palace, 1764–1765. Prague owes the design of the Estates Theatre (Stavovské divadlo), realized between 1781 and 1783 by Anton Haffenecker, to the cavalier architect Count von Künigl. It was here that Mozart's *Don Giovanni* was first performed in 1787.

◀ Sculpture

The leading sculptors in the third quarter of the 18th century in Prague were Johann Anton Quittainer (1709–1765), Ignaz Platzer the Elder (1717–1787), whose works included the design for the façade ornamentation of the archbishop's palace, and Richard Prachner (1705–1782). The Church of St Nicholas in Malá Strana has works by Platzer and Prachner.
The painter Norbert Grund (1717–1767), a proponent of the »Feinmaler« technique, made a name for himself well beyond Bohemia; during his lifetime his works were forged and several times they were reproduced by means of engravings.

19th Century

Classicism

Unlike the Baroque, to which Bohemians clung longer, and more passionately, than did other central Europeans, Classicism was relatively insignificant, at least as far as fine arts were concerned. The former Customs House, U hybernú, (▶Municipal House), was given its Empire façade in 1808–1811 by **Georg Fischer**. It is one of the most remarkable architectural achievements of the period.
Romanticism was the first movement to be kindled in Bohemia after Herder's ideas had contributed to the awakening of the Czech nation. Yet the Czechs' attainment of cultural independence resulted also in the decline of supranational »Bohemian art«; from the second half of the 19th century there was an increasingly decisive drift into separate Czech and German components. The most important of the Romantic and post-Romantic

? DID YOU KNOW …?

■ what the goddess Minerva's gladiator team high up on Prague's National Theatre is called? The Triga (team of three) – the Quadriga is in Berlin.

painters were Joseph von Führich (1800–1876), **Josef Mánes** (1820–1871) and **Mikoláš Aleš** (1852–1913), as well as Gabriel Max, pupil of Piloty, and Václav Brožik.

Important representatives of neo-Gothic were Joseph Kranner (high altar in St Vitus Cathedral, 1868–1873) and Joseph Mocker (extension of St Vitus Cathedral, 1859–1929). The Czech pupil of Semper, **Josef Zítek**, designed the magnificent National Theatre (1868–1881) in ostentatious Czech neo-Renaissance style, but after a great fire it had to be replaced by architect **Josef Schulz** (1840–1917); it reopened in 1883. Josef Schulz also directed the building of the »Rudolfinum«, arguably the most important building of this era in Prague.

In sculpture, a school influenced by French art was founded by **Josef Václav Myslbek** (1848–1922; equestrian statue of St Wenceslas on Wenceslas Square, bronze statue of cardinal Schwarzenberg in St Vitus Cathedral). Distinguished students included Jan Štursa (1880–1925), and Bohumil Kafka (1878–1942; Mánes memorial in front of the Rudolfinum), and Otto Gutfreund (1889–1927).

20th Century

Art Nouveau architecture
Scarcely any other city can rival Prague for Art Nouveau buildings. The best example of »Prague Secession style« is the splendid Municipal House (Obecní dům), built 1906–1911 according to plans by Osvald Polívka and Antonín Balšanek.

Modernism ▶
Among the forerunners of modern architecture in the 20th century were Josef Maria Olbrich (1867–1908), Josef Hoffmann (1870–1956) and Adolf Loos (1870–1933), whose main work, however, was carried out in Darmstadt (Olbrich) or Vienna (Hoffmann and Loos). »House Müller« by **Adolf Loos**, in Prague-Střešovice, was built between 1928 and 1930. In it Loos realized for the first time his »space plan« – a concept of living-space based on the principle of individual rooms varying in height, arranged round the central axis of the house.

Cubism ▶
The final move to modern architecture in Prague was made by **Josef Gočár** (1880–1945), who built the Cubist »House of the Black Madonna« (dům U černé Matky Boží) on Celetná in 1911/1912; **Pavel Janák** and **Josef Chochol**. Chochol's Cubist architecture is a Prague speciality that can be interpreted as a counter-trend to Functionalism. Villa Kovařovič at Libušina 3 or the residential building Neklanova 30 (▶Sights from A to Z, Vyšehrad) transfer the vividness and dimensionality of Picasso's paintings to architecture. The Functionalist Trade Fair Palace (Veletržní palác) by Oldřich Tyl and Josef Fuchs today houses part of Prague's National Gallery; the monumental building was erected between 1925 and 1928, and it impressed even Le Corbusier.

Prague Castle ▶
The architect **Josip Plečnik** was commissioned by Thomáš Garrigue Masaryk, co-founder of the (first) Republic of Czechoslovakia, to

modernize Prague Castle – an undertaking that was not completed until 1928. He adapted historic elements and aimed for a dialogue between past and present, tending towards a style that might now be described as postmodern.

The Futurist television tower (1987–1990) by David Èerny was initially hugely controversial; it is a vital component of Žižkov's skyline today. The highlight of contemporary architecture in the city is the »Dancing House« (Tančící dům) of 1996 by architects **Frank O. Gehry** and **Vlado Milunič**, which stands on the corner of Jirásek Square (Jiráskovo náměstí) and Rašín Quay (Rašínovo nábřeží) (► Dancing House). The eccentric glass and concrete building, also called »Ginger & Fred« after the fleet-footed stars of the Hollywood musical, filled a gap on the bank of the Vltava left by World War II. The undulating façade of the seven-storey building fits in very cleverly alongside Rococo, Renaissance and Art Nouveau façades.

◄ The present

Art Nouveau ornamentation, Hotel Evropa

Frenchman Jean Nouvel is another architect of international renown who has left his mark on Prague. His »Golden Angel« building (Zlatý Anděl), with offices and commercial premises, was completed in November 2000 and is in various ways a superb achievement and has brought the area to life.

Conservative art trends in Prague are represented, for instance, by the painter and illustrator Max Švabinský(1873–1962), whose works include beautiful glass paintings in St Vitus Cathedral (1946–1948); and Heinrich Hönich, a pupil of Wilhelm Leibl.

There were important exponents of **Expressionism** as well as Cubism. German-speaking artists were more numerous among the Expressionists (Oskar Kokoschka, Alfred Kubin, Josef Hegenbarth), Czechs among the Cubists (Emil Filla, Václav Špála). The monumental Jan Hus memorial of 1915 on Old Town Square is by Ladislav Šaloun, who also designed allegorical sculptures for several buildings in Prague.

The art pedagogue and theoretician Adolf Hölzel (1853–1934) from Olomouc is one of the founders of abstract painting.

OPEN THE WINDOWS TO EUROPE

1891 was an important year for Prague, both in politics and in architecture. In this year Letná Gardens played host to the »Bohemian National Exhibition«, a trade fair designed not only to document Bohemia's ascent to industrial nation status, but also to make visible the Czech national movement.

The buildings constructed for this exhibition were clearly designed with an eye cast towards England, Europe's »first« industrial nation, and to the culturally pre-eminent France: the **Hanavský Pavilion**, moved in 1898 to its current position on the Letná plateau, was constructed from pieces of wrought-iron, as were the modern glass and iron constructions of English exhibition architecture; and the 60m/200ft viewing-tower built by the Czech tourist club on Petrín hill was nothing other than a **copy of the Eiffel Tower in Paris**.

Prague Art Nouveau

Yet in spite of these progressive signs at the beginning of the 1890s, Art Nouveau did not become widely established in Prague until the turn of the century – relatively late. Art Nouveau architects active from the very beginning included Otto Wagner's pupil **Jan Kotěra**, who exerted an enormous influence on the younger generation, both as architect (for instance, of Peterk v d m erected in 1899/1900 at 12 Wenceslas Square), and as teacher. »Open the windows to Europe« was his motto, and it fired Prague's artists with enthusiasm for the most recent developments in western Europe. Art Nouveau architecture spread in Prague from the turn of the century, especially along Wenceslas Square, which had been developing into a generous metropolitan boulevard from the mid-19th century, and along neighbouring Na p ikop (On the Moat) – the two together forming the »Golden Cross«.

A whole generation of artists was involved in creating the Municipal House.

Art Nouveau spread to architecture as well as decorative arts. Alfons Mucha designed this plate in 1897; it is one of the exhibits in the Mucha Museum, close to Wenceslas Square.

The new style was used in hotels and cafés, insurance offices, large stores, ornate assembly rooms and association headquarters. One of the best addresses on the square was number 29, the »Archduke Stephen«, built in 1903, now the **Grand Hotel Evropa**; its gabled façade is distinguished by clear structure and lavish moulded decoration. The sumptuous interior of the coffee house on the ground floor is still (almost) entirely authentic. Two years before the hotel opened, in 1901, the building of **Prague's main railway station** had begun. In spite of various later alterations, there is still no denying its Secession character.

Pomp and ceremony

House Koruna, on the corner of Wenceslas Square and Na příkop ,was built between 1911 and 1914 from plans by **Antonín Pfeiffer**, and is

The observant visitor walking through Prague will find many Art Nouveau details on the façades.

clearly recognisable by its lofty tower. It houses offices and business premises, and embodies the more Constructivist version of Prague Art Nouveau. On Národní are two particularly good Secession buildings by **Osvald Polívka**: the Topic publishing-house; and directly adjacent, the former **»Praha« Insurance Company** (1903–1905), whose name is prominently inscribed in large letters artistically looped around the oval windows on the façade. At the east end of Na příkop the Municipal House, built between 1906 and 1911 according to plans by **Antonín Balšánek** and **Osvald Polívka**, takes up a whole block. However, the magnificence of this building cannot disguise the fact that it is just as close to late 19th-century neo-Baroque as it is to Art Nouveau, which in fact had passed its peak by the time the Municipal House was completed. One of those involved in the design was **Alfons Mucha**, who had already made a name for himself in Paris as painter, illustrator and poster designer. Just behind the Municipal House is the luxury hotel **Paříž** (U obecního domu 1), which has an impeccable, elaborately restored Art Nouveau interior; a look at the elegant entrance hall should not be passed up. The hotel was returned to the original owner's family after the Velvet Revolution and is now being run by them.

Famous People

Why did Franz Kafka have such a difficult relationship with his father? How is Peter Parler remembered in Prague? Why has a statue of St John Nepomuk been standing on Charles Bridge for more than 300 years? The following biographies are memorials in miniature for those whose names are inseparably linked with the city.

Tycho Brahe (1546–1601)

When the Danish astronomer Tycho Brahe came to Prague in 1597 he was already famous; from 1599 he served as Emperor Rudolf II's court astronomer. Brahe had built an observatory in Denmark; his astronomical instruments were the largest of the time – the telescope had not yet been discovered. Though his observations yielded the empirical foundations for Kepler's laws of planetary motion, he remained an opponent of the heliocentric world picture. For a long time Tycho Brahe's system of the world, which continued to make the earth the centre of the universe, competed with that of Copernicus. Tycho Brahe is portrayed on his tomb in Týn Church.

Charles IV (1316–1378)

Charles IV became German king in 1346 and King of Bohemia the same year; in 1355 he was declared Roman emperor. He intended that Prague, as his seat of residence, should become the intellectual and artistic centre of the empire, the »Rome of the North«: the university of Prague (Karolinum) was founded in 1348, the first university in central Europe, and important master builders and artists were invited to Prague. Under his rule, architecture rose to consummate heights: he commissioned the Charles Bridge, St Vitus Cathedral and Nové Město (Prague's New Town), as well as Karlštejn Castle – as repository for the imperial crown jewels and coronation insignia. Poets such as Petrarch and Rienzo were in Prague during Charles's reign. Indeed Charles IV was a writer himself: he composed an account of his rise to power in Latin (*Vita Caroli*), wrote a Wenceslas legend, and is supposedly the author of a *Mirror for Princes*.

Bohemian king with an eye for the arts

Christoph (1655–1722) and Kilian Ignaz Dientzenhofer (1689–1751)

Christoph Dientzenhofer came from a large family network of Bavarian architects. Having moved to Prague, he never worked anywhere else. With his genius son Kilian Ignaz he created Dientzenhofer Baroque, a synthesis of the early Bavarian wall-pillar system and the baldachin principle of Italian Guarino Guarini. This was the prerequisite for the final, supreme phase of Baroque sacral architecture in central Europe. The father's works were often begun in a rather conventional manner and then brought to architectural and stylistic perfection by the son. This is the case, for instance, in Břevnov Monastery, in the Church of the Nativity of Our Lord (behind the Loreta), and especially in St Nicholas Church in Malá Strana, one of the most significant late Baroque sacral buildings anywhere in central Europe with regard to historical development and urban architecture.

Architect family

← *A memorial to Jan Hus stands on Old Town Square.*

Consummate architecture The overall view of Prague and the wider Baroque cultural landscape of Bohemia would be unthinkable without Kilian Ignaz Dientzenhofer's contribution. Further important buildings of his are: Villa Amerika, the Church of St Nicholas in Staré Město, the Church of St John Nepomuk on the Rock and the Ursuline nunnery in Kutná Hora; furthermore, he was responsible for the re-modelling of the Church of St Thomas in Malá Strana. He also designed the plans for Sylva-Taroucca Palace and Goltz-Kinský Palace (► Sights from A to Z, Na přikopě / Old Town Square).

Antonín Dvořák (1841–1904)

Composer Antonín Dvořák is regarded as trailblazer for an independent Slav music, with his numerous chamber music compositions and great symphonies. The composer was born in Nelahozeves close to Prague; in 1875 he was awarded an Austrian state scholarship, thanks in large part to a recommendation from Johannes Brahms.

Style synthesis From 1884 Dvořák travelled to England several times, and from 1891 he was professor at the Prague Conservatory. During his three-year stay in America as head of the National Conservatory in New York (1892–1895) he influenced many young American composers. His most famous *New World Symphony* (1893) is full of impressions garnered at this time; elements of American folklore are blended with Bohemian and Moravian folk music. Dvořák also made a name for himself as a composer of operas (*The Jacobin*, 1889; *Rusalka*, 1901; *Armida*, 1904; and others).

Jaroslav Hašek (1883–1923)

Author »Hašek? He must have come into the world on the neck of a beer-bottle – he was no politician, he was drunk ... Again there are stories of such breathtakingly crazy audacity in the book that they could only be the inventions of some monstrous beer and schnaps soak in the dead of night ...«

That was the judgement passed by Kurt Tucholsky in 1926 on the Prague writer Hašek and the major work that made him world famous: *The Good Soldier Švejk*. Hašek created in Josef Švejk an immortal figure whose disarming simplicity exposes the stupidity of the world; the work is a satire on the Austro-Hungarian monarchy and at the same time a profoundly anti-militarist and pacifist work.

Hašek, inventor of Švejk

In the »Cowshed« bar, located in the Vinohrady district, Hašek ran a cabaret with friends; in the afternoons each one wrote the parts he intended to play in the evening. Hašek's talent for improvisation proved very useful when he appeared as chairman, candidate and main speaker for the »Party of Moderate Progress within the Bounds of Law«, which he had founded. He spent the money collected at the end of every meeting on alcohol in the Cowshed the very same evening. In 1915 he was conscripted into the 91st Infantry Regiment, but defected to the Russian side before the year was out. He returned to Prague under a false name in 1921, and the first chapter of *Švejk*, created out of his experiences of the war, appeared in March the same year. Initially no publisher could be found, so Hašek published it himself and hawked it around in pubs. Each week he produced a new chapter. *Švejk* was still not finished when he died in January 1923 as a result of many years of inordinate alcohol consumption; Hašek's name became famous only after his death.

Václav Havel (born 1936)

From politically persecuted author and dissident to first representative of his Czech homeland – the career of Václav Havel, native of Prague, reads like a modern fairy-tale. During the Prague Spring, Havel was chairman of the »Club of Independent Writers« and became the most prominent spokesman of dissident intellectuals. After their attempts at reform had been crushed he was forbidden to publish in his own country, though his plays for theatre and radio were performed to great acclaim elsewhere in Europe.

Prominent politician

From dissident to president

His activities as spokesman for and co-founder of »Charter 77« led to harassment, house arrest, and a total of 50 months in prison. Yet despite health problems Havel would not budge. In 1989 he was elected chairman of the newly founded Civic Forum, and 40 days later he was unanimously chosen as the first democratically elected state president of the ČSSR. Although he was elected to this office a second time in the Czech Republic, and enjoys international esteem, at home the »poet-president« was beset by dwindling support, and in 2003 his period of office as president came to an end. In the past it has mainly been events in Havel's private life that have hit the headlines – from life-threatening lung disease to his marriage to actress Dagmar Veškrnová, 17 years younger than himself.

Jan Hus (c1370–1415)

Reformer The Czech church reformer Jan Hus was born in 1370 of peasant stock in Husinec. Ordained as priest in 1400, Master Jan Hus taught at Charles University and preached in Bethlehem Chapel against papal authority, criticized the secular possessions of the church and demanded a Bohemian national church. He consolidated his ideas for reform in culture by helping to bring more Czech emphasis to Prague's university, where he was the first rector from 1409–1410.

Charged with heresy The reformer was supported by the people as well as by King Wenceslas, but he was excommunicated by the pope in 1411. In his polemic *De ecclesia* (*Regarding the Church*) of 1413, Hus painted a picture of the church as a non-hierarchical assembly of believers who recognized as their leader only Christ, not the pope. With a guarantee of safe conduct from the German king Sigismund, Hus answered a summons to the Council of Constance in 1414, where he was charged with heresy. Since Hus did not recant, he was burnt at the stake in Constance in 1415. His death sparked off violent conflict in Bohemia between the Hussites (moderate Utraquists and radical Taborites) and the country's Catholics, who supported the king, and in 1420, after the first Prague defenestration, the conflict finally led to the bloody Hussite Wars.

Statues in Old Town Square and in the Karolinum memorial court commemorate the reformer. Alongside Bethlehem Chapel stands a reconstruction of the house where Jan Hus lived.

Milena Jesenská (1896–1944)

Milena Jesenská's name is usually mentioned in connection with Franz Kafka, but it is unfair for him to overshadow his Prague-based

friend. She deserves to be recognized as a journalist who worked for equal rights for women and on behalf of German immigrants, and who declared: »One should write political articles just as one writes love-letters.«

Milena grew up in Prague. Her father, a violent and angry nationalist, was a failure as a parent; her mother died when Milena was seventeen years old. In order to end her relationship with the writer Ernst Polak, her father had her sent to an asylum. Nevertheless, she married Polak and went with him to Vienna. The unhappy relationship inspired Milena to start writing in 1919. She translated Kafka's tale *The Boilerman* into Czech and started to correspond with him. On her return to Prague in 1925 – Kafka died in 1924 in Klosterneuburg – she gained in self-confidence after the separation from Polak, and was commissioned by the highly regarded Prague newspaper *Národní listy* to run the women's page. She joined the

Communist party and in 1926 she re-married: her new husband was the Bauhaus architect Jaromír Krejcar. She fell ill while pregnant and became addicted to morphium. This second marriage, too, was a failure.

In 1939 Milena was arrested by the Gestapo for helping people to escape; she died in 1944 in Ravensbrück concentration camp. A committed Czech, she wrote in one of her last articles: »Of course I am a Czech, but above all I try to be a decent human being.«

Franz Kafka (1883–1924)

The prose writing of the insurance clerk Franz Kafka met with little recognition during his lifetime. Kafka was the son of a German-Jewish Prague businessman. A problematic relationship with his father, whom he feared, was a life-long influence, and this is reflected in works such as *The Judgement* (1916) or *Letter to His Father* (1919). In 1906 Kafka completed his study of jurisprudence, and in 1908 he became an employee of the Prague Worker-Accident Insurance Agency. Close friends of the highly sensitive loner included the writers Max Brod and Franz ► Werfel. In 1917 Kafka developed tuberculosis, and five years later he retired on health grounds; in the summer of 1924 he died of tuberculosis of the larynx.

Unrecognized genius

Many of Kafka's tales, three fragmentary novels (*America*, 1912–1914; *The Trial*, 1914–1915; *The Castle*, 1921–1922), and the diaries and letters which are so important for the understanding of his work were edited posthumously by Max Brod – contrary to Kafka's explicit wishes.

Franz Kafka, lonely genius

Not until World War II was over did Kafka's work find worldwide recognition. With regard to both form and content his prose defies classification into any literary genre; time and time again it presents a precise and vivid portrayal of the fruitless fight of the individual against anonymous powers, of unnerving insecurity and anxiety. There have been various approaches – psychoanalytical, existential, theological and philosophical – to the interpretation of the »Kafka-esque« world. Researchers are redoubling their efforts to understand the exact biographical context of the work. The writer was buried in the New Jewish Cemetery on Israelská / Jana Želivského (Metro: Želivského in Žižkov; open: Sun–Thu, 9am–5pm; Fri 9am–2pm).

Alfons Mucha (1860–1939)

Graphic artist and craftsman The graphic artist and craftsman Alfons Mucha first worked as a decorative artist in Vienna, then studied in Munich and, from 1888, in Paris, where he became famous above all for his posters for actress Sarah Bernhardt. Mucha is known as an artist capable of turning his hand to many a decorative challenge; he designed interiors, arts-and-crafts items, and book ornamentation. He had a decisive influence on Art Nouveau. After a period in the United States (1904–1910) he returned to Bohemia where he spent the rest of his life creating 20 paintings for the *Slav Epic*, also undertaking work such as the decoration of Lord Mayor's Hall in the Municipal House and poster designs for theatrical productions. Mucha was buried in Vyšehrad. A museum devoted to his work is located close to Wenceslas Square (►Sights from A to Z).

Jan Neruda (1834–1891)

Journalist and poet The journalist and poet Jan Neruda was born in Prague's Malá Strana; the cobbled street Nerudova is named after him. He soon abandoned the study of jurisprudence and philosophy, begun in 1853, in favour of a literary career, and at the age of 22 he became feature section editor of the newspaper *Národní listy*. In 1866 he founded the periodical *Květy* (*Flowers*) with Hálek, and in 1873 *Lumír*, for a long time the leader in the field. Neruda is considered the founder of Czech feature writing. He also published several volumes of poetry, plays and travel sketches. His lively *Tales of the Little Quarter* (1878) tell of little people and great destinies in the old Prague district below Hradčany.

Peter Parler (c1330–1399)

Master builder and sculptor The sculptor and master builder Peter Parler was a key figure in the development of Gothic art in central Europe. He was born in Schwäbisch Gmünd, son of a respected cathedral architect, and in 1353 he was summoned to Prague by Charles IV in order to continue work on the choir of St Vitus Cathedral. Parler also built All Saints Chapel in the castle, and between 1380 and 1390 he designed Charles Bridge with the Old Town Bridge Tower. Its sculptures are also products of the Parler workshop, which can be shown to have influenced the development of the »Soft« style. Examples of the individual Parler style are also found in the 21 portrait busts on the triforium of St Vitus Cathedral, which include a self-portrait of the artist.

Parler's sons **Wenzel and Johann** continued work on St Vitus Cathedral. His nephew Heinrich Parler was a sculptor in Prague. Amongst other properties, Parler owned Hrzán Palace on Loretánská ulička and the Parler house on Hradčany Square.

Rainer Maria Rilke (1875–1926)

Rainer (actually René) Maria Rilke was born in Prague, at Jindřišská 17/899. His career as an army officer was cut short by ill health, and he went on to study art, philosophy and literature in Prague, Munich and Berlin. In 1899–1900 two lengthy journeys took him to Italy and Russia, where he got to know Leo Tolstoy. In 1900 Rilke settled in Worpswede and married the sculptress Clara Westhoff; however the marriage lasted only one year. In Paris he worked as Rodin's secretary, under whose influence he moved from the dreamy emotional lyric to the »object« poem. After the break he travelled through Europe, North Africa, Egypt and Spain. From 1911–1912 he lived as guest of the Princess of Thurn and Taxis in Duino Castle close to Trieste, where he wrote his first *Duino Elegies*. He completed them in 1923 in Muzot in Switzerland, where he died in 1926, having made it his home.

Many of the works of this important German-language lyricist bear the mark of his Prague home. His *Two Prague Stories* of 1899 recall the politically turbulent times around 1900, Czech-German discord, and the latter-day Austrian Prague of the declining Danube monarchy.

Bedřich Smetana (1824–1884)

The Czech composer Bedřich (Frederick) Smetana studied piano and music theory in Prague; in 1848 he founded his own music school. After a five-year spell in Sweden he returned to his native city in 1861, where he was conductor at the National Theatre from 1866. Smetana founded a Czech national style in opera (*The Bartered Bride*, 1866; *Libuše*, 1881; *The Devil's Wall*, 1882) and in symphonic poems (*My Country*, *The Vltava*, *Vyšehrad*). During his lifetime Smetana's work was controversial; he was accused of taking his lead too much from Wagner and Liszt, and his independent achievements were not recognized. Although he became deaf when he was 50 years old, Smetana did not give up composing. From 1882, however, he displayed symptoms of mental illness, and by the time of his death he had lost his mind entirely.

Controversial composer in his day

His grave is in the memorial cemetery in Vyšehrad. In Staré Město (at Novotného lávka 1) there is a Smetana museum (▶Sights from A to Z).

Franz Werfel (1890–1945)

Franz Werfel was one of Prague's great writers, alongside Max Brod, Franz ▶Kafka and Egon Erwin Kisch. Son of a wealthy Jewish merchant family, he began with Expressionist lyric poetry and Symbolist drama, and later moved to historico-political realism. Among his best-known works are the novels *Embezzled Heaven* (1939) and *Star of the Unborn* (1945). Since 1990, there has been a memorial plaque on the house where Werfel was born in Nové Město (Havlíčova 11).

Expressionist writer

Practicalities

WHAT MUST ON NO ACCOUNT GET LEFT BEHIND? WHERE CAN YOU GET TICKETS FOR THE PRAGUE SPRING MUSIC FESTIVAL? WHERE ARE DUMPLINGS ON THE MENU? CHECK IT OUT HERE – PREFERABLY BEFORE THE TRIP!

Accommodation

Hotels Since most Prague hotels have either opened or been completely renovated within the last decade, almost all come up to western standards and many even exceed them. This fact is reflected however in the extremely high prices. During festivals prices are raised further, while out of season they are reduced. There is also accommodation on floating hotels, the »botels« moored on the Vltava. The increasing popularity of the so-called »Pearl on the Vltava« makes it advisable to book ahead. Hotels can be booked on the internet at www.prague.nethotels.com and www.travel.cz.

Apartments Holiday apartments with hotel service and 24-hour reception are available even for single-night stopovers from Prague City Apartments, Divadelni 24, Praha 1, tel. 224 990 990, fax 224 990 999, www.prague-city-apartments.cz.

Camping It is only possible to list a limited selection of campsites in and around Prague (see below). Detailed information is available from Prague Information Service (PIS). The sites are usually 5–10km/3–6mi outside the city. A brief overview is available at www.camp.cz.

▶ RECOMMENDED HOTELS

- ▶ ① etc. see map p.60/61
- ▶ **Price categories for a double room**
  Luxury: from £180/US$350/€251
  Mid-range: £106–179/US$200–349/€151–250
  Budget: less than £105/US$200/€150

LUXURY

▶ ③ **Aria**
Praha 1, Tržiště 9
Tel. 225 334 111, fax 257 535 357
Email: stay@ariahotel.net
www.ariahotel.net
Music-inspired ambience. 52 rooms individually fitted to themes of classical music, jazz, musical or opera. Visitors can choose a bed according to their favourite composer. The interior décor is by New York designers. There is a magical view of Petřín hill's Baroque gardens from the terrace.

▶ ㉚ **Boscolo Hotel Carlo IV**
Praha 1, Senovážné náměstí 13
Tel. 224 593 033, fax 224 223 960
Email: congress@carloIV.boscolo.com
www.boscolohotels.com
A hotel of truly majestic class. Originally a bank palace, it competes with the National Museum for splendour and scale. Upgraded by Roman luxury hotel group Boscolo, there is heavy leather furniture in the hall. Magnificent pilasters, crystal candelabras and exquisite Art Deco create an exalted atmosphere. The 152 spacious rooms are furnished with

antiques: it's like sleeping in the royal treasury. Gourmet cuisine with Italian flair.

▶ ㉗ **Esplanade**

Praha 1, Washingtonova 19
Tel. 224 50 11 11, fax 224 22 93 06
Email: esplanade@esplanade.cz
www.esplanade.cz
The fine French restaurant alone may well inspire a visit to this exclusive 64-room hotel. Renovated in 1930s style, it is situated in a quiet spot opposite a part, near the main railway station.

▶ ⑩ **Four Seasons**

Praha 1, Veleslavínova 2 a
Tel. 221 42 70 00
Fax 221 42 77 88
Email: prg.reservation@
fourseasons.com
www.fourseasons.com
Three buildings, Gothic, Renaissance and Baroque, are linked by contemporary design. Centrally located on the Vltava, the hotel is just a few steps from Charles Bridge and Prague's Old Town. More than 162 rooms and suites are on offer. The Allegro restaurant, combining Italian cuisine with Czech specialities, is part of the hotel; an inviting riverside terrace is open in summer.

▶ ㉛ **Hilton Atrium**

Praha 8, Pobřežní 1
Tel. 224 84 11 11, fax 224 84 23 78
Email: book-prague@hilton.com
www.hilton.com
The ultra-modern glass palace located east of Staré Město is the largest hotel in Prague, with 788 rooms. Restaurants, cafés, business centre, conference rooms, swimming-pool, disco, casino and a fitness suite await the guest.

Four Seasons with view of Prague Castle

▶ ㉘ **Le Palais**

Praha 2, U Zvonařky 1
Tel. 234 634 111 , fax 234 634 635
Email: info@palaishotel.cz
www.palaishotel.cz
Located in Prague's once very high-class residential district of Vinohrady (meaning vineyards). Belle Époque atmosphere. Painter Luděk Marold – famous for his gigantic painting of the Hussite battle of Lipany, the largest historical battle painting in the world – lived here, and created the interior decoration in 1898 for the then owner. With 72 luxury rooms, this establishment makes the prestigious »Leading Small Hotels of the World« list.

Prague Hotels and Restaurants

© Baedeker

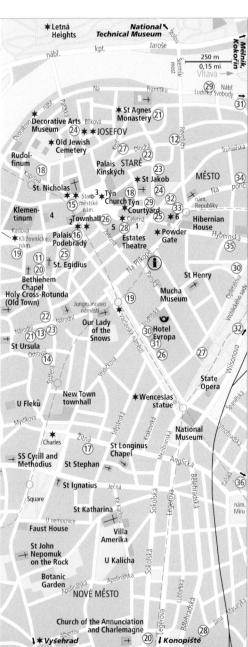

1 House of the Black Madonna
2 Minute House
3 Hus monument
4 Palais Clam-Gallas
5 Karolinum
6 Representation House

Where to eat

① Peklo
② U Černého Vola
③ U Kolovrata
④ Petřinké sady
⑤ Nebozízek
⑥ U Maliru
⑦ U Mecenáše
⑧ Square - Malostranská kavárna
⑨ Pálffy Palác
⑩ U tří pštrosů
⑪ Rybářský Klub
⑫ Kampapark
⑬ Hoffmeister
⑭ Žofín
⑮ Hanavský pavilon
⑯ Kristian Marco
⑰ Slavia
⑱ Le Café Colonial
⑲ V Zátiší
⑳ Klub architektů
㉑ Louvre
㉒ Monarch
㉓ Le Patio
㉔ Pravda
㉕ Vysmátý zajíc
㉖ Grand Café Praha
㉗ Kolkovna
㉘ Kogo
㉙ La Provence
㉚ Titanic
㉛ Evropa
㉜ Paříž
㉝ Obecní dům
㉞ Imperial
㉟ Arco
㊱ TV Tower

Where to sleep

① Dům U velké boty
② Neruda
③ Aria
④ Hostel Sokol
⑤ Roma
⑥ Kampa - Stará Zbrojnice
⑦ U červené sklenice
⑧ U tří pštrosů
⑨ Admirál
⑩ Four Seasons
⑪ Husova Pension & Hostel
⑫ Dlouhá Pension & Hostel
⑬ Unitas
⑭ Élite
⑮ Černá liška
⑯ U železných vrat
⑰ Juniorhotel
⑱ Ungelt
⑲ Ambassador-Zlatá Husa
⑳ Březina Pension
㉑ Maximilian
㉒ Antik
㉓ Josef
㉔ Central
㉕ Paříž
㉖ Evropa
㉗ Esplanade
㉘ Le Palais
㉙ Albatros
㉚ Boscolo Hotel Carlo IV.
㉛ Hilton Atrium
㉜ Arcotel Teatrino

ℹ FOR A GOOD NIGHT'S SLEEP

- Boscolo Hotel Carlo IV: former bank palace with modern design
- Le Palais: top class, with personal service
- U železných vrat (At the Iron Gate): romantic, in the heart of Staré Město
- Antik: Old Town idyll, not too expensive
- Roma: new hotel in Malá Strana, decent prices
- Grand Hotel Evropa: Art Nouveau with patina on Wenceslas Square
- Botel Admirál: stylish floating hotel on the Vltava

► ㉕ Paříž
Praha 1, U Obecního domu 1
Tel. 222 19 51 95, fax 222 195 907
Email: booking@hotel-pariz.cz
www.hotel-pariz.cz
This venerable luxury hotel of 1907, situated behind the Municipal House, has 100 generously-sized rooms, two conference rooms and a stylish fin-de-siècle restaurant.

► ⑧ U tří pštrosů (The Three Ostriches)
Praha 1,
Dražického náměstí 12
Tel. 257 288 888, fax 257 533 217
Email: info@upstrosu.cz
www.upstrosu.cz
»The Three Ostriches« is just a few yards from Charles Bridge. Early booking necessary in order to secure one of the 18 romantic rooms, which are very sought after! Good Bohemian food in the restaurant.

► ⑯ U železných vrat (The Iron Gate)
Praha 1, Michalská 19
Tel: 225 777 777, fax 225 777 778
Email: hotel@irongate.cz

www.irongate.cz
A chic Baroque residence with 14th-century foundation walls. Romantic courtyard café, wall-paintings in 44 sumptuous rooms. Frescoes, artwork and antique furniture, plus Staré Město's loveliest attic suite, with a view of all 100 spires. This is how Mozart would live in Prague today.

MID-RANGE

► ⑲ Ambassador – Zlatá Husa
Praha 1, Václavské náměstí 5
Tel. 224 19 31 11, fax 224 22 61 67
Email: hotel@ambassador.cz
www.ambassador.cz
This Art Nouveau house is a delight, not only because of the Louis XIV furnishings in some of the 118 rooms and its location on Wenceslas Square, but also because of the especially good food in Halali restaurant.

► ㉒ Antik
Praha 1, Dlouhá 22
Tel. 222 322 288
Fax 222 328 540
Email: info@hotelantik.cz
www.antikhotels.com/antik.php
Live like the 19th-century bourgeoisie in a renovated historic house. Twelve rooms, café and a shop with antiques, in atmospheric Josefov setting.

► ㉜ Arcotel Teatrino
► Žižkov, Baedeker Tip p.204.

► ㉔ Centrál
Praha 1, Rybná 8
Tel. 224 812 041
Fax 22 32 84 04
As its name indicates, this hotel is in the middle of Staré Město. Now renovated, it has 55 rooms and a restaurant.

▶ ⑭ **Élite**
Praha 1, Ostrovní 1
Tel. 224 932 250, fax 224 930 787
Email: sales@hotelelite.cz
www.hotelelite.cz
A restored Renaissance palace
with 77 rooms in the middle of
historic Nové Město, not far from
the National Theatre. Ancient
walls in the inner courtyard,
beams and divine frescoes in the
rooms, ducal suite with romantic
vaulting. Restaurant and music
club in the cellar.

▶ ㉓ **Josef**
Praha 1, Rybná 20
Tel: 221 700 111, fax 221 700 999
Email: reservation@hoteljosef.-
com, www.hoteljosef.com
Icy cool. Ultimate London design
with white walls, gleaming stainless steel surfaces, orange lounge
furniture. Guests sit like fish in an
aquarium behind the restaurant's
reinforced green glass. This is how
models and the movers and shak-
ers of fashion like it – cold.

▶ ⑥ **Kampa – Stará Zbrojnice**
Praha 1, Všehrdova 16
Tel. 271 090 851, fax 271 090 870
www.hotel-kampa.info.
This Best Western hotel with 84
rooms lies hidden on Kampa
Island, 5 minutes walk from
Charles Bridge.

▶ ㉑ **Maximilian**
Praha 1, Haštalská 14
Tel. 225 303 111, fax 225 303 110
Email: reservations@maximilian-
hotel.com
www.maximilianhotel.com
The hotel is close to the Convent
of St Agnes. The 72 rooms are
exquisitely appointed, with air-
conditioning and fax; there are

seminar rooms, and the hotel has
its own underground garage. Ex-
plore the sights of the Old Town
with ease on foot from here.

In Staré Město: Maximilian

▶ ② **Neruda**
Praha 1, Nerudova 44
Tel. 257 53 55 57, fax 257 53 14 92
Email: info@
hotelneruda-praha.cz
www. hotelneruda-praha.cz
This charming little hotel (20
rooms) located on the street of the
same name in Malá Strana is
tastefully furnished and decorated
in a building that dates back to
1348. The Carolina café-restau-
rant, with home baking and a
range of international and Czech
specialities, is part of the establishment.

▶ ⑤ **Roma**
Praha 1, Malá Strana, Újezd 24
Tel. 222 500 222, fax 222 500 333
Email: recepce@hotelroma.cz
www.hotelroma.cz
Close to Kampa Island, this friendly hotel of the Mozart era is a listed building, which has been renovated with meticulous attention to detail. Modern atrium and designer wing. Total of 87 rooms, eight furnished with antiques. Underground garage.

▶ ⑱ **Ungelt**
Praha 1, Malá Štupartská 1
Tel. 224 82 86 86, fax 224 82 81 81
www.ungelt.cz
Small apartment hotel with nine units in a building dating from the 10th century. Not far from Old Town Square; parking right outside the hotel in season.

BUDGET

▶ ⑳ **Březina Pension**
Praha 2, Legerova 39 - 41
Tel. 224 266 779
Fax 224 266 777
Email: info@brezina.cz
www.brezina.cz
In one of Prague's wonderful patrician houses of the 19th-century age of industrial expansion. Copious stucco, curlicues, and façade ornamentation. The 35 rooms are equipped for business guests, with internet access for the laptop.

▶ ⑮ **Černá liška**
Praha 1, U Mikulášská 1
Tel. 224 23 22 50, fax 224 23 22 49
www.cernaliska.cz
This small, select hotel with twelve rooms is located right on Old Town Square, next to the Church of St Nicholas. The rooms are elegantly appointed; there is a summer terrace, and an à-la-carte restaurant in the Gothic vaulted cellar.

▶ ① **Dům U velké boty**
▶ Lobkowicz Palace, Baedeker Tip p.177.

▶ ㉖ **Evropa**
Praha 1, Václavské náměstí 25
Tel. 224 215 387, fax 224 224 544
Email: reception@evropahotel.cz
www. evropahotel.cz
No-one should expect old-fashioned comfort in this hotel in classic Art Nouveau style: time has left its mark on the 115 rooms. Robust nostalgia is required; otherwise, try the Art Nouveau café.

▶ ⑰ **Junior Hotel**
Praha 2, Žitná 12
Tel. 224 231 754, fax 271 750 274
Very central, but also seriously noisy, accommodation at a budget price in this 22-room hotel.

▶ ⑬ **Unitas**
Praha 1, Bartolomějská 9
Tel. 224 21 10 20, fax 224 21 08 00
www.unitas.cz/
This central guesthouse, due for renovation by 2008, has 34 simply appointed rooms (2–6 beds) with shared showers and WC. A fee is charged for parking (with surveillance). All rooms are non-smoking.

BOTELS

▶ ⑨ **Admirál**
Praha 5, Hořejší nábřeží
Tel. 257 32 13 02, fax 257 319 516
Email: info@admiral-botel.cz
www.admiral-botel.cz
This floating hotel moored on the Vltava riverside offers 88 small

double-bed cabins, sun deck, a restaurant and a bar – all with a pitching floor. A special kind of experience!

► ㉙ **Albatros**
Praha 1, nábřeží Ludvíka Svobody
Tel. 224 810 547
Fax 224 81 12 14
Email: info@botelalbatros.cz
www.botelalbatros.cz
This botel (86 cabins, restaurant) is more centrally located and also noisier than the »Admirál«. Friday and Saturday disco!

YOUTH HOSTELS AND PRIVATE ACCOMMODATION

A different sort of accommodation, a botel

► ⑪ **Husova Guesthouse & Hostel**
Praha 1, Husova 3
Tel. 222 220 078, fax 224 826 665
Email: hostel@travellers.cz
www.travellers.cz, open 29 June–25 August

► ⑫ **Dlouhá Guesthouse & Hotel**
Praha 1, Dlouhá 33
Tel. 224 826 662
Fax 224 826 665
Email: hostel@travellers.cz
www.travellers.cz, open all year
Youth hotel, 300m/330yd from Old Town Square

► ④ **Hostel Sokol**
Praha 1, Nosticova 2
Tel. 257 007 397, fax 257 007 340
www.sokol-cos.cz
Clean dormitories, 7–14 beds per room

CAMPING

► **Sportcamp Motol**
nad Hliníkem 1202
CZ-15000 Praha

Tel. 257 213 080, fax 257 215 084
April–Oct
8km/5mi west of the city, grass pitches, trees, shopping, take-away, restaurant

► **Sokol Troja**
Trojská 171 a
CZ-17100 Praha 7
www.camp-sokol-troja.cz
Tel. 228 542 908, fax 283 850 486
Open all year.
5km/3mi north of the city centre, grass pitches with trees beside busy road, shopping and snacks on site

► **Sokol Dolní Počernice**
Národních hrdinu 290
CZ-19012 Praha 9
Tel./fax 281 931 368
Email: info@campingsokol.cz
www.campingsokol.cz
April–Oct
East of Prague, also offers bunga-low accommodation, restaurant and food shop, sports facilities, suitable for children

Arrival · Before the Journey

How to get there

By car Any journey from the UK to Prague involves crossing the Channel, and the quickest way across is via the Channel Tunnel. Fares can be expensive; taking the ferry is often cheaper. The most direct route from Calais to Prague is via Lille, Brussels, Cologne, Frankfurt and Nuremberg, entering the Czech Republic at the Rozvadov (Waidhaus) border crossing; the motorway in the direction of Pilsen and Prague starts just across the frontier. The journey of just over 1000km/620mi is likely to take about 14 hours. Another option is to travel via Dresden, crossing the border at Cínovec (Zinnwald) (E 55), but this route is a favourite of lorry drivers, too.

Prague is also easily reached via South or East Germany, or Austria. There are about a dozen border crossings from Germany, and about the same number from Austria, and the Czech Republic is relatively well supplied with roads. The motorways converge on Prague in star formation.

A toll is payable on Czech motorways: it is best to buy a vignette at the frontier (▶Transport).

By bus or coach Eurolines (tel.: 01582 400694) offer a service to Prague from London Victoria. Coaches arrive at Prague's Florenc bus station, next to the

Art Nouveau ambience welcomes new arrivals.

ADDRESSES

BUS COMPANIES

▶ **Eurolines Ltd.**
52 Grosvenor Gardens
London SW1W 0UA
Tel. 0870 514 3219
www.eurolines.com

▶ **Bohemia Euroexpress**
Florenc bus station
Křižikova 6
CZ-186 00 Praha 8
Tel. 224 218 680, fax 224 814 821
Reservations for
departures from Prague

TIMETABLE INFORMATION

▶ **České Dráhy**
Czech Railways
Tel. 972 211 111 (24 Stunden)
www.cd.cz

▶ **International Rail**
08700 84 14 10
www.internationalrail.com

▶ **Seat 61**
(online journey planning)
www.seat61.com

Metro station of the same name. The journey takes about 23 hours, a few hours longer than taking the train. Fares however are considerably cheaper.

There are good rail connections between London and Prague. The most direct routes are via Germany, passing through either Cologne or Berlin. For the former, take an afternoon Eurostar to Brussels and a connecting train to Cologne, then the »Kopernikus« sleeper train to Prague. Some sleepers on this train are even equipped with a private shower and toilet. Alternatively take a Eurostar from London to Brussels early in the evening to connect with the overnight sleeper to Berlin, then a scenic EuroCity journey from Berlin to Prague – those who wish to can enjoy lunch in the restaurant car. Both routes take about 19 hours.
Since rail travel is significantly cheaper in the Czech Republic than in neighbouring countries in the west, it is a good idea to buy a ticket only as far as the border, and get another there.
Most trains from abroad arrive at Prague's **main railway station** (Hlavní nádraží, Praha 2, Wilsonova 16), which adjoins the Metro station Hlavní nádraží. However, trains to and from Berlin usually stop only at the new station **Praha-Holešovice**. **Tickets** are available at the stations, and also in the Čedok offices (▶Information). | By train

Czech Airlines (www.csa.cz) offers direct flights to Prague from a variety of European cities, including London and Edinburgh, as well as from the USA (New York) and Canada (Toronto). British Airways fly direct to Prague from London Gatwick. Reasonably priced flights from the UK and Republic of Ireland are listed at www.cheapflights.co.uk. | By air

Ruzyně Airport ▸ Ruzyně Airport is 10km/6mi west of Prague, on the road to Kladno. There is a bus service from the airport to the city centre: Czech Airlines (ČSA) runs buses to the travel agent Vltava (Revoluční 25), via the last stop on Metro Line A, Dejvická; buses no. 254 and 119 go to the last stop on Metro Line A, Dejvická; no. 108 goes to Metro stop Hradčanská (Line A). Tickets are available from the public transport (DP) information desk at the airport.

Entry and Departure Regulations

Travel documents
In order to enter the Czech Republic, citizens of EU countries require a valid **identity card** or **passport**; children under 16 need either their own passport with a photograph or they can be entered on a parent's passport. While EU citizens require no visa, regardless of the length or purpose of the visit, citizens of the USA, Canada, Australia and New Zealand need a visa for a stay exceeding 90 days. In the case of non-EU citizens, it is possible that officials will demand evidence on entry of adequate financial means to cover the duration of the planned stay and the return journey: cash, credit cards, travellers' cheques, air or rail tickets are acceptable.

Documents for drivers ▸
Drivers require their driving licence, vehicle registration document, and green international insurance card. Vehicles must display an oval plaque indicating nationality, or EU plaque.

Pets
The new EU regulations, from July 2004, require dogs and cats to have an official veterinary **pet passport** for journeys within the EU. This contains an official veterinary health certificate (issued not more than 30 days before travelling), a rabies vaccination certificate issued at least 20 days and not more than eleven months before entering the country, and a passport photograph. In addition, the animal must be identified by microchip or tattoo. A muzzle and a lead are compulsory. Hotel accommodation can be a problem – many hotels will not accept pets, or they make an extra charge. Dogs must be kept on a lead on all beaches and in nature reserves.

Customs regulations
Since 2004 the Czech Republic has been a member of the EU, and therefore belongs to the European common market. From 1.1.2008 travellers over 17 years of age may bring into the country, for their own private use, 10 litres/2.6 US gal of spirits, 90 litres/24 US gal of wine, 110 litres/30 US gal of beer and 800 cigarettes. For travellers from non-EU countries, the allowance for people over 17 is 200 cigarettes (or 100 cigarillos, 50 cigars or 250g/9oz tobacco); 2 litres/0.5 US gal of wine and 2 litres/0.5 US gal of sparkling wine or 1 litre/0.26 US gal of spirits with more than 22% alcohol content, or 2 litres/0.5 US gal of spirits with less than 22% alcohol content, 500g/1.1lb of coffee or 200g/7oz of coffee extract, 100g/3.5oz of tea or 40g/1.4oz of tea extract, 50g/1.75oz of perfume or 0.25 litres/8.5 US fl oz of eau de toilette, plus presents to a value of £124/€175/US$255.

Travel Insurance

Citizens of EU countries are entitled to treatment in Italy under the local regulations in case of illness on production of their **European health insurance card**. Even with this card, in most cases some of the costs for medical care and prescribed medication must be paid by the patient. Upon presentation of receipts the health insurance at home covers the costs – but not for all treatments. Citizens of non-EU countries must pay for medical treatment and medicine themselves and should take out private health insurance.

Health insurance

Electricity

Main voltage is 220 AC, in some old residential buildings still 120 AC. An adapter is generally necessary.

Emergency

Emergency: tel. 112
Police: tel. 158
Fire service: tel. 150
Breakdown service ▶Transport
Medical emergency ▶Health

Entertainment

Concerts, theatre performances and films start at 7pm and usually last till about 10pm. Pubs usually close at 11pm, while some wine bars are open till midnight. After that, night-owls can choose between jazz cellars, nightclubs in the big hotels, and various discos.

Nightlife

 ADDRESSES

NIGHT CLUBS

▶ **Goldfinger in Hotel Ambassador**
Praha 1, Václavské náměstí 5
Fri and Sat 8pm–3am

»Black light« theatre, revue and vaudeville

▶ **Duplex**
Praha 1, Václavské náměstí 21

www.duplexduplex.cz
10pm–5am
Dance over the roofs of Wenceslas Square. Mick Jagger celebrated his 60th here; among the party guests was ex-president Václav Havel. Hot themed parties with model casting. DJs with Funk'n Motion, Groove & Rave.

► **Darling Cabaret**
Praha 1,
Ve Smečkách 32 a (corner of Wenceslas Square)
www.kabaret.cz
daily midnight–5am
A touch of Las Vegas. Go-go girls, table dance, cabaret with Pink Panther.

► **Hergetova cihelna**
Praha 1, Malá Strana
Cihelná 2 b
www.cihelna.com
daily 11.30pm–1am
Champagne with romance. The terrace of the restored tileworks on the Vltava waterfront is the most beautiful place for lovers. View of Charles Bridge lit by flares, designer lounge with leather seating, 12m/39ft-long mahogany bar, vinotheque and top-class pizzas, chill-out music live or with DJs.

► **U vystřeleného oka**
Praha 3, Žižkov,
U božích
bojovníků 3
www.uvystrelenehooka.cz
Live music from 7pm
Prague, letting it all hang out. Beer and music in authentic symbiosis. Traditionally decorated walls. Every weekend a hive of anything from dripping, sweating rock groups to Dixie bands with wicked shrapnel sound. The venue name

»The Shot-Out Eye« refers to the one-eyed Hussite leader Jan Žižka. His equestrian statue keeps an eye on proceedings on Vítkov hill.

KLUBS

► **Klub lávka**
Praha 1, Staré Město, Novotného lávka 1, www.lavka.cz
Disco daily 9.30pm–5am, theatre performances begin at 8pm
Club theatre, disco, tequila bar. Beneath the dance floor flows the Vltava; the club is located on a barrage. Stroll out onto the terrace beneath Charles Bridge.

► **RadostFX**
Praha 2, Bělehradská 120
www.radostfx.cz
Wed–Sun 10pm–6am
One of Prague's hottest clubs, the meeting place of »beautiful people«, lounge, restaurant.

► **Roxy**
Praha 1, Dlouhá 33
www.roxy.cz
daily from 8pm
Not only a club, also a rendezvous for Prague film students, theatre, concerts, DJ workshops ...

Etiquette and Customs

There is refined English humour, black humour and gallows humour. But Prague humour tops them all. It starts off in fine British spirit, turns black, and finally hangs like a rogue on the gallows. Don't be quick to take offense in Prague; after all, as the saying goes: »Czechs aren't friendly, but they are human.« So though you may often encounter rudeness, you will never see inhumanity.

Prague humour and other niceties

All Czechs love the king! It is rather a long time since the glory days of Charles IV, father of the nation. Yet in the national consciousness he is just as much part of life as the royals are in Britain. And sometimes Czechs really yearn for their monarchy. So the visitor is well advised to enthuse over the great Charles and his architecture (and not just in Prague).

In spite of EU expansion towards the east, the exact geographical position of this nation needs to be observed. The Czechs do not regard themselves as belonging to the east. Indeed, they insist that »in Eastern Europe, we are closest to the west«. Links with the west are constantly emphasized, as is Prague's position at »the heart of central Europe«. Attending to these nuances of geography enhances that feeling of togetherness.

Anyone who knows that »Rosamunde«, the world's most famous polka, really comes from Bohemia

The modern and the historic on display on Karlova

will immediately find favour. Any proud Czech will refuse to hear a word said against their country's folk music. Brass is as essential a part of Czech culture as the bagpipes are to Scotland's. Moreover, the polka is immortal!

»I'm not stupid!« is a slogan on the lips of all true Czechs. It is a good idea to take note of this, and behave accordingly. Czechs don't like to have anything explained twice; in any case, they'll do it their way, often rather stubbornly. Flexibility is not exactly a national strength, whereas improvisation is. Czechs may rank as the best in the world at finding provisional solutions. As they say, »No-one is stupid here.«

»Cheers« in Czech is »na zdraví«. This is on no account to be mixed up with the Russian »Nazdarovje«. Confusion here may provoke allergic reactions.

To be avoided at all costs
For some time now, Prague has been a popular destination for stag nights. Groups of young British men descending on the city to take advantage of the cheap beer and other nocturnal attractions have earned a bad reputation among the locals. Stag parties are increasingly being banned from the bars of the Old Town. Walking shirtless and inebriated through the city centre chanting football slogans is, to say the least, frowned upon. Having said that, there is some tolerance of the mostly harmless if raucous Brits: »They drink, they spend money, they go home,« is the philosophical reaction of many Prague residents. Even as august a figure as Prague's chief of police is on record as saying that he »prefers drunken Britons to sober Germans«.

It is not the done thing to criticize Czech cooking. Even when the culinary offering in front of you doesn't quite come up to scratch, it's best not to compare it unfavourably with the cuisine at home. Naturally though, Czech beer is the best in the world! No arguments there.

Berating the Communists is passé. That topic is closed. Political evaluation, if it is to be indulged in at all, should be left to historians.

Lastly, comparing Prague with other cities is also unnecessary: Prague is, and always will be, unique!

Festivals, Holidays and Events

National Holidays

1 January (New Year's Day)
Easter Monday
1 May (Labour Day)
8 May (Day of the Liberation of Prague, 1945)
5 July (Day of the Apostles to the Slavs, SS Cyril and Methodius)
6 July (Death of Jan Hus: burnt at the stake in Constance, 1415)
28 September (Day of Bohemian patron saint Wenceslas)
28 October (Founding of Czechoslovakia, 1918)
17 November (Day of the Struggle for Freedom and Democracy)
24 December (Christmas Eve)
25 and 26 December (Christmas)

⏵ HOLIDAYS AND EVENTS

JANUARY

► **Carnival**
Traditions, costumes and masks from all over the world: from Basel carnival via Rio samba to Venetian masks. Visiting parades in Prague.

www.pis.cz,
tickets: www.bohemiaticket.cz

FEBRUARY

► **Žižkovský masopust**
Here comes the Prussian Guard!

Carnival in Prague's »black district« of Žižkov. With home-made sausages and a masked parade. Main venues are »U vystřeleného oka« (The Shot-Out Eye), U božích bojovníků 3; and Palác Akropolis. Last weekend in the month. Tel. 723 370 944, www.praha3.cz

MARCH

► Mozart Open

Theatre festival with a mix of arias and opera intended as an ironic counterpart to Salzburg (every year March–October). In Club Lávka, National Puppet Theatre. www.mozart.cz

► Agharta Prague Jazz Festival

The syncopated season begins in March and lasts until October. The Agharta Club and Lucerna Bar have become cult venues of international repute. www.agharta.cz

APRIL

► Bohemia Žofin Cup

Dance competition and performances by the best couples in the world. Golden Hall in Žofín Cultural Centre. www.cokdyvpraze.cz. Special dance homepage: www.praguedancefestival.cz

MAY

► Prague Spring (Pražské jaro)

The festival opens in the Municipal House (Obecní dům) on 8 May. Traditional finale (approx. mid-June) is »Beethoven's Ninth« in the Rudolfinum. With Schiller's ode »all people become brothers«. Pražské jaro, Malá Strana, Hellichova 18, tel. 257 312 547, 257 311 921, email: info@festival.cz, www.festival.cz

► Prague Marathon

Start and finish on Old Town Square, 41.2km/26mi, time limit: 6 hours. Last Sunday before Whitsun. Registration form online: www.pim.cz. Information: Tel. 224 919 209 Fax 224 923 355.

JUNE

► Kmochův Kolín

Don't forget to pack that hat! František Kmoch was Bohemia's well-loved composer of marches, deeply rooted in Czech tradition, folklore and folk music. The big brass starts blowing on the second weekend in June. Also in Kutná Hora with spectacular St Barbara's Cathedral. Tel./fax 233 378 657 www.kmochuv-kolin.cz

JULY

► Karlovy Vary (Karlsbad) film festival

Not so full of themselves: here, the Hollywood stars are approachable. This competition was started in 1946, and is a category A event, up there with Cannes, Berlin and Venice. Here the Oscar is called the Crystal Globe. Filmovy Festival Karlovy Vary, Panská 1 Tel. 221 411 011/22, fax 221 411 033, www.kviff.cz

AUGUST

► Audite Organum

International organ festival in St James' Basilica (Staré Město, Malá Štupartská 6) – until the last Sunday in September. Acoustics to send shivers down the spine. Tel. 257 317 269 www.auditeorganum.cz

► **Prague Autumn
(Pražský podzim)**
International concert series in the
Rudolfinum. Centred around
works by Smetana, Dvořák, Fibich,
Janáček, and Martinů (the Vltava
Debussy).
CZ-13006 Praha 3
Příběnická 20
Tel. 222 540 484
Fax 222 540 415
www.pragueautumn.cz

OCTOBER

► **Festival Musica Judaica**
Jewish music, drawing on folklore,
religion and ancient custom.
Kulturní zentrum ZMP
CZ-11001 Praha 1
Maiselova 15
Tel. 224 819 352
Fax 222 325 172
www.jewishmuseum.cz

NOVEMBER

► **Seasonal music for
Advent and Christmas**
In all Prague churches. www.pis.cz
Tickets: www.bohemiaticket.cz

DECEMBER

► **»Hey, Master«**
Traditional Bohemian Christmas
from the heart of the nation:
oratorio by Jan Jakub Ryba and
Baroque church music (Mysli-
veček, Stamitz, Vranický) in
churches and cathedrals.
www.pis.cz
tickets: www.bohemiaticket.cz

► **Christmas market on
Old Town Square**
Medieval crafts, wrought-iron
work, glassblowers, puppet players
and gingerbread. To top it all, God
sings down from heaven – Karel,
the »golden voice«. Traditional
live event on Christmas Eve.

Food and Drink

Bohemian cuisine is well known far beyond the frontiers of the
country. It is lauded for its tasty and filling dishes and for the variety
of pancake-type desserts. Relatively little importance is attached to
vegetables and salads.

Food

Meat The favourite meat of the Czechs is pork, prepared in many different
ways. Roast pork may be regarded as the national dish, served with
cabbage and dumplings. On festive occasions pork is replaced by
crisp roast goose or duck, with the same side dishes. Game is often
excellent, be it haunch of venison or larded hare. Further very important specialities are steamed beef, boiled pork belly, roast lung
and various sorts of sausage (roast sausages, bacon sausages, Prague
sausages, smoked sausages and spiced knackwurst). Prague's boiled
ham is famous all over the world.

Less frequently seen on the menu are **fish dishes**. However, scarcely any family can get by without the traditional carp at Christmas.

For all main dishes, **sauces** are considered very important. Sometimes this is seasoned gravy, possibly refined by the addition of cream. Both meat and vegetables are often accompanied by a white sauce, given a special flavour by marjoram and caraway seeds.

Bohemian cuisine is unthinkable without **dumplings**. There are many varieties. Alongside semolina dumplings and noodles, dumplings made of potato or white bread are the most frequent side dishes. Bacon dumplings filled with cabbage or spinach, served with fried

Cabbage dumpling with goulash: a typical Czech dish

onions, are a favourite main dish, but the high point of Bohemian dumpling specialities is undoubtedly the fruit dumpling made with yeast dough, to which Franz Werfel (►Famous People) devotes more than 1000 words in his novel *The Pure in Heart*. They can be filled with cherries, apricots, apples, blueberries or, most especially, plums. The dumplings are topped with hard, grated cream cheese or poppy seeds, and, last of all, melted butter.

There is a wide range of flour-based foods. Apfelstrudel and the variety of small cakes and doughnuts may be tempting, but the pancakes (palačinky) surpass them all. Made with egg-batter and filled with cream cheese, jam or chocolate, these pancakes are not as paper-thin as French crêpes, but just as delicious.

Pancakes

Drinks

►Badeker Special p.76.

Beer

Prague wine bars do serve wines with an international name, but principally home-grown wines are on offer. Among these are the famous »Ludmila« wine from the banks of the Elbe close to Mělník, and the Žernosecké and Primatorské varieties. Good-quality wines also come from the southern Moravian areas of Znaim, Mikulov (Nikolsburg), Velkopavlovické (Grosspawlowitz) and Valtické (Feldsberg), as well as from the region around Bratislava (Pressburg) in Slovakia.

Wine

Pivo means beer in Czech, and in Prague it's the stuff that dreams are made of. Czechs are world leaders in per capita consumption.

CZECH PASSIONS

In Prague, especially at lunchtime, it is still possible to see people heading for the nearest pub with carrier rack in hand, to emerge with six freshly-filled mugs and hurry back to the office. Beer is the Czech national drink, and Prague offers countless opportunities to sample the products of the country's brewing skills. Some Prague beer cellars still store their beer in Gothic vaults, from which it flows incomparably fresh from rarely closed taps.

Czech beer owes its world reputation above all to the unique »Bohemian hops« grown today in northern Bohemia around Saaz, Raudnitz, Auscha and Dauba, and exported to all parts of the world. As early as the ninth century, chronicles make mention of hop-growing in Bohemia, and from the twelfth century hops were exported via the river Elbe to the famous hop-market in Hamburg. For centuries the export of hop-plants carried the death penalty. Beers were brewed from barley, wheat and even oats, with the country's especially soft brewery water, and flavoured with the highly esteemed hops; the beers were already famous for their variety and quality in medieval Europe.

Pale or dark

Czech beers are usually bottom-fermented. A basic distinction is made between light (»světlé«) and dark (»tmavé«) beers. Beer is not classed according to alcohol content, but rather according to the Balling scale, which measures the proportion of soluble ingredients present before fermentation (similar to the original wort of German beers). The most famous Bohemian beer is Pilsner Urquell (»Plzeňský Prazdroj«) from Plzeň (Pilsen), which has been brewed since 1842 and has become the model for all beers of this type throughout the world. The first beer tavern in Prague to serve pils, or pilsener, was »U Pinkas« (Chez Pinkas, Praha 1, Jungmannovo náměstí 15), founded by the tailor Pinkas in 1843, and still in existence. Further well-known pils taverns are »U Schnellů« (Chez Schnell, Praha 1, Tomášská 2) and »U dvou coček« (The Two Cats, Praha 1, Uhelný trh 10).

The milder and slightly sweetish Budweiser (Budvar) is rather overshadowed by pils, but unjustly so. It has been brewed in the southern Bohemian town of České Budějovice (Budweis) since 1531.

The best place to sample it in Prague is »U medvidk« (The Little Bear, Praha 1, Na Perštýně 7), which was a brewery in medieval times. The Velké Popovice brewery in central Bohemia produces two beers, a fine light lager (Velkopopovický kozel) and a dark special. The place to sample these beers in Prague is »U černého vola« (The Black Ox, Praha 1, Loretánské náměstí 1).

Prague breweries

There are still four breweries in Prague. The largest of them is the one in Smíchov district, which produces a light lager (Staropramen = Old Spring). Smíchover is served, for instance, in »U Glaubiců« (Praha 1, Malostranské náměstí 5) and in »U dvou srdci« (The Two Hearts, Praha 1, U lužického semináře 38).

In Braník district a light and a dark beer are brewed. Both are available in »U svatého Tomáše« (St Thomas, Praha 1, Letenská 12), the cellar of the former Augustinian brewery, which produced its own beer up to 1950 (currently undergoing refurbishment). In »U supa« (The Vulture, Praha 1, Celetná 22), which has been serving beer since the 14th century, the light beer is on tap. In Holešovice brewery a 10% cask beer, »Měštan«, is brewed.

A real Prague institution is the city's last genuine house-brewery, »U Fleků« (Praha 1, Křemencova 11), which has been brewing a strong dark beer since 1299. However, these days the place is turning into a tourist trap. Beware the waiter's pressing offer of a – apparently gratis – drink (e.g. becherovka): everything will appear on the bill, at a hefty price. Moreover, listed prices do not include service. Nonetheless, »U Fleků« offers an unparalleled atmosphere with its rambling, smoke-filled tap-rooms, and beer garden in summer. The tavern is also famous for its traditional Czech cabaret.

Author Jaroslav Hašek and his hero Švejk were regulars at the beer tavern »U Kalicha« (Praha 2, Na bojišti 13), which unfortunately is usually overcrowded nowadays.

Spirits »Hard« spirits produced in the country include: slivovice (plum schnaps) from Moravian Slovakia, meruňkovice (made from apricots), žitná or režná (corn schnaps) and jalovcová or borovička (juniper schnaps). After a heavy meal many people swear by Karlovy Vary becherovka, an excellent digestive liqueur.

Coffee and tea Coffee is prepared and served in Turkish style (complete with grounds). Espresso has to be specially requested; Viennese coffee with lashings of whipped cream may also be available. Tea (čaj), milk (mléko) and »juice« are on offer everywhere.

Restaurants

In Prague the gastronomy scene has become more colourful, as has the range of hotels: in addition to traditional Bohemian eateries (▸ Food and Drink), there are now international restaurants throughout the city. Many wine bars and taverns also offer hot food.
In most places the kitchen is **open all day**, usually 10am–11pm.
Service is included in all prices; but for good service it is customary to give a **tip** of 5–10 %.

▶ RECOMMENDED RESTAURANTS

EXPENSIVE

▸ ① **etc. see map p.60/61.**

▸ **Price categories**
Expensive:
from CZK1000 (£27/US$50)
Moderate:
CZK500 – CZK1000
(£13.50/US$25/–£27/US$50/)
Inexpensive:
under CZK500 (£13.50/US$25)

▸ ⑥ **U Malířů
(Painters' House)**
Praha 1
Maltézské náměstí 11
Tel. 257 530 000, 257 530 318
www.umaliru.cz
daily 11.30am–midnight
Brightly-coloured 1930s frescoes adorn the medieval vaulting in the dining-room. Haute cuisine delights are served – try the guinea fowl risotto with truffles.

▸ ⑬ **Hoffmeister**
Praha 1, Pod Bruskou 7
Tel. 251 017 133
www.hoffmeister.cz
daily noon–3pm,
6.30pm–11.30pm
French culinary creations as well as traditional Bohemian fare – and artwork by the owner's father, whose original drawings adorn the elaborately decorated diningroom.

▸ ⑫ **Kampa Park**
Praha 1, Na Kampě 8 b
Tel. 257 532 685
www.kampapark.cz
daily 11am–1am
Restaurant with view of the Vltava. Light crossover cooking and Czech wines are served. Illustrious guest-list has included Václav Havel, as well as Hillary Clinton, Michael Douglas, Madonna ...

Dinner by candlelight chez Pálffy

⑨ **Pálffy Palác**
Praha 1, Malá Strana,
Valdštejnská 14
Tel. 257 530 522,
www.palffy.cz
daily 11am–midnight
Waiting for Mozart! Salon with
stucco ceiling, recorded music and
candlelight. The romantic atmosphere and view from the garden
up to the castle wall has over-
whelmed Sean Connery, Tom
Cruise and Pavarotti. Traditional
Bohemian recipes with bacon,
game and sheatfish, refined with
thyme, rosemary and cream.
Tempting aromas from the starred
chefs!

① **Peklo (Hell)**
Praha 1, Strahovské nádvoří 1
Tel. 220 516 652
www.peklo.cz
daily noon–11.30pm,
Mon from 6pm
This wine cellar is right next to
Strahov Monastery, in mysterious
catacombs and grottoes.

▶Strahov Monastery, Baedeker
Tip p.243.

㉔ **Pravda**
Praha 1, Pařížská 17
Tel. 222 326 203
www.pravdarestaurant.cz
daily 11am–1am
Eat elegantly in a stylish atmosphere. The Art Deco interior
decoration is in black-and-white
and glitter tones. Cross-cultural
cuisine. Right next to Old-New
Synagogue. Seating outside in
summer.

---

i GOOD VALUE MEALS

- Le Café Colonial: steak paradise with Raj
  ambience
- Pálffy Palác: dinner with Mozart
- Kogo: best Italian restaurant, classy design
- Žofín: Bohemian cooking just like grand-
  mother used to make
- Kolkovna: duck, pork & cabbage in mini-
  brewery
- Rybářský club: for fish, on the waterfront
  (a tip for those in the know)

▸ ⑦ **U Mecenáše (Maecenas)**
Praha 1, Malostranské náměstí 10
Tel. 257 531 631
daily noon–11pm
Excellent Bohemian cooking,
choice wines and a cosy atmosphere are the hallmarks of this
first-class 400-year-old establishment. It is said that in the 17th
century Prague's executioner was a
regular; after the day's work he
liked to enjoy his well-earned
evening respite at the table in the
first room. It is advisable to make a
reservation in the stylishly decorated vault and popular restaurant.

▸ ⑩ **U tří pštrosů
(The Three Ostriches)**
Praha 1, Dražického náměstí 6
Tel. 257 288 888
daily 11.30am–1am
This house, close to Charles
Bridge, belonged to an Armenian
merchant and purveyor to the
court; around 1700, following the
spirit of the times, he traded busily
in ostrich feathers, and founded
Prague's first coffee-house on this
spot. Both hotel and restaurant
still deserve their recommendation.

▸ ⑲ **V Zátiší (Still Life)**
Praha 1, Liliová 1
Tel. 222 220 627
daily noon–3pm,
5pm–11pm
International cuisine, served in two
charming rooms, celebrity venue.
Speciality: duck in lavender sauce.

MODERATE

▸ ⑮ **Hanavský pavilon**
Praha 7, Letenské sady 173
Tel. 233 323 641

Goods on display in Staré Město arcades

www.hanavskypavilon.cz
daily 11am–1am
On Letná hill: a circular panorama terrace over the curve of the Vltava, with view of Charles Bridge in the distance. The cast-iron pavilion, gifted by steel baron Hanavský in 1891, is an Art Nouveau gem, with crystal interior decoration. Speciality: monkfish in pepper sauce.

► ㉙ **La Provence**
Praha 1, Štupartská 9
Tel. 296 826 155
daily noon–11pm
Top restaurant with wines and exquisite cuisine from Provence. Duck breast in honey sauce or coq au vin is served with a quality wine from the extensive list; though it will not come cheap.

► ⑱ **Le Café Colonial**
Praha 1, Široká 6
Tel. 224 818 322
daily 10am–midnight
This café & restaurant in colonial style opposite Pinkasova Synagogue offers an international menu with Asiatic touch and offers good value for money. Young clientele: the university is nearby.

► ⑤ **Nebozízek (Little Drill)**
Praha 1, Petřínské sady 411
Tel. 257 315 329
daily 10am–10pm
Get to this restaurant on Petřín hill (►Petřín) on foot or by the funicular. The excellent food and a wonderful view of Prague are ready and waiting. Book in good time!

► ㉓ **Le Patio**
Praha 1, Staré Město, Národní 22
Tel. 224 934 375
www.lepatio.cz

daily 11am–11pm
The exotic flair of a Moroccan fishing village. Mediterranean cuisine, salads and trendy clientèle.

► ⑧ **Square – Malostranská kavárna**
Praha 1, Malá Strana
Malostranské náměstí 5
Tel. 800 152 672
www.squarerestaurant.cz
daily 8am–1am
Below the massive Baroque splendour of St Nicholas Church: elegant design in historic rooms of Viennese »Café Radetzky«, founded in 1874; graced by Neruda, Kafka and legendary soprano Ema Destinnová. Now painted in trendy wash, with green reinforced glass and stainless steel fittings, a chic venue for mannequin salads, gourmet pizza, pasta and various types of strudel. Atmospheric seating on the terrace alongside the comings and goings of the tram-stop.

► ㉚ **Titanic (in Grand Hotel Evropa)**
Praha 1, Václavské náměstí 29
Tel. 224 228 117
This Art Nouveau restaurant in the hotel basement offers stylish ambience and interior decoration that is well worth a look. The menu features French and Bohemian dishes.
► Wenceslas Square, Baedeker Tip p.260.

► ㉕ **Vysmátý zajíc (The Mischievous Hare)**
Praha 1, Staré Město
Michalská 13
Tel. 224 216 993
www.vysmatyzajic.cz
daily 11am–midnight

Cocktail bar 6pm–3am
A gastronomic experience, staged in old Prague tavern style. Furniture ranging from antique to high-class junk. Czech-Italian specialities: rabbit in garlic, and pasta with poppy seeds and mango. Late-night live music in the bar.

▶ ③ **U Kolovrata**
Praha 1, Valdštejnská 18
Tel. 257 530 729
daily 11am–11pm
Very good wines accompany international and Bohemian food.

▶ ⑭ **Žofín**
Praha 1, Slovanský ostrov 226
Tel. 224 934 548
daily 11.30am–midnight, terrace in summer from 10am
On the Vltava island: waiting for »Daddy«, Emperor Franz Josef – that's what it feels like. Gold plush monarchy ambience, Bohemian food just like grandmother used to make. Divine pancakes strewn with poppy seeds, caramel and cinnamon.

INEXPENSIVE

▶ ⑳ **Klub architekt**
Praha 1, Betlémské náměstí 5a
Tel. 224 401 214
daily 11am–midnight
Stylish cellar vault with modern fittings close to Bethlehem Chapel.
▶Bethlehem Chapel, Baedeker Tip p.125.

▶ ⑯ **Kristian Marco**
Praha 1, Hollar Mooring, Smetanovo nábřeží
Tel. 222 227 330
www.kristian-marco.cz
daily 11am–midnight
Not far from Charles Bridge, the Kristian Marco is the right place

for fish enthusiasts and connoisseurs. Whether carp, pike or trout, everything is served on the upper deck – prepared in all sorts of different ways.

▶ ㉘ **Kogo**
Praha 1, Staré Město
Havelská 499/29
Tel. 224 210 259
www.kogo.cz
Mon–Fri 8am–11pm; Sat, Sun 9am–11pm
1930s portal, designer ambience in black and orange. Best pizza and pasta in town. Chic clientèle, Italian-style.

▶ ㉗ **Kolkovna**
(Revenue Stamp Centre)
Praha 1, Josefov, V Kolkovně 8
Tel. 224 819 701
www.kolkovna.cz
daily 11am–midnight
Yuppies in executive suits favour the good old times: a nostalgic micro-brewery with lots of Monarchy brass and mahogany. Earthy odours of blood and cabbage linger under the green lampshades. Pilsner Urquell foams.

▶ ㉒ **Monarch**
Praha 1, Staré Město
Na Perštýně 15
Tel. 224 239 602
Wine shop: Mon–Fri noon–8pm, Wine bar: Mon–Sat noon–midnight
Wine-dealer, bar and bistro Parisian-style. In the wine-tasting cellar, a select clientèle of Frenchmen, Italians and Spaniards sip and gargle. A strapping lady vintner introduces the top Czech wines in the selection. On the counter is a tempting display of delicious cheeses, ham and bacon, as well as

fondu and quiches. Don't forget
the espresso with your digestive
liqueur!

▶ ④ **Petřinské sady**
Praha 1, Seminářská zahrada 13
Tel. 257 320 688
daily noon–11pm
On the slopes of Petřín hill, set in a
cherry orchard. Panoramic view
from the castle to the Vltava
promenade, the red roofs of Malá
Strana look close enough to touch.
The fiery »Petřín sword« (skew-
ered meat) is grilled on charcoal.

▶ ⑪ **Rybářský klub**
Praha 1, Malá Strana, U Sovových
mlýnů 1, Tel. 257 534 200
daily noon–3pm
6.30pm–10.30pm
A jolly little fisherman's house
right on the Vltava. Perch, trout,
pike, carp, sheatfish, zander specialities, deliciously prepared. Ex-
president Havel's secret tip: sal-
mon with wild mushrooms and
polenta.

▶ ② **U Černého Vola
(The Black Ox)**
Praha 1, Hradčany, Loretánské
náměstí 1
Tel. 220 513 481

daily 10am–11pm
As medieval as it gets, permeated
by the fragrance of Loreta. Royal
coats-of-arms on the walls. Food
here only serves to »support« the
beer – like »utopence« (bacon
sausages drenched in an oily
vinegar decoction). The regulars,
organized as part-owners in a
share company, drink for a good
cause: the net profits go to a home
for the blind. The neighbourhood
share company ensures that
everything stays just the way it was
in olden times.

WHERE TO DRINK BEER
▶Baedeker Special p.76

CAFÉS

▶ ㉟ **Arco**
Praha 1, Hybernská 16/1004
Tel. 974 886 542
Mon–Fri 3pm–9pm, Sat, Sun
10am–9.30pm
Café Arco, like many of the
famous coffee-houses, lives on its
legendary tradition. In the 1920s
Prague's German-speaking authors used to meet here. Today the
café is part of the police canteen.

▶ ㉛ **Evropa**
▶ Restaurants, Wenceslas Square,
Baedeker Tip p.260

▶ ㉞ **Imperial**
Praha 1, Na poříčí 15/1072
Tel. 222 316 012
daily 10am–10pm
The locals' favourite café. The
interior is like Cleopatra's grave,
tiled with lion, sphinx and palm
decoration. Fusion cuisine com-
bines dumplings, vegetarian bur-
gers and strawberry pancakes.
With cream, please! Steamy Dixie
vibes from 9pm.

Egyptian décor in the Imperial

formerly named after the Prague journalist Milena Jesenská (►Famous People), well-known as friend of Franz Kafka. The direct view of the hourly procession of apostles on the Astronomical Clock, over a cup of coffee, is unbeatable.

► ㉝ **Obecní dům**
Praha 1, náměstí Republiky 5
Tel. 222 002 763
daily 7.30am–11pm
The café in the Municipal House has to be seen. The Art Nouveau interior is particularly inviting. In summer there is outside seating, too.

► ㉜ **Paříž**
Praha 1, U obecního domu 1
Tel. 222 195 900
daily 8am–midnight
Another notable hotel café with plenty of atmosphere. Seating at high windows in authentic Art Nouveau ambience. Gold-rimmed plates and cups.

► ㉗ **Slavia**
Praha 1, Národní třída 1
Tel. 224 218 493
daily 8am–midnight
Legendary café opposite the National Theatre, since 1891.
►National Theatre, Baedeker Tip p.196.

► ㊱ **TV Tower**
Praha 3, Mahlerovy sady 1
Tel. 267 005 778
daily 11am–11pm
Delight in sampling the pinnacle of Prague's coffee up on the television tower, along with snacks and apple pie. 120 metres (nearly 400ft) below, the whole city lies at your feet.

► ㉑ **Louvre**
Praha 1, Národní třída 22
Tel. 224 930 949
Mon–Fri 8am–11.30pm,
Sat, Sun from 9am
First-floor café, pleasant mix of Czechs with just a few tourists. The high pastel-coloured walls create a cosy atmosphere. The café is rich in tradition and was closed in 1948, considered a symbol of bourgeois lifestyle; it reopened in 1992. The restaurant offers a varied menu to suit all tastes. There is also a billiard room.

► ㉖ **Grand Café Praha**
Praha 1, Staroměstské náměstí 22
Tel. 221 632 602, www.grandcafe.cz
daily 10am–9pm
This café on Old Town Square was

Health

In the event of illness, consult your hotel reception or tour leader in the first instance. Seriously ill foreign visitors are treated in outpatient clinics, general or specialist hospitals (Czech = nemocnice). The standard of medical care is on the whole adequate. — Medical assistance

 USEFUL ADDRESSES

EMERGENCY SERVICES

▶ **Medical emergency service**
Tel. 1 55

▶ **Accident emergency service**
Tel. 12 30, 12 40

▶ **Emergency**
▶Emergency

▶ **Doctors on call**
Praha 1, Palackého 5
Tel. 224 949 181

▶ **Dentists on call**
Praha 1, Palackého 5
Tel. 224 946 981, 1 41 22
Mon–Fri 7pm–7am,
Sat, Sun 24-hour service

EMERGENCY HOSPITALS

▶ **Na Homolce**
Praha 5, Roentgenova 2
Tel. 257 271 111, www.homolka.cz
In the event of illness any patient receives treatment in any hospital; in Na Homolce hospital there is a special department for foreign private patients, with swimming pool and cafeteria.

PHARMACIES WITH 24-HOUR SERVICE

▶ **Lékarna U Svaté Ludmily**
Praha 2, Belgická 37
Tel. 224 237 207 31

▶ **Lékarna Palackého**
Praha 1, Palackého 5
Tel. 224 94 69 82

Information

 IMPORTANT ADDRESSES

UK (AND REPUBLIC OF IRELAND)

▶ **Czech Tourism**
13 Harley St, London W1G 9QG
Tel. 020 7631 0427
Tel. 09063 640641 for brochures
www.czechtourism.com

USA

▶ **Czech Tourism**
1109 Madison Ave
New York
NY 10028
Tel. 212 288 0830
www.czechtourism.com

CANADA

▸ **Czech Tourist Authority**
2 Bloor Street West, Suite 1500
Toronto, Ontario M4W 3E2
Tel. 416 363 9928
www.czechtourism.com

PRAGUE

▸ **Čedok**
Na příkopě 18, CZ-11135 Praha 1
Tel. 224 197 641
Fax 224 216 324 387
Enquiries of all sorts, reservations
for rail, bus and airline tickets;
bureau de change, city tours,
excursions and tickets for cultural
events; meeting-place for morning
tour »Historic Prague«, day trips
and guided walks.

▸ **Prague Information Service**
Passage Lucerna, Vodičkova 36
Staroměstská radnice
(Old Town Hall)
Staroměstské náměstí 1
postal address:
Betlémské náměstí 2
CZ-11698 Praha 1
Tel. 1 24 44, www.prague-info.cz
There are further information
offices at the main railway station
(Hlavní nádraží) and, from April
to October, in Malá Strana Bridge
Tower (Malostranská mostecká
věž).

Listings are given monthly in
Downtown magazine, with information on cinema and theatre
programmes, concerts, exhibitions
and other events. Prague's cinema
listings and details of other events
can be found at www.prague.tv.
Prague in your pocket appears
every three months; it is a good
guide, with useful addresses, news
of events and tips:
www.in-yourpocket.com.

CZECH EMBASSIES

▸ **In the UK**
26-30 Kensington Palace Gardens
London W8 4QY
Tel. 020 7243 1115
Fax 020 7727 9654
Email: london@embassy.mzv.cz
www.mzv.cz/london/

▸ **In Australia**
8 Culgoa Circuit, O'Malley
Canberra, ACT 2606
Tel. (61-2) 62901386
Fax (61-2) 62900006
Email:
canberra@embassy.mzv.cz

▸ **In Canada**
251 Cooper St.
Ottawa, Ontario K2P0G2
Tel. (613) 562-3875
Fax (613) 562-3878
Email: ottawa@embassy.mzv.cz

▸ **In the Republic of Ireland**
57 Northumberland Road
Ballsbridge, Dublin 4
Tel. +353 1 668 1135
Fax +353 1 668 1660
Email: dublin@embassy.mzv.cz

▸ **In New Zealand**
Honorary Consulate of the Czech
Republic
Level 3, BMW Mini Centre
11-15 Great South Road, New-
market
PO Box 7448 Wellesley Street
Auckland
Tel. +64-9-522-8736

▸ **In the USA**
3900 Spring of Freedom St. NW
Washington, DC 20008
Tel. (202) 274-9100
Fax (202) 966-8540
Email:
washington@embassy.mzv.cz

FOREIGN EMBASSIES IN PRAGUE

► **British embassy**
Thunovská 14, Malá Strana
Tel. 257 402 111, www.britain.cz

► **Australian embassy**
6th floor, Klimentská 10,
Nové Město, tel. 296 578 350
www.embassy.gov.au/cz.html

► **Canadian embassy**
Muchova 6, Bubeneč
Tel. 272 101 800, www.canada.cz

► **Irish embassy**
Tržiště 13, Malá Strana
Tel. 257 530 061
Email: pragueembassy@dfa.ie

► **New Zealand embassy**
Dykova 19, Vinohrady
Tel. 222 514 672
Email: egermayer@nzconsul.cz

► **United States embassy**
Tržiště 15, Malá Strana
Tel. 257 022 000, www.usembassy.cz

INTERNET

► **www.mzv.cz**
The ministry for foreign affairs

homepage offers basic information
about the country.

► **www.prague-hotel-guide.net**
An overview in English of exhibitions and museums can be found
on this site.

► **www.zamky-hrady.cz**
Information about castles and
palaces in the vicinity of Prague;
supplements the list at www.pis.cz.

INTERNET CAFÉS

► **PG Cyber Café**
Praha 5, Village Cinemas, Andel
Tel. 420 774 225 500
www.pgcybercafe.cz
Mon–Fri 9am–5pm, Sat, Sun from
10am

► **Spika**
Praha 1, Dlážděná 4
Tel. 224 21 15 21, fax 224 23 83 87
http://netcafé.spika.cz
Surf the internet during the week for
CZK20 (£0.50/US$1) per 15 min.

► **U Zlaté růže**
Praha 1, Thunovská 21
Tel./fax 575 33 974
www.dafe@internetpoint.cz

Language

In Czech the main stress is always on the first syllable, whereby l and
r as semi-vowels also carry a stress, even when vowels follow (e.g.
Vltava; Brno). In words without a vowel, r carries the stress (e.g.
prst/finger). Czech distinguishes clearly between long and short
vowels. Long vowels have an accent (á, é, í) or a small ring (ů). Y is
always pronounced i. A hook above the letter ě indicates the pronunciation ye (as in yet). Both parts of diphthongs (aj, áj, ej, au, ou)
are pronounced distinctly, stressed on the first part, with j as semi-
vowel y (e.g. kraj/land, auto/car).

Rules of pronunciation

The diacritics are characteristic of Czech; these are: č (pronounced ch), š (like sh), ž (like s in treasure), ř (like r + ž).

CZECH LANGUAGE GUIDE

At a glance

Say ...?	mluvíte ...?
... English?	... anglicky?
... French?	... francouzsky?
... German?	... německy?
I don't understand	nerozumín
yes, indeed	ano
no	ne
please!	prosím!
thank you!	děkuji!
excuse me!/sorry	promiňte!
can you please help me?	Prosím vás, můžete mi pomoci?
good morning!	dobré jitro!
good evening!	dobrý večer!
good night!	dobrou noc!
goodbye!	na shledanou!
man/woman	pán/paní

Out and about

where is ...?	kde je ...?
street, lane	třída/ulice
road to ...	cesta do ...
square	náměstí
travel agent	cestovní kancelář
bank	banka
bureau de change	směnárna
railway station	nádraží
church	kostel
cathedral	chrám
museum	muzeum
when?	kdy?
castle	zámek
open	otevřeno
closed	zavřeno

Accommodation

hotel	hotel

I would like ...	cht lbych/cht labych
room	pokoj
single room	jednolžkový pokoj
twin-bed room	dvoulžkový pokoj
key	kli
toilet	toaleta, záchod
bath	koupelna
guesthouse	hostinec

Illness

doctor	léka
chemist	lékárna
I have a temperature.	Mám hore ku.
It hurts here.	Mám bolesti tady.

Traffic

no entry!	pr jezd zakázán!
one-way traffic	jednosm ná ulice
diversion	objížd'ka
beware!	pozor!
There has been an accident!	stala se nehoda!
right	napravo, vpravo
left	nalevo, vlevo
straight on	pímo
above	naho e
below	dole

Weekdays

Monday	pond l
Tuesday	úterý
Wednesday	st eda
Thursday	tvrtek
Friday	pátek
Saturday	sobota
Sunday	ned le
public holiday	svátek

Numerals

1	jeden, jedna, jedno	3	trí
2	dva, dvě, dvě	4	čtyři

5	pět	18	osmnáct
6	šest	19	devatenáct
7	sedm	20	dvacet
8	osm	30	třicet
9	devět	40	čyřicet
10	deset	50	padesát
11	jedenáct	60	šedesát
12	dvanáct	70	sedmdesát
13	třínáct	80	osmdesát
14	čtrnáct	90	devadesát
15	patnáct	100	sto
16	šestnáct	1000	tisíc
17	sedmnást	million	milión

Breakfast (snidaně)

black coffee	erná káva
coffee with milk	bílá káva
tea with milk	ajs mlékem
hot chocolate	okoĺıda
fruit-juice	džus
eggs and bacon	vejce na slanin
bread	chleba
butter	máslo
sliced sausage	salám
jam	džem

Soups (polévky)

potato soup	bramborová polévka
white cabbage soup with sausage	zelná s klobásou
onion soup	cibulová

Main dishes

roast pork	vep ová
roast duck	kachna pe ená
Wiener schnitzel	smažený ízek
breaded carp	kapr smaženy
roast goose	pe ená husa
goulash	guláš
fish	ryby
... zigane/gipsy-style (with vegetables)	... po cikánsku
trout	pstruh

Side dishes

sauerkraut	zelí
red cabbage	ervené zelí
potato dumplings	bramborové knedlíky
bacon dumplings	špekové knedlíky
boiled potatoes	va erné brambory
chips/fries	smažené hranolky
potato salad	bramborový salát
white cabbage salad	zelný
mixed salad	míchaný

Desserts

fruit dumplings	ovocné knedlíky
pancakes	pala irky
... with fruit and cream	... s ovocem a se šleha kou
cream puff	V rník se šleha kou

Literature & Film

Brod, Max, *Tycho Brahe's Path to God*; Northwestern University Press; New Ed edition (2007)
This historical novel appeared in 1916; Max Brod presents Johannes Kepler and Tycho Brahe not as historic individuals, but as representatives of opposing cosmologies.

Hašek, Jaroslav, *The Good Soldier Švejk*; Penguin Classics (2005)
Under the guise of imbecility Švejk confuses everything and reduces war to absurdity – a symbol of resistance against authority.

Hrabal, Bohumil, *I Served the King of England*; New Directions (2007)
First-person narrative of a gradual ascent to hotel ownership, from Czechoslovakia in the 1930s till shortly after the end of the Communist regime. Realizing that it is worth lifting himself above his lowly origins, the protagonist's claim to have served the king of England eventually leads to his serving the emperor of Abyssinia.

Kisch, Egon Erwin, *The Raging Reporter*; Purdue University Press (1987)

Novels and stories

The journalistic style Kisch developed between 1906 and 1913 as local reporter in Prague is characterized by a certain distance and objectivity. In the early 1920s he travelled widely in Europe, aiming to report on ordinary people, the »hoi polloi«. At the same time, for Kisch the reporter, journalistic activity involved commitment to humanity. His collection of »most remarkable reports« paints a racy picture of the times.

i THE BEST CLASSIC FILMS

- *Kafka* with Jeremy Irons and Theresa Russell (director: Steven Soderbergh): very free interpretation of Kafka's *The Castle*.
- *Amadeus* directed by Prague's Miloš Forman; the city stands in for Vienna.
- *Kolja* (director: Jan Svěrák) is an Oscar-winning tale from Prague; it tells the story of a Russian boy, Kolja, who gets left behind in Prague while his mother tries her luck with a man in the west. A Czech Philharmonic musician plays the »transitional father«.
- *Pan Tau*: the gentleman with umbrella and bowler, always up to his tricks, was a big favourite with the kids. Made in Barrandov film studios.

Kundera, Milan, *The Unbearable Lightness of Being*; Harper Perennial Modern Classics (1999); ISIS Audio Books; Unabridged edition (1999), read by Jonathan Oliver
Against the backdrop of political events and the invasion of Warsaw Pact troops, the love story of Prague surgeon Tomaš and waitress Teresa leads to Zürich and back. The novel gave Milan Kundera his international breakthrough. In 1979 he lost Czech citizenship, as critic of the regime; since then he has lived in France.

Meyrink, Gustav, *The Golem*; Dedalus (2000)
Like many other writers before him who in one way or another used the Golem legend as subject matter, Prague writer Meyrink (1868–1932) also tackled the myth of the artificially created, dumb human being. Created from clay by Rabbi Löw, in Meyrink's novel it becomes a symbol of the Jewish people; the book, written in 1915, ranks among the world's great literary works. ▶ Josefov, Baedeker Tip p.161.

Neruda, Jan, *Tales of the Little Quarter*, ▶Baedeker Tip p.199.

Sherwood, Frances, *The Book of Splendour*; W. W. Norton & Company (2003)
While Emperor Rudolf II, residing in Prague Castle, has scholars search for the elixir of immortality, the sage Rabbi Löw creates Golem. But Jossel, as he calls him, is no soulless lump of clay. When he falls in love with Jewish dressmaker Rachel, there are consequences for the whole of Prague. Set in 1601.

Topol, Jáchym, *City, Sister, Silver*; Catbird Press (2000). Topol's challenging debut captures the post-communist world and its social dislocation. Dark, horrific and hallucinatory, this three parter is influenced by Meyrink's *The Golem* and Dante's *Inferno*.

Keane, John, *Václav Havel*; Basic Books (2001)   Biography
More than 70 people, including Havel's brother Ivan, contributed over a six-year period to the meticulous assembling of dates, details and documents. This is Havel's life as mirror image of political events, and at the same time a close-up view of the Czech nation's inner life. Well researched and well written, a thought-provoking contribution to understanding.

Media

The most popular Czech daily is *Blesk* (Lightning), a typical tabloid.   Czech daily
Other papers with a big circulation are *Mladá fronta Dnes* (Today)   newspapers
and *Lidové Noviny* (People's Paper). Almost all the dailies belong to Swiss, German or French publishing houses.

The critical commentary of the English-language *Prague Post* appears   Newspapers in
weekly on a Wednesday. The *Prague Daily Monitor*provides daily   English
news in English on Czech politics, business and markets, sports, and Prague events. The *Prague Tribune* is a monthly magazine focusing on lifestyle and business in the Czech Republic.

Money

The national currency is called the Koruna Česka (Czech koruna or   Currency
crown, plural koruny), abbreviated to CZK or Kč. The crown is freely convertible. The following banknotes are in circulation: CZK20, 50, 100, 200, 500, 1000, 2000 and 5000. There are coins for CZK1, 2, 5, 10, 20 and 50; and also for 10, 20 and 50 haléř (heller). There are 100 haléř to the crown.

i EXCHANGE RATES

- CZK100 = £2,72
- £1 = CZK36,78
- CZK100 = US$5,47
- US$1 = CZK18,27

Up to CZK200,000 can be **taken in and out of the country free**. Higher sums have to be approved by frontier controls. Other freely convertible currencies are not subject to restrictions. It is expected that the euro will be adopted in 2012.

It is worth comparing charges before changing money: bureaux de   Exchanging
change, travel agents and hotels often charge very high fees – but the-   money
re are exceptions! Misleading »no fee« promotion usually goes hand-in-hand with an unfavourable exchange rate.

Cashpoints/
credit cards
It is possible to get money round the clock at the numerous cash-points in Prague with credit cards and bank cards – combined, of course, with your PIN. Most international credit cards are accepted by banks, hotels, restaurants, car-hire firms and many retailers. If a card is lost, get it stopped at once!

Museums and Exhibitions

Opening times
In general Tue–Sun 10am–5pm, but see the different opening hours given for some museums. The Jewish Museum is open on Monday, closed on Saturday.

▶ PRAGUE'S MUSEUMS

ART

▶ **Prague City Gallery**
  ▶Prague City Gallery

▶ **Galerie D in Dientzenhofer Pavilion**
  ▶Smíchov
  Praha 5, Matoušova 9
  Tue–Sun 10am–1pm
  2pm–6 pm

▶ **»House of the Stone Bell«**
  ▶Old Town Square

▶ **»House at the Black Madonna«**
  ▶Celetná
  Praha 1, Celetná 34
  Tue–Sun 10am–6pm
  Permanent exhibition of Czech Cubism

▶ **Hergertova Cihelna – Prague Jewellery Collection**
  Praha 1, Cihelná 2 b
  Tel. 221 451 400
  daily 10am–6pm
  Luxury goods from 17th century to present day, including Fabergé eggs and Tiffany jewels

▶ **Kampa Museum**
  Praha 1, Kampa Island, U Sovových mlýnů 503
  www.museumkampa.cz
  daily 10am–6pm
  Forbidden art. A Czech million-aire, Jan Mládek, has collected in America what the Communists deemed degenerate. In 2002 an old Renaissance mill was renovated, in an experimental way, to house his collection. A glass balcony allows visitors to hover over the Vltava, while a chair for giants makes for an odd view of Charles Bridge. The interior courtyard features an exciting combination of steel and stone. Relax on the gourmet terrace.

▶ **Museum of Decorative Arts**
  ▶Museum of Decorative Arts

▶ **Lapidarium**
  ▶Stromovka Park

▶ **Mánes Gallery**
  ▶Mánes Exhibition Hall

▶ **Mucha Museum**
  ▶Wenceslas Square

The Museum of Decorative Arts has some splendid items on display.

▶ **Prague City Museum**
  ▶Prague City Museum

▶ **National Gallery**
  ▶Convent of St Agnes, St George's
  Convent in Prague castle, Veletržní Palace, Sternberg Palace,
  www.ngprague.cz

▶ **National Museum**
  ▶National Museum

▶ **Wallenstein Riding School**
  ▶Wallenstein Palace
  Praha 1, Valdštejnská 2

▶ **Strahov Picture Gallery**
  ▶Strahov Monastery

CULTURAL HISTORY/
HISTORY

▶ **Historical Museum**
  ▶National Museum

▶ **Jewish Museum**
  ▶Josefov

▶ **Museum of Communism**
  ▶Na příkopě
  Baedeker Tip p.102.

▶ **Náprstek Museum**
  Praha 1, Betlémské náměstí 1
  Tues–Sun 9am–12.15pm,
  1pm–5.30pm
  free entry on first Friday of the
  month
  Ethnological collection from
  Asian, African and American cultures

▶ **National memorial for victims
  of Heydrich reprisals**
  ▶Charles Square, SS Cyril and
  Methodius

LITERATURE, THEATRE
AND MUSIC

▶ **Dvořák Museum**
  ▶Villa Amerika

▶ **Franz Kafka exhibition**
  Praha 1

náměstí Franze Kafky 5
Tue–Fri 10am–6pm,
Sat 10am–5pm

► **Franz Kafka Museum**
Praha 1, Hergetova Cihelna,
Cihelná 2 b, www.kafkamuseum.cz
March–Dec daily 10am–6pm, Jan/
Feb till 5pm
In the former tile-works on Vltava
waterfront in Malá Strana, this 3-
language display entitled »K's City.
Franz Kafka and Prague« exam-
ines the places where Kafka lived
and the topography of his writing.

► **Mozart Museum**
►Villa Bertramka

► **Museum of Czech Literature**
►White Mountain with Star
Summer Palace

► **Smetana Museum**
►Smetana Museum

MILITARY

► **Military History Museum**
►Hradčany Square

► **Military Museum**
Praha 3, U památníku 2
Nov–April Mon–Fri 9.30am–5pm;
May–Oct Tue–Sun 10am–6pm,
www.militarymuseum.cz

OTHER

► **Museum of the Infant Jesus of Prague**
►Church of our Lady Victorious

► **Museum of Physical Education and Sport**
►Tyrš House

► **Natural Science Museum**
►National Museum

► **National Technical Museum**
►National Technical Museum

► **Pedagogical Museum Komenského**
Praha 1, Valdštejnská 20
Tue–Sun 10am–12.30pm
1pm–5pm, www.pmjak.cz
This museum is dedicated to
humanist pedagogue and philosopher Jan Amos Comenius
(1592–1670)

► **Police Museum**
Praha 2, Ke Karlova 1
Tue–Sun 10am–5pm
The Police Museum and parts of
the State Archive collection are
housed in the Gothic-Baroque
Karlov Monastery; www.mvcr.cz.

► **Post Museum**
Praha 1, Nové mlýny 2
Tue–Sun 9am–11am
2pm–5pm, www.cpost.cz
Display of postage stamps

► **Puppet Museum**
Praha 1, Karlova 12
May–Oct 10am–8pm
Nov–April noon–6pm
Collections of important Czech
wood-carvers' work, and samples
of traditional and modern puppet-
making from home and abroad.

► **Toy Museum**
►Prague Castle, Baedeker Tip
p.235

► **Wax Museum**
Praha 1, Melantrichova 5
www.waxmuseumprague.cz
daily 9am–8pm
Smetana, Dvořák, Mucha and
other illustrious personalities from
politics, sport, music and show
business.

Post and Communications

Postage stamps (známky) are obtainable from post offices, tobacconists and newsagents. Postage to all European countries for letters up to 20g/0.7oz and postcards is CZK11 (£0.30/€0.41).

Telephone

Phone cards are supplied by I-Call, Karta X, NetCall 55 and Smartcall. Cards with different numbers of units (for CZK200, CZK320, CZK400, CZK460 and CZK600) are obtainable from newsagents, post offices, hotels and travel agents. Local calls from public telephone kiosks cost CZK4.

Mobile phones

The Czech mobile networks function throughout the country with providers T-Mobile CZ, Eurotel and OskarVodafone. Sometimes it is worth comparing prices and connecting manually, in order to minimize roaming charges.

DIALLING CODES

▶ **Dialling codes to Prague**
from the Czech Republic 0
from the UK and Republic of Ireland:
Tel. 00 42 0
from the USA, Canada and Australia:
Tel. 00 11 42 0

▶ **Dialling codes from Prague**
to the UK:
tel. 00 44

to the Republic of Ireland:
Tel. 00 353
to the USA and Canada: tel. 00 1
to Australia: tel. 00 61
The 0 that precedes the subsequent local area code is omitted.

DIRECTORY ENQUIRIES

▶ **National**
Tel. 11 80

▶ **International**
Tel. 11 81

Prices and Discounts

EU expansion to the east, prices from the west

The days of art and entertainment costing next-to-nothing are over in Prague. Museum and gallery prices in particular are now quite high. So it is worth investing in a »gift entry card« (dárková vstupenka): it gives access to all locations of the multi-site National Gallery for CZK500 (£13.50/US$25) per person, or CZK900 (£24/US$45) for two. Cultural organizations celebrate their anniversaries or special jubilees by offering free entry (details online). The tourist card offers a favourable rate for metro, tram and bus: 24 hours for CZK80/£2/US$4 (obtainable from ticket machines), 3 days for CZK220 (£6/

▶ WHAT DOES IT COST?

3-course meal from £18/ CZK660	**Simple meal** from £6/ CZK210	**Cup of coffee** £1.50/ CZK50	**Metro ride** from £0,35/ CZK13	**Double room** from £57/ CZK2000

US$11), and weekly ticket for CZK280 (£7.50/US$14). The charge for two weeks is almost a »free gift« – just CZK320 (£9/US$1). Obtainable from metro stations, kiosks and hotels.

Shopping

Paris, London, Prague

Stroll along luxury boulevards. Shop in glamourous palaces. Hunt for top brands in revamped department stores. With the aroma of cappuccino wafting around, shopping in Prague is up there with Paris and London. A typical feature in the city are the embedded shopping arcades: labyrinths with high ceilings, arches and wide steps. Nostalgic Art Nouveau architecture has been modernized with reinforced glass and stainless steel. Cool colours and bold structures contrast excitingly with old façades. The designer interior sets the tone. With Renaissance stucco ceilings, wrought-iron balustrades and original Art Deco lamps, some international stores (H & M, Mango, Bogner, Versace) offer shops in Prague's city centre boasting the best atmosphere of their entire chain.

Presents

Bohemian glass is famous all over the world; it can come as beautifully cut glass, and in glorious colours. Bohemian porcelain and garnet jewellery are also very popular. Other favourite souvenirs are pewter jewellery, ceramics, pillow-lace items, all sorts of wood carvings, splendidly embroidered mats, cloths and traditional clothing, toys, Christmas cribs, books, artwork, puppets, sports items, and the typical drinks (▶ Beer; also plum schnaps »slivovice«, digestive liqueur »becherovka«) and food items (Prague ham, Znaim pickled gherkins, sausages etc) from Prague and the surrounding region. Second-hand bookshops and antique shops are also much lauded.

Antiques

Since export duties may be payable on antiques, it is advisable to make enquiries at the airport customs office (Celní úřad Praha, Praha 6, tel. 166 090 996, www.cs.mfcr.cz).

SHOPPING ADDRESSES

ANTIQUE DEALERS

► **Art Décoratif**
Praha 1, Melantrichova 5
www.artdecoratif.cz
Designs based on exhibits in
Prague museums

► **Dorotheum Prag**
Praha 1, Ovocný trh 580/2
www.dorotheum.cz
Europe's largest auction house
came to Prague in 2003.

► **Pod Kinskou**
Praha 5, Náměstí Kinských 7
www.antiques-shop.cz
Specializing in paintings and antique furniture

DEPARTMENT STORES

► **Anděl City**
Praha 5, Smíchov, Radlická 1 b
daily 7am–midnight
Hip! French shopping at Carre-
four, boutiques with top Italian
brands. Trendy corners offering
cappuccino, bubbly and sushi.
Right next to the metro: line B,
Andel

► **Tesco**
Praha 1, Národní třída 26
8am–9pm, Sat 9am–8pm
Sun 10am–7pm

Right beside metro station Národní třída, this is a good place to
do some quick shopping at almost
any time, especially for food.

► **Kotva**
Praha 1, náměstí Republiky 8
www.od-kotva.cz
9am–8pm, Sat 9am–6pm
Sun 10am–6pm
»Kotva« (Anchor), the one-time
consumer flagship of Socialism,
still a good place for a little
schnaps. With gourmet paradise
in the basement.

Searching for top brands

»Your business is your home« – Prague has adapted its opening
hours to this old Jewish saying. Most shops are open till 8pm; large
stores till 10pm; supermarkets and hypermarkets in the new shopping centres till midnight. Moreover, the early morning shift starts
here at 7am. On Saturdays the large stores close at 7pm. On Sunday
most shops are open again from noon, at least till 6pm; in the centre,
longer. There is no law on closing times in tourist areas. Shops close
when the last customer leaves.

Opening hours

Sport and Outdoors

Ice hockey Winners of Olympic gold in 1998 in Nagano, the Czech team (without Slovakia) have been world champions four times. Together with Ostrava, Prague hosted the World Championships of 2004, but the Czechs were knocked out. Ice hockey has a long tradition for the Czechs, and is as popular as football with the general public. During the Communist era, games against the Soviet Union were seen as covert »wars of resistance«. On two occasions the ČSSR team succeeded in beating the Russian »Zbornaja kommanda«, winning the World Championships of 1972 in Prague, and even winning in Moscow in 1985, the latter victory being regarded as a good omen for the impending end of Kremlin domination. Two Czech ice hockey heroes became legends in North America's National Hockey League: goalkeeper Hašek and forward Jágr.

In the Czech league (Extraliga ledního hokeje), 14 teams compete.

 SPECTATOR SPORT

ICE HOCKEY

▶ **HC Sparta Praha (Paegas Aréna)**
Praha 7, Za Elektrárnou 419
Tel. 266 727 454
www.hcsparta.cz

▶ **SK Slavia**
Praha 10, Vladivostocká 10
Tel. 267 311 102, www.skslavia.cz

STADIUM

▶ **Sazka Arena**
Praha 9, Ocelářská 2
Tickets tel. 266 121 122
www.sazkaticket.cz
Round as a saucer: the most modern multi-purpose venue in Europe, built for the ice hockey World Championship of 2004, in the record time of only two years. The ice-rink can be transformed overnight into a stage.

FOOTBALL

▶ **AC Sparta Praha**
Praha 7, Milady Horákové 98
Tickets tel. 296 111 336, 296 111 400, www.sparta.cz
Entry prices: National League CZK60–210 (£1.60–5.60/US$3–10); European games, Champions' League CZK400–900 (£10.75–24/US$20–45). Sparta is traditionally top of the table, with a success rate comparable to Manchester United.

▶ **FK Viktoria Žižkov**
Praha 3, Seifertova
Tel. 222 712 503
www.fkviktoriazizkov.cz
Nicknamed »Viktorka«, the people's club in working-class district of Žižkov. Usually fighting relegation.

▶ **SK Slavia Praha**
Praha 10
Vladivostocká 2
Tel. 267 311 102, 233 081 753
www.skslavia.cz
Sparta's rival, and likewise one of the top five in the table.

There are 16 teams competing for the National League cup, and Pra-   Football
gue has three teams in the competition: Sparta, Slavia and Viktoria.
A fourth eleven, the legendary Bohemia, is labouring in the regional
league. Altogether Prague has 125 associations registered for competitions. The beautiful game is Prague's life.

Theatre · Concerts

Theatre, opera and concert tickets should be purchased in advance,   Tickets in
either at the theatre itself or from agents, who will take a fee. The of-   advance
fices of Prague Information Office (PIS, ►Information) also sell tickets. Take care with tickets offered for sale on the street.

 INFORMATION

TICKETS IN ADVANCE

► **Bohemia Ticket
International**
Praha 1, Na příkopě 16
Tel. 224 215 031
www.bohemiaticket.cz
Mon–Fri 10am–7pm
Sat until 5pm, Sun until 3pm

► **Ticketpro**
Praha 1, Salvátorská 10
Tel. 224 816 020
www.ticketpro.cz
Mon–Fri 9am–noon
1pm–5.15pm

MUSIC · CLASSICAL

► **National Theatre
(Národní divadlo)**
Praha 1, Národní třída 2
Tel. 224 901 668
www.narodni-divadlo.cz
www.national-theater.cz
Czech works, avant-garde and
Verdi. The latest hit: *Nagano*, the
1998 Olympic gold medal for ice
hockey in Nagano presented as
opera.

► **State Opera
(Státní opera Praha)**
Praha 1, Vinohrady, Legerova 75
Tel 296 117 111, www.opera.cz

► **Estates Theatre
(Stavovské divadlo)**
Praha 1, Staré Město
Ovocný trh 1
Tel. 224 215 001
www.stavovskedivadlo.cz

CONCERTS

Good acoustics in Prague
churches: concerts take place in
the Convent of St Agnes, St
George's Basilica, the churches of
St Gall, St Ursula and St Nicholas,
and in St James.

► **Rudolfinum
(Dvořák and Suk Hall)**
Praha 1, Staré Město
Alšovo nábřeži 12
Tel. 227 059 352
www.ceskafilharmonie.cz
Home of the Czech Philharmonic,
final concert of »Prague Spring«
given here every year.

Magnificent Estates Theatre

▶ **U kamenného zvonu**
(»House of the Stone Bell«)
Praha 1, Staroměstské náměstí 13
Tel. 224 827 526
Early music, medieval to Baroque,
including unknown masters.

▶ **Obecní dům**
(Municipal House)
Praha 1, Staré Město
náměsti republiky 5
Tel. 222 312 048
www.obecnidum.cz
Opening concert of »Prague
Spring« in Smetana Hall. Finest
Art Nouveau ambience.

▶ **Villa Bertramka**
Praha 5, Mozartova 169
Tel. 257 316 753
www.betramka.cz
Mozart concerts with gold dress-
coat and wig.
Violins float upon Prague's sum-
mer breeze. Malá Strana palaces
open their gardens for serenades:
Wallenstein, Ledeburg, Pálffy,

Royal Gardens Ballroom, Belvedere Pavilion, and the courtyard in
Villa Amerika (Dvorák Museum).
Information and tickets: www.via-
musica.cz, www.bohemiaticket.cz;
email: order@bohemiaticket.cz

PRAGUE SPRING

The »Prague Spring« music festival
(mid-May – early June) has an
international reputation. Festival
concerts take place in Artists'
House, Culture Palace, churches
or other historic
settings, some even in Prague's
Baroque gardens (information by
poster).

MUSIC/CABARET

▶ **Rococo Theatre**
(Divadlo Rokoko)
Praha 1, Václavské náměstí 38

JAZZ

▶ **Reduta**
Praha 1, Národní třída 20
Tel. 224 933 487

www.redutajazzclub.cz
Oldest jazz club in Europe still in existence. Special distinction: Bill Clinton's saxophone.

▶ **Agharta Jazz Centrum**
Praha 1, Železná 16
Tel. 222 211 275
www.agharta.cz
Best jazz club, according to many locals; live music daily 9pm–midnight

▶ **Lucerna**
Praha 1, Vodičkova 36
Tel. 224 215 186
www.hospodalucerna.cz
International jazz scene, stars and sessions. Start: 9pm. The longest nights of music finally fade here.

▶ **Metropolitan Jazz Club**
Praha 1, Jungmannova 14
Tel. 224 947 777
For »Fats Blues«, evergreens, swing, bebop. The golden oldies can swing.

ROCK AND POP CONCERTS

▶ **Křižikova fontana**
Praha 7, Výstaviště (Exhibition Grounds), Tel. 220 103 224
www.krizikovafontana.cz
From Orff to Orpheus: Carmina Burana, Dance of the Vampire and U 2. Hourly light & sound show by the fountains in summer 8pm–11pm.

▶ **Rock Café**
Praha 1, Národní 20
Tel. 224 933 947
www.rockcafe.cz
daily 10am–3am, Rock concerts from 9pm

THEATRE

▶ **Culture Palace (Kongresové Centrum)**
Praha 4, 5. května 65
Mixed programme

▶ **Laterna Magica**
Praha 1, Národní třída 4
www.laterna.cz
Multi-vision laser, »black light«

Laterna Magica: between illusion and reality

theatre, video, mobiles, mime, ballet and dance. Gold medal at Expo 1958 in Brussels. Newly staged in the style of the times. Casanova, Graffiti and Star Wars.

▶ **Music Theatre in Karlín (Hudební divadlo v Karlíně)**
Praha 8, Křižíkova 10
www.hdk.cz
Operetta, musicals

▶ **National Theatre (Národní divadlo)**
Praha 1, Národní třída 2
www.narodni-divadlo.cz
Opera, ballet, theatre

▶ **Nová scéna**
Praha 1, Národní třída 4
Ballet, theatre

▶ **Semafore Theatre (Divadlo Semafor)**
Praha 1, Jungmannova 1
www.semafor.cz
Musical comedy

▶ **Prague State Opera (Státní opera Praha)**
Praha 1, Wilsonova 4
www.opera.cz
Opera, ballet

TOP EVENTS

- Agharta Jazz Centrum: jazz and syncopation »east meets west«
- Estates Theatre (Stavovské divadlo): Mozart's *Don Giovanni*
- Křižikova fontana: light & sound show by the fountain
- Villa Bertramka: *A Little Night Music* in Mozart costume
- Obecní dům (Municipal House): classical music in Prague's most beautiful Art Nouveau hall

▶ **Estates Theatre (Stavovské divadlo)**
Praha 1, Ovocný trh 1
www.stavovskedivadlo.cz
Opera, ballet, theatre

▶ **Theatre on the Balustrade (Divadlo na zábradlí)**
Praha 1, Anenské náměstí 5
www.nazabradli.cz
Theatre and mime in the tradition of Ladislav Fialka (died 1991)

▶ **Kolowrat Theatre (Divadlo Kolowrat)**
Praha 1, Ovocný trh 6
Opera, ballet, theatre

SATIRICAL THEATRE · CABARET

▶ **Rococo Theatre (Divadlo Rokoko)**
Praha 1, Václavské náměstí 38
Music and theatre

▶ **U Fleků**
Praha 1, Křemencova 11
www.ufleku.cz
Traditional Czech cabaret

▶ **Varieté Praga**
Praha 1, Vodičkova 30

▶ **Viola's Wine Bar**
Praha 1, Národní třída 7
Poetry readings, jazz

CHILDREN AND YOUNG PEOPLE'S THEATRE

▶ **Puppet World (Říše loutek) National Puppet Theatre**
Praha 1, Žatecká 1

▶ **Spejbl and Hurvínek (Divadlo Spejbla a Hurvínka)**
Praha 6, Dejvická 38
www.speijbl-hurvinek.cz
Puppet theatre

Time

In the winter half-year Prague follows **Central European time (CET)**. For the period from April to September, the Czech Republic has introduced **summer time** (Central European time + 1 h).

Tours and Guides

Local travel agents organize numerous bus-tours and walks to the loveliest places in the Golden City. Prague Information Service (PIS) can also provide guides for individual tours.

The bus-tour »Historic Prague« is very impressive; it ends with a walk through Prague castle. A ride on the little sightseeing train or in one of the horse-drawn coaches, both starting from Old Town Square, can be rewarding. Another good alternative is a leisurely walk through the historic city centre, followed by a ride on the funicular up Petřín hill, and a further walk to Strahov Monastery, Loreta and Prague Castle.

⏵ TOUR ORGANIZERS

► **Prague Information Service (PIS)**
Old Town Hall
Tel. 224 482 562, 221 444
Fax 224 482 380
www.pis.cz

► **Bohemia Travel Service (BTS)**
Gray Line Prague, Palác Vltava, Revolucni 25, Praha 1
Tel. 224 826 262, fax 224 826 261
Individual and group tours; Prague by night, excursions to Karlštejn, Konopiště, Kutná Hora etc. Guests are picked up at their hotel.

► **Daily Walks in Prague**
Tel./fax 281 917 642
www.walks.cz
Meeting-point by the Astronomical Clock on ►Old Town Hall. In addition to standard city tours there are Prague pub walks, tours with music as their theme, and a »Traces of Communism« trail.

► **Precious Legacy Tours**
Praha 1, Kaprová 13
Tel. 222 321 954
Fax 224 721 068
Alongside the usual sightseeing tours, there is a strong emphasis on Jewish life in Prague: guided tours of the Jewish quarter; Jewish Prague by night; Prague from the viewpoint of famous Jewish personalities, from Rabbi Löw to Franz Kafka.

► **Trip on the Vltava**
►Transport, by boat

Transport

By Car

Vignette For travel on motorways or comparable expressways a vignette is required, obtainable at border crossings, some petrol stations and post offices. A vignette lasting a year currently costs CZK900 (£24/US$45/€34), one month CZK300 (£8/US$15/€11) and seven days CZK200 (£5.40/US$10/€7.50). Anyone caught without a vignette should expect a hefty fine.

Traffic regulations Traffic regulations in the Czech Republic are the same as in most other European countries. There are heavy penalties for non-compliance. There is a **zero** alcohol limit. The **maximum speed** on motorways and expressways for cars, motorcycles and camper vans up to 3.5t is 80mph/130kmh (camper vans over 3.5t and cars with trailer 50mph/80kmh); on country roads for cars, motorcycles and camper vans up to 3.5t, 55mph/90kmh (camper vans over 3.5t and cars with trailer 50mph/80kmh); in built-up areas the limit is 30mph/50kmh unless otherwise indicated.

! *Baedeker* TIP

Beware of unofficial taxis

In order to avoid potentially difficult situations, it is best when hailing a taxi to avoid any that are not officially licensed, especially at tourist hotspots. Taxis ordered by phone are preferable (see main text). Many hotels offer a special taxi service.

Taxis can be hired at taxi ranks, hailed as they pass or ordered by phone. As a tourist in Prague it is essential to ensure that the driver has turned on the taximeter; alternatively, agree a fixed price beforehand. Taxi drivers, and others, usually have at least basic English and do not take advantage of tourists. The initial charge is CZK30 (£0.80/US$1.50/€1.25), each additional kilometre costs CZK22 (£0.60/US$1/€0.80). (AAA Radiotaxi tel. 1 40 14; Citytaxi tel. 233 103 310 and Halotaxi tel. 244 114 411.)

By Boat

Boat trips on the Vltava The landing-stage for Vltava passenger ships is close to Palacký Bridge (Palackého most), on Rašínovo nábřež quay. From May to September boat tours organized by the Prague steamship company (Pražská paroplavební společnost) leave here every half-hour; they offer a good overview of Prague (tel. 224 931 013, fax 224 930 022). In addition, motor boats depart from Palacký Bridge for recreational destinations around Prague with delightful scenery, such as Slapy Reservoir on the Vltava or Roztoky Castle.

In addition to conventional boat trips on the Vltava, »Evropská Vodní Doprava«, with its landing-stage by Čechův most opposite

Hotel Intercontinental, offers night cruises; it also hires out boats for special tours or private parties by arrangement (tel. 224 810 030, fax 224 810 003, www.evd.cz).

Public Transport in the City

Adult tickets for tram, city bus and metro cost CZK20 (£0.50/US$1/ €0.75). Short journey tickets for CZK14 (£0.38/US$0.70/€0.50) are valid for tram or bus journeys lasting a maximum of 20 minutes, with no changing; and for a metro journey of a maximum of five stops, line change permitted. Tickets (jízdenky) are obtainable at metro stations, in most hotels, at railway stations, newspaper stands, newsagents and transport company offices. Tickets have to be stamped at the start of the journey. Day tickets are valid for 24 hours; tickets for 3, 7 or 15 days are also available.

Bus, tram

On the main routes, trams and buses operate round the clock at intervals of 7–15 minutes; at night every 20–40 minutes. Red city buses link metro stations with the new residential areas on the outskirts of the city.

For the **underground railway (metro)**, use the same tickets as for the tram (see ▸above). Single tickets, like those for tram and bus, are valid for one hour. The first metro departs at 5am, the last shortly before midnight, from each end of each line.

Prague Metro

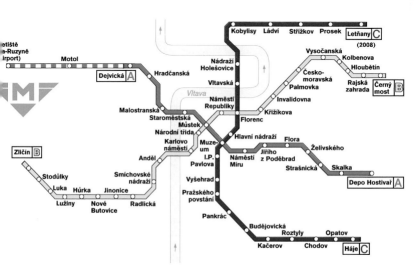

USEFUL ADDRESSES

HELP ON THE ROAD

▶ **Ústřední automotoklub (UAMK)**
Na strži 9, CZ-14002 Praha 4
Tel. 261 10 43 33
Tel. 12 30 (breakdown service)
Fax 261 10 43 78
Email: turist@uamk.cz
www.uamk.cz

▶ **Road maintenance (Silňiční Služba)**
Opletalova 21
CZ-11000 Praha 1
Tel. 2 22 24, 12 57

BUS & RAIL

▶ **www.dpp.cz**
Official homepage of Prague public transport, also in English

▶ **www.jizdnirady.cz**
Timetables and ticket offices of Czech bus companies

▶ **www.vlak-bus.cz**
Official website of Czech rail and bus companies, with timetable, rail connections and bus prices for the entire Czech Republic.

Travellers with Disabilities

A number of institutions offer information about places that make suitable provision for disabled travellers, organize group travel, find trained travel assistants, and provide help with individual travel arrangements.

Prague is not yet very well geared to those with special needs. Many public buildings are accessible only via steps. The Prague association for the disabled, »Sdružení zdravotně postižených«, does however offer wheelchairs on loan and hires out specially adapted cars.

 ADDRESSES

▶ **RADAR (UK)**
12 City Forum, 250 City Road
London EC1V 8AF
Tel. 020 7250 3222
Fax: 020 7250 0212
www.radar.org.uk

▶ **Mobility International USA**
132 E. Broadway, Suite 343
Eugene, Oregon USA 97401
Tel. (541) 343-1284

Fax: (541) 343-6812
www.miusa.org

▶ **Sdružení zdravotně postižených**
Praha 8, Karlínské náměstí 12
Tel. 224 81 69 07

▶ **Czech Rail**
Tel. 224 61 56 33
www.cd.cz

Czech Rail also provides help for travellers with disabilities, makes special compartments available, and organizes travel to the railway station. These services have to be booked at least four days in advance.

When to Go

In spring, from about mid-April, Prague has a special charm, with flowering fruit trees on the slopes beside the Vltava. An additional attraction at this time of year is the traditional annual »Prague Spring« music festival (▶Theatre, Concerts, Musicals). The temperature in summer is as would be expected in central Europe, whereby the highest average temperature is in July; but that is also the month with the heaviest downpours because of frequent storms (maximum temperature 24°C/75°F, rainfall 70mm/ 2.75in). Autumn, with temperate weather, is also a very good time to visit the Golden City. The coldest month in the not very snowy winter is January, with an average minimum temperature of -4°C/25°F.

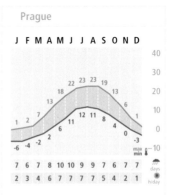

Tours

NO NEED FOR A LIMOUSINE TO
GET AROUND THE CITY. THE
BEST WAY TO SEE PRAGUE IS
ON FOOT.

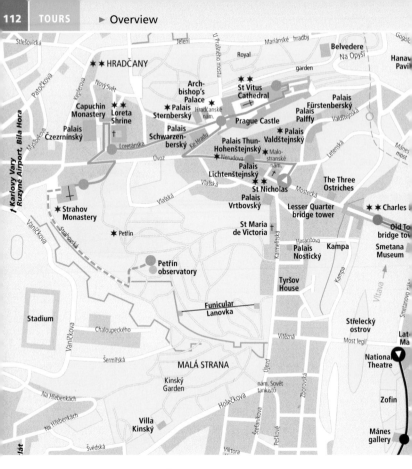

Three walks – when you've taken these you will have seen the most important sights in Prague. But a few side trips are worthwhile, too.

━━━ **TOUR 1**   **From the Lesser Quarter to the Petřín**
Prague's Lesser Quarter, rich in history, along with Hradčany Square, Loreta and Strahov Monastery are the best way to start a visit to the city.   ▶ **page 115**

━━━ **TOUR 2**   **From Wenceslas Square to Charles Bridge**
Wenceslas Square, Old Town Square, Josefov and Charles Bridge are the highlights of the second tour.   ▶ **page 117**

━━━ **TOUR 3**   **From the National Theatre to Vyšehrad**
Off the beaten paths ... that's what this third walk through Prague could be called, for the new city beyond the historic centre also has something to offer...   ▶ **page 119**

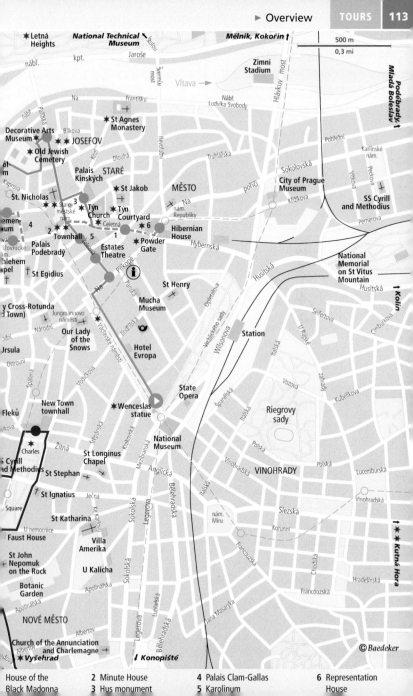

House of the
Black Madonna

2 Minute House
3 Hus monument

4 Palais Clam-Gallas
5 Karolinum

6 Representation
House

Getting Around in Prague

A trip to Prague is becoming ever more inviting – thanks to cheap flights – and is worthwhile even for a short weekend break. The average visitor to Prague stays three or four days. One of the things that make the modern metropolis attractive is that all the sights are very centrally located, and can easily be reached on foot. A good tip for anyone who wants to enjoy a first look at Prague in comfort is to take a ride on the number 22 tram, which goes past Prague Castle, Malá Strana Square (Malostranské náměstí), the National Theatre (Národní divadlo) and the New Town Hall in Nové Město in less than 20 minutes. It is possible to get off and take a closer look at anything of particular interest. The Metro underground railway is quicker, and the network plan is clearly displayed, but there is far less to look at. All the same, the Metro is a useful alternative on occasion. The bus is the best means of transport for the outer suburbs. There is little point driving a car in Prague. Finding somewhere to park is problematic, and most places are well served by public transport. It is best to be cautious with taxis, and advisable to call a radio taxi. Prague, the furthest west of the capital cities in the former eastern bloc, is changing at a pace scarcely matched in any other European metropolis – and this started well before the country joined the EU. Try to plan a visit before the last façade has been restored, so as not to miss the charm of the rapidly fading past.

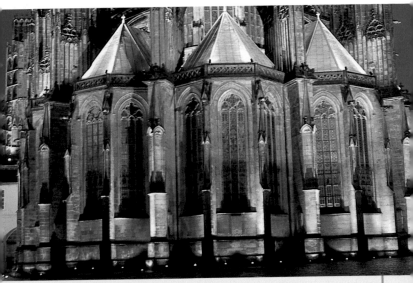

The genius Pater Parler immortalized himself in the radiating chapels on St Vitus Cathedral.

Tour 1 Malá Strana (Lesser Quarter)

Duration: 1 day
Destination: Petřín

Start: Malá Strana Square

The best way to begin a visit to Prague is with a tour of Malá Strana (the Lesser or Little Quarter), taking in Prague Castle (Pražský hrad), the city's undisputed highlight, which alone requires half a day. Add to it Malá Strana Square (Malostranské náměsti), the Loreta, and Strahov Monastery (Strahovský klášter), and the day is full.

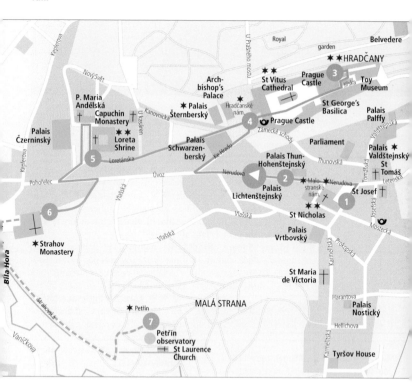

Idyllic Malá Strana spreads out along the left bank of the Vltava. The imposing ✷ ✷ **Church of St Nicholas (Sv Mikuláš)** in the middle of ❶ ✷ **Malá Strana Square** is considered a prime example of High Baroque architecture. The cobbled street ❷ ✷ **Nerudova** is named after Jan Neruda, Czech author of *Tales of the Little Quarter*. It runs

Beautifully located: Strahov Monastery

west from the square and is lined with magnificent late-Baroque burgher houses. Stroll along it as far as the turning »Ke Hradu«; these steps lead up to Prague Castle. ➌ ✸ ✸ **Prague Castle** (Pražský hrad; since 1918 the official seat of the president of the republic) is the high point of the tour, with the ✸ ✸ **Royal Palace**, ✸ ✸ **St Vitus Cathedral**, St George's Basilica, the valuable Bohemian Mannerism and Baroque collection in the adjacent Benedictine nunnery, and the famous Golden Lane (Zlatá ulička).

➍ ✸ **Hradčany Square (Hradčanské náměstí)** is flanked by the Archbishop's Palace and the former Schwarzenberský Palace with the Military History Museum (Vojenské historické muzeum). Not yet tired? A short detour via Loretánská ulička can take in the ➎ ✸ ✸ **Loreta pilgrimage shrine on Loreta Square (Loretánské náměstí)**. Those who still haven't seen enough can take a look at ➏ ✸ **Strahov Monastery (Strahovský klášter)**, highly recommended for its two ✸ ✸ libraries. If the stay in Prague is to last more than a couple of days, then this first day's tour can be shortened, reserving the visit to ➌ ✸ ✸ **Prague Castle** and the pilgrimage shrine ➎ ✸ ✸ **Loreta** for the

! *Baedeker* TIP

The royal route

Why not follow the traditional coronation route taken by the Bohemian kings and emperors? Such processions began at Vyšehrad and led to the Powder Gate, continued on Celetná diagonally across Old Town Square, over Charles Bridge and on to St Vitus Cathedral in Hradany.

morning of the second day. Then the afternoon can be spent on a visit to the famous library of ⑥ ✳ **Strahov Monastery,** followed by a walk on the wooded ⑦ ✳ **Petřín** hill. Look down from the Petřín lookout tower (Prague's Eiffel Tower) at all the sights seen so far.

Tour 2   Staré Město (Old Town)

Duration: 1 day   **Start:** Wenceslas Square
Destination: Charles Bridge

This second tour is devoted to the sights of Staré Město, with Wenceslas Square (Václavské náměsti, very important in the city's recent past), historic Old Town Square (Staroměstské náměsti), the interesting Josefov district, and Charles Bridge (Karlův most).

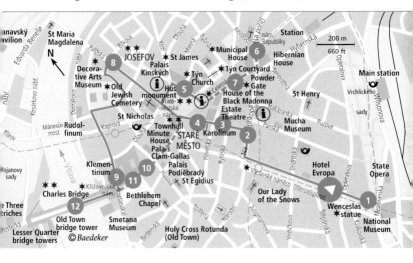

The recommended starting-point is ❶ ✳ **Wenceslas Square** where so much has happened, in the »Golden Cross«. A good meeting-place in this »boulevard« is the bronze Wenceslas monument (Pomník svatého Václava) opposite the **National Museum (Národní muzeum)**. Historic Staré Město begins at the north end of the square, from which point the popular pedestrian zone ❷ **Na přikopě (On the Moat)** runs east. Železná runs from the ❸ **Estates Theatre (Stavovské divadlo)**, in which Mozart's *Don Giovanni* was first performed in 1787, to the ❹ **Karolinum**, founded by Charles IV in 1348 and the oldest university in central Europe, and on to historic ❺ ✳ ✳ **Old Town Square (Staroměstské náměsti)**.

An alternative starting-point is the Square of the Republic (Náměstí Republiky), with arguably the best Art Nouveau building in Prague, to which a whole generation of artists contributed: the ❻ ✳ **Municipal House (Obecní dům/Representační dům)**. From behind the eighbouring Powder Gate (Prašná brána), which formed part of the Old Town fortifications, runs ❼ ✳ **Celetná**, a pedestrian zone and shopping street lined by Baroque mansions. Celetná also leads straight to the magnificent ❺ ✳ ✳ **Old Town Square (Staroměstské náměstí)** with the Gothic ✳ **Týn Church** (Týnský kostel), Goltz-Kinských Palace, the Church of St Nicholas (Kostel sv Mikuláše) and the legendary ✳ ✳ **Astronomical Clock** by Master Hanuš on Staré Město's ✳ ✳ **town hall** (Staroměstská radnice). In the middle of the square stands the statue of Jan Hus, who was burnt at the stake for »heresy« in Constance in 1415. Numerous cafés invite the passer-by to linger, and it is worth spending a little time watching the lively goings-on in this busy square. From the northwest corner of the square follow the Art Nouveau avenue Pařížská to ❽ ✳ ✳ **Josefov** with the State Jewish Museum (Státní Židovské muzeum), encompassing the six surviving Prague synagogues, the Jewish town hall and theOld Jewish Cemetery with ceremonial hall. Although Jews settled here from the 13th century onward, usually engaging in business and commerce, they did not gain civil rights and could not live outside Josefov until 1848. World War II in effect meant the end of Josefov; most of its inhabitants were killed. On the western edge of Josefov is the ✳ **Museum of Decorative Arts** (Umělecko průmyslové muzeum), which is well worth a visit and boasts a famous collection of glass and porcelain; also the **Rudolfinum**, home of the Czech Philharmonic.

Continuing parallel to the Vltava waterfront the route leads to ❾ ✳ **Knights of the Cross Square (Křižovnické náměstí)**, with the Church of St Salvator on the east side, the Baroque church of the Knights of the Cross to the north, and the cast-iron Charles IV monument. It is also possible to approach the square direct from Old Town Square, following the route taken by the traditional coronation procession along ❿ **Karlova**, past the former Jesuit college, the ⓫ **Klementinum**. The Gothic Old Town Bridge Tower (Staroměstská mostecká věž) on Knights of the Cross Square gives access to the east end of ⓬ ✳ ✳ **Charles Bridge (Karlův most)**, from which there is a splendid view of the Vltava valley. Under the gaze of the saintly bridge figures, people stroll between musicians and cartoonists towards Malá Strana, where several places to eat are within easy walking distance.

! *Baedeker* TIP

Sightseeing

Still a useful tip: in order to discover historic Prague, get on the number 22 tram! It takes less than 20 minutes to cross the city and goes past Prague Castle, Malá Strana Square, the National Theatre and Charles Square. However, a popular name for the number 22 is the »Pickpocket-Express« – so be warned!

Tour 3 Nové Město (New Town)

Duration: 1/2 day   **Start:** National Theatre
Destination: Vyšehrad

The tours of Malá Strana and Staré Město have already taken in
many of Prague's main sights, which are all in close proximity to
one another. The third walk goes further afield, but is no less interesting.

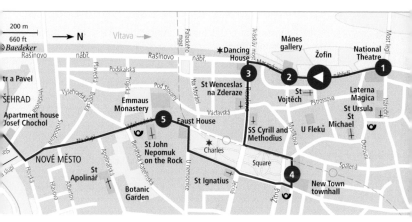

The tour starts at the ❶ **National Theatre**. Should the opportunity
arise, it is worth taking a look at the interior, to which all Prague's
leading 19th-century artists made their contribution. The walk continues south along the Vltava, passing the island of Žofín/Slovanský
ostrov, formed in the 18th century by natural silting, and the ❷ **Ma-
nés gallery** with Šítka water tower. Today the Functionalist gallery
puts on exhibitions of modern art. The ❸ ✳ **Dancing House** by architects Frank O. Gehry and Vlado Milunič is the next landmark on
the walk, a Prague gem of contemporary architecture. Pause here,
then turn east into Resslova, and pass the two churches of St Wenceslas on Na Zderaze (a 14th-century Gothic building) and SS Cyril
and Methodius (a Baroque church by Kilian Ignaz Dientzenhofer; a
national monument), to arrive finally at ❹ **Charles Square** (Karlovo
náměstí). This is the largest square in Prague, a traffic intersection
point, yet more like a park than a square with all its greenery, and
plenty of sights worth seeing: the Faustus House, the Baroque
Church of St Ignatius by Carlo Lurago – especially the interior – and
the New Town Hall, no longer used for its original purpose, but serving as a venue mostly for grand civic functions.

Vyšehradská continues south from here, past ❺**Emmaus Monastery (Klášter Emauzy)**, the Church of St John of Nepomuk on the Rock and the botanical garden. Have a look, in passing, at the Cubist apartment house by Josef Chochol below the fortress of Vyšehrad. Many myths have been spun around❻ ✳ **Vyšehrad**. It offers a wonderful view of the city and the Vltava valley; it also has the Romanesque round chapel of St Martin, the collegiate church of SS Peter und Paul, and the ✳ ✳ memorial cemetery, all worth seeing.

Excursions

Outside the city   A few excursions in the vicinity of Prague can be rewarding, for instance to **Chateau Troja**, where 19th-century Czech painting is exhibited today, or to the Baroque **Bevnov Monastery**, or to the most famous medieval castle in Bohemia, ✳ ✳ **Karlštejn Castle**. On the **White Mountain**, where in 1620 the battle took place that determined the destiny of the Bohemian lands, stands **Star Summer Palace**, a hunting-lodge set in a delightful park.

A little further afield   Within a radius of 70km/45mi around Prague there are castles and fortresses very well worth seeing, situated in wonderful countryside, as well as UNESCO world heritage locations and memorial sites.

✳

Konopiště Chateau ►   Konopiště Chateau (Zámek Konopiště) is located approximately 44km/28mi south of Prague. The Gothic chateau, based on French chateaus, was reconstructed in late-Gothic style, after which a Renaissance palace was added. Baroque elements were introduced in the 18th century. In 1887 Konopiště passed into the hands of Archduke Franz Ferdinand d'Este, later heir to the throne of Austria. He had the chateau remodelled as a magnificent palace. The exquisite interior decoration dates from that time, including the artefacts in the curious St George's Museum where there are numerous portrayals and images of the saint.

✳ ✳

Kutná Hora ►   The picturesque mountain town of Kutná Hora, which became famous and wealthy through the discovery of silver deposits, lies approximately 70 km/44mi east of Prague; it has been listed as a protected heritage area by UNESCO. From 1300, the Kutná Hora silver mines were the basis for the minting of the Prague groschen, the most stable and best-known Bohemian coin of the Middle Ages. This era of economic prosperity has left traces in the form of unique masterpieces of Gothic architecture, such as the »**Stone House**« (Kamenný dům), which now houses the town museum. The Baroque **Ursuline nunnery** was built according to plans by Kilian Ignaz Dientzenhofer; František Maximilian Kaňka built the Baroque **Church of St John Nepomuk** (Kostel svatého Jana Nepomuckého). The **Italian Court** (Vlašský dvůr), the mint built in around 1300 and named after the first minters who came from Florence, was later a royal resi-

Kutná Hora is a UNESCO world heritage site.

dence. The **fort** (Hrádek) was set up as a second mint shortly after it was built. The late Gothic ✱ ✱**Church of St Barbara** (Chrám svaté Barbory) was begun by Peter Parler's workshop and completed in 1585. The ribbed vaulting in the impressive interior displays Renaissance influence and features numerous coats-of-arms.

The skyline of Mělník, the centre of Bohemia's wine-growing industry 38km/25mi north of Prague, is dominated by the Gothic **Church of SS Peter und Paul**, and extensive castle grounds. Approximately 7km/4mi northwest, surrounded by vineyards on the right bank of the river Elbe, stands **Libchov** with its 16th-century **castle**. 17km/10.5mi northeast, the Romantic/neo-Gothic **Kokořín Castle** rises up from dense woods above the charming Kokořín valley (Kokořínský důl). The river Pšovka flows through the valley, with cleft chalk cliffs on either side. ◀ Mlník

The fortress town of **Terezín** was built by Maria Theresa and Joseph II – a prime Bohemian example of Classicist and Empire urban planning. During World War II the inhabitants were driven out by the Nazis and the town was turned into the Terezín ghetto. Starting in 1940, more than 140,000 Jews from all over Europe were deported to this concentration camp. Near the entrance to the fortress is a large national cemetery.

In the second half of the 13th century, Otokar II had a hunting-lodge with chapel built at the confluence of the rivers Vltava and Beraun, approximately 10km/6mi south of Prague; under King Wenceslas (Václav) II it was converted into a Cistercian monastery. Destroyed in the Hussite Wars, the monastery was rebuilt at the beginning of the 18th century, and turned into a three-part castle complex at the beginning of the 20th century. The National Gallery's collection of Asian art is housed externally in Zbraslav Castle (www.ngprague.cz). Open: Tue–Sun 10am–6pm; Metro: Smíchovské, Bus: 129, 241, 243, 360, 255. ◀ Zbraslav Castle (Zámek Zbraslav)

Sights from A to Z

CHARLES BRIDGE, MORE THAN 500M/550YD LONG AND ONE OF 18 BRIDGES OVER THE VLTAVA, LINKS STARÉ MĚSTO WITH MALÁ STRANA. DURING THE DAY IT IS TAKEN OVER BY PERFORMERS, CARICATURISTS AND TOURISTS.

Belvedere (Královský letohrádek)

D 3

Location: Praha 1, Hradčany **Metro:** Malostranská, Hradčanská
Tram: 22

Ferdinand I had Belvedere, or the Summer Palace, built (1538–1563) for his wife Anna at the same time as the Royal Garden. Designed by Paolo della Stella, the Summer Palace is one of the finest examples of Italian Renaissance style north of the Alps. The arches of the arcade running right round the building rest on slender columns with voluted capitals. They are decorated with tendril moulding and reliefs with scenes from Greek mythology, hunting and rustic life. On the west side, between the second and third arches, there is an interesting scene: Ferdinand I presents his wife with a fig branch. The novel construction of the curved roof in the form of a ship's hull takes its lead from shipbuilding technology.

The palace was put at the disposal of the army at the end of the 18th century, and even used as an artillery laboratory until 1838, so the interior space has been altered to a considerable degree. Temporary exhibitions are currently on show in the palace.

Singing Fountain West of Belvedere is the »Singing Fountain«. It was designed in the years 1564–1568 by **Tomáš Jaroš** and cast in bronze. When drops of water fall on it, the resonating cavities of the bowl make a sound; lay an ear against the rim of the fountain to hear this special acoustic effect.

Belvedere: in the foreground, the Singing Fountain

The Ball-Game Court was constructed between 1567and 1569 by Bo- **Ball-Game Court**
nifaz Wohlmut. The sgraffiti on the exterior show allegories of the elements, virtues and liberal arts. In front of the ball-game court is the
statue group *Night* by **Matthias Bernhard Braun** (c1730); its companion piece (*Day*) was destroyed shortly after it was made, during the
Prussian bombardment of Prague.

South of Belvedere is Chotek Park (Chotkovy sady). This, Prague's **Chotek Park**
second public park, was created in the years 1833–1841 on the initiative of city governor Count Chotek.

Bethlehem Chapel (Betlémská kaple)

E 4

Location: Praha 1, Staré Město, **Tram:** 6, 9, 18, 21, 22, 23
Betlémské n. **Metro:** Národní třída

Bethlehem Chapel is a simple, originally Gothic building. Between ☉
1950 and 1953 it was rebuilt according to the original plan as found Opening hours:
in old prints, descriptions and views, using designs by architect Jaro- April–Oct
slav Fragner. This sacral building was declared a national monument daily 9am–6pm
of culture in 1962, and is one of the Czech Republic's most impor- Nov–March
tant historical religious monuments. daily 9am–5pm

In 1391 Prague citizens wanted to found a church in which Mass
would be celebrated in Czech. The Catholic authorities agreed only
to the building of a Gothic chapel. This, however, could accommodate 3000; and its centre was not the altar, but the pulpit. Czech reformer Jan Hus preached here between 1402 and 1413. After his
death in 1415 the chapel continued to be the spiritual centre of the
Hussite movement. It was from this pulpit in 1521 that the German
peasant leader Thomas Müntzer
preached the establishment of a
state of God, based on equality and
common property, and issued his
Prague manifesto. During the years
1609–1620 the chapel belonged to
the community of Bohemian
Brothers. One of those active here
was Senior Jan Cyrillus, later the
father-in-law of the great educator
of the people, Jan Amos Comenius.
After Ferdinand II had defeated
the »Winter King« Friedrich V of
the Palatinate in 1620 at the Battle
of the White Mountain – Roman
Catholicism was the only religious

> ! *Baedeker* TIP
>
> **Read... and feed**
> Klub architektů is a favourite haunt of all
> Prague's keen readers. This multi-purpose oasis
> in Staré Msto boasts a view of the Gothic
> Bethlehem Chapel where Jan Hus once preached.
> The specialist bookshop offers nourishment for
> the mind, while the medieval cellar caters for the
> body. In summer, guests can sit in the airy
> courtyard – and it won't break the bank.
> Reservation recommended! Tel. 224 401 214,
> daily 11.30am–midnight.

faith allowed from 1627 – the Jesuits bought the chapel. In 1773 the order was dissolved; in 1786 the chapel was demolished down to its outer walls.

On the **inside of the church walls** fragments of tracts by Masters Jan Hus and Jakoubek ze Stříbra can still be seen. In recent times students from the Academy of Visual Arts have decorated the walls with paintings, working from miniatures in the *Jena Codex*, *Richenthal Chronicle* and *Velislav Bible*. The reconstructed wooden pulpit, choir and oratory are also new.

In Jan Hus's **preacher's house** above the chapel are exhibits documenting the reformer's life and work, and the architectural history of the chapel.

Church of St Giles (Kostel svatého Jiljí)

Husova třída leads north from Bethlehem Square. A short distance along on the right hand side is the Church of St Giles. The Romanesque building was remodelled in Gothic style between 1339 and 1371. Originally in the hands of Hussite Utraquists, the church was given to the Dominicans by Ferdinand II in 1625, after the Battle of the White Mountain.

In 1733 the building was converted into Baroque style, probably according to designs by **Kilian Ignaz Dientzenhofer**. Wenzel Lorenz Reiner was responsible for the *Glorification of the Dominican Order of Preachers* ceiling fresco. The subject enabled him to display the full range of his skills: he created a triumph of trompe-l'oeil architecture, with cupola and triangular portico in the process of collapsing, yet supported by St Dominic. Reiner also painted the altar picture in the left side-aisle chapel. Here, too, is his tomb. The ornate confessionals are from the workshop of Richard Prachner.

Church concerts regularly take place in St Giles'.

Břevnov Monastery (Klášter Břevnov)

Location: Praha 6, Břevnov, Markétská 28	**Bus:** 108, 174, 180 **Tram:** 8, 22, 23

5km/3mi from the city centre in the direction of Karlovy Vary (road no. 6) lies the district of Břevnov, with its Benedictine monastery of the same name. It was founded in 993 by Prince Boleslav II and St Adalbert (later bishop of Prague), and is the second Benedictine abbey and earliest monastery in Bohemia. All that remained of the original Romanesque monastery church, built in the 11th century, was the chancel crypt. The Baroque complex seen today arose under master builder **Christoph Dientzenhofer**. First, St Margaret's Church was built (by 1716); four years later the monastery was completed.

In order to visit the monastery it is necessary to join one of the guided tours, which take place only at weekends (Sat, Sun between 10am and 4pm). Groups can also book a tour during the week (tel. 220 406 111, fax 233 351 566 or internet: www.brevnov.cz). Unfortunately tours are conducted only in Czech, though a detailed brochure is available in English.

Monastery site

Entry to the monastery courtyard is through a beautiful portal (1740) by **Kilian Ignaz Dientzenhofer**. A statue of St Benedict (by Karl Josef Hiernle) stands in the courtyard. The Baroque monastery buildings were begun in 1708 by **Paul Ignaz Bayer** and completed c1715 by Christoph Dientzenhofer. Inside, the prelates' hall is particularly notable; its ceiling fresco (*St Günther's Peacock Miracle*, 1727) is by Cosmas Damian Asam; Bernardo Spinetti designed the stucco work. There are fine paintings by A. Tuvora in the reception hall and Chinese salon.

Church of St Margaret

The monastery site's central point is the Church of St Margaret (Kostel svaté Markéty). It, too, was built by **Christoph Dientzenhofer** (completed c1720). The ceiling frescoes are by Johann Jakob Steinfels; the altar paintings by Peter Brandl. The depiction of St Margaret on the main altar is by Matthias Wenceslas Jäckel. A statue of St John Nepomuk outside the church (by Karl Josef Hiernle) commemorates Bohemia's patron saint.
From Břevnov Monastery, the no. 8 and no. 22 trams go direct to Star Summer Palace on ▶White Mountain.

✹ Celetná

E 4

Location: Praha 1, Staré Město, Celetná (pedestrian zone)

Metro: Staroměstská, Můstek, Náměstí Republiky

Named after the medieval bakers of bread rolls, »calty «, Celetná has always been part of the link between Vltava ford, the Staré Město marketplaces, and the east of the Staré Město district. It was along this route the »coronation procession« once ran, from the ▶Powder Gate via ▶Old Town Square and Charles Bridge, up to ▶Prague Castle.
Celetná has been very well restored (restorations were completed in 1987), and is lined by many important city palaces of Romanesque and Gothic origin, remodelled in Baroque style.
No. 12 is one of the finest. The former **Hrzán Palace** was probably given its high Baroque appearance by **Giovanni Battista Alliprandi** in 1702. The sculptures on the front are thought to be from the workshop of **Ferdinand Maximilian Brokoff**.
The Attica figures at no. 2, the **Sixt House**, close to Old Town Square, are attributed to **Anton Braun**.

SLANTS AND DIAGONALS, OR CUBISM BOHEMIAN-STYLE

Celetná, with its carefully restored Baroque and Rococo palaces, is among the most beautiful streets in Prague's historic centre. One of the few buildings that does not fit the pattern is the house on the corner of the fruit market, named »The House at the Black Madonna« after the Marian plaque on its façade – the house-sign from the Baroque building that used to stand here.

The building makes a sober, functionalist first impression; it was designed by Josef Gočár in 1911/1912 as a retail store for wholesaler František Josef Herbst. Constructed with steel skeleton – discernible in the large, scarcely interrupted surfaces of the windows and the variable disposition of interior spaces – it represents the most modern architecture in Prague at the beginning of the 20th century.

Yet that is not all. Closer inspection reveals various details that cannot easily be slotted into any architectural style, such as the rounded windows, slanting eaves, and deeply recessed entrance which is framed by a pair of pillars with pointed tops and hexagonal capitals. The round stairwell with its glass dome is also unusual for its wrought-iron stair-rail, and creates an illusion of plasticity with its spiralling, twisting cubes.

Prague speciality

Improvements of the postmodern age? By no means. Rather, these curious details express a style known otherwise only from painting – Cubism. For a few years in Prague – and only here – there arose Cubist architecture and Cubist design. The new style had arisen in 1906/1907 in Paris, where Picasso and Braque brought about the break with traditional conventions of painting.

One of Cubism's most important formal innovations was the departure from central perspective in favour of a presentation that brought different views of an object into the picture. Since the Cubists held that every object could be reduced to a few basic cubic forms, they dissolved the object into individual geometrical and plastic forms, which were anchored in the painting without spatial coherence.

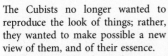

Former Legio bank by Josef Gočár, Na poříčí 24, built 1921–1923

A prime example of Cubist architecture is the »House at the Black Madonna«.

The Cubists no longer wanted to reproduce the look of things; rather, they wanted to make possible a new view of them, and of their essence.

In Prague, as elsewhere, there were heated discussions about the new art from France. People were familiar with paintings by the famous Picasso and Braque either from journeys to Paris or through the collection of art historian Vincenc Kramar, who systematically bought French avant-garde works from 1910. In Prague it was above all the younger generation who were enthusiastic about Cubism, men such as sculptor **Otto Gutfreund**, architects **Josef Gočár, Josef Chochol** and **Pavel Janák**, and painters **Emil Filla, Bohumil Kubišta** and **Václav Špála**. »The House at the Black Madonna« is not the only architectural legacy of Prague's Cubists. Between 1920 and 1925 more than 30 Cubist houses were built in the city, of which 27 still survive. Only a small distance from the centre, in Vyšehrad district, several apartment blocks and villas were built with Cubist façades designed by **Josef Chochol** (Neklanova 30 and Libušina 49, among others).

The peak of his achievement is the apartment block at Neklanova 30, completed in 1914. Like the objects in a Cubist painting, this building flouts a one-dimensional view. The formal centre is the corner of the building, simultaneously the corner of two streets, where the sides converge at an acute angle, as in a ship's prow. Wherever the eye seeks the order of a right angle and the restfulness of a smooth wall, it has to relinquish its hold to slants and diagonals, encountering faceted triangles and rhomboids that curve out of the surface, variegated through light and shadow.

In the home

Like the Art Nouveau architects, so also Prague's Cubists designed complete interiors – from the doorknob, through balustrades and lamps, to sofas, cupboards, desks and carpets. Nor did avant-garde design stop there: vases, sugar bowls and coat hooks were also given the treatment. The Prague Workshops founded in 1912 produced avant-garde **furniture**. A showpiece rediscovered in the 1980s by postmodern furniture designers is the massive, expressive sofa by **Josef Gočár**, with its jagged frame of black stained oak. The exhibition displays a few of Pavel Janák's wooden chairs – the horror of any bourgeois drawing-room with their triangular backs and buckled legs. Whether one would choose (or be able) to sit on them, however, is quite another matter.

»Golden Angel« as house emblem, Celetná

The family coat of arms above the doorway at no. 13 recall the one-time owner of the **Baroque Caretto-Millesimo Palace**.

Nos. 17 and 20: the Menhart House, now has the **»Spider«** (U pavouka) wine tavern, while **Buquoyský Palace** (no. 20) has belonged to Prague's Charles University since it was re-styled in the 18th century.

No. 22, the Classicist house next door known as **»The Vulture«** (U zlatého supa), is also used by the university.

A statue of the Madonna (c1730) by **Matthias Bernhard Braun** adorns the Baroque façade of no. 23, **»U Schönfloku«**.

No. 31, **Pachtovský Palace**, remodelled in the mid-18th century in Dientzenhofer Baroque style, is now an administrative building.

The house-sign of the »Madonna behind Bars« at no. 34 is a favourite photo motif. It is the only remaining evidence of the former Baroque façade of the Cubist **»House at the Black Madonna«** (U černé Matky boží of 1911–1912 (►Baedeker Special p.128). The house, designed by Josef Gočár with two recessed top floors, attests Prague's own brand of Cubism, which – unlike in Paris – extended to architecture. Almost contemporary with the ► Municipal House, whose decorative surfaces also owe a lot to Art Nouveau, the House at the Black Madonna is more progressive, with large front windows only possible within a ferroconcrete construction. Nevertheless, its sculptural emphasis preserves architectural harmony with the surrounding Baroque houses. On the ground floor there was originally a café, popular with artists; the office space above was created with freely movable partitioning.

⏱ Opening hours: Tue–Sun 10am–6pm

The permanent exhibition of Czech Cubism 1911–1919 on the top floors has been closed since 2007 for technical reasons.

The Mint No. 36, where in the 14th century part of the Bohemian royal court was located, was a mint from the 16th century on. The current building, »The Mint« (U Mincovna), was built by mintmaster František Josef Pachta of Rájov in the 18th century. A hundred years later the building was extended and given a neo-Baroque appearance. Celetná ends at the monumental **Powder Gate** (►Municipal House), part of the earlier Staré Město fortifications.

Charles Bridge (Karlův most)

Location: Praha 1, Staré Město,   **Metro:** Staroměstská, Malostranská
Karlův most   **Tram:** 17, 18

Charles Bridge is reserved for pedestrians; it links the two sides of the Vltava, Staré Město (Old Town) and Malá Strana (Lesser Quarter). From the bridge there is a wonderful view of the Vltava valley with its numerous bridges, of Shooters' Island and Slav Island (Žofín), and of Staré Město and Malá Strana themselves with ►Prague Castle. Beneath the west piers lies►Kampa Island, which is separated from Malá Strana by the narrow Čertovka branch of the Vltava (»Prague's Venice«).

In summer, the bridge is populated by painters, musicians, and arts and crafts vendors. It rests on 16 piers and is 520m/570yd long and 10m/11yd wide. It was begun in 1357 under Charles IV by **J. Ottl** and completed in the early 15th century under Wenceslas IV by **Peter Parler**. The massive bridge towers on both banks, as well as the bridge itself, once served defensive purposes.

Flood disasters have often damaged the fabric of the bridge – two arches had to be replaced in 1890 – yet have never caused it to collapse. In recent times, however, structural damage has been discovered. But although restoration work is planned for the coming years, the bridge will remain accessible. Part of the estimated cost of £7.3 million/€11.25 million/US$15.2 million is to be raised through donations.

Charles Bridge makes an enormous impact, largely because of its rich sculptural ornamentation. This **»statue promenade«**, which originated for the most part in the Baroque era, is one of Prague's loveliest architectural achievements and that, combined with the strict Gothic architecture of the bridge, gives it a high degree of artistic appeal. In 1657 a bronze crucifix that had stood here since the 14th century was renovated; between 1706 and 1714, 26 statues were erected by famous artists (**Matthias Bernhard Braun**, **Johann Brokoff** and **his sons Michael Josef and Ferdinand Maximilian**) and other sculptors. In the mid-19th century these were followed by five further statues (by **Josef Max** and **Emanuel Max**); in 1938 the stone group of SS Cyril and Methodius (by **Karel Dvořák**) was added. The sandstone figures have suffered greatly through the ravages of time and environmental impact; in the meantime almost all have been replaced by copies. The only marble statue is that of St Philip Benizi. The most valuable artistically is the chiselled sandstone figure of St Luitgard, a picture of mercy and grace: Christ leans down from the Cross to St Luitgard and allows her to kiss his wounds. The only statue cast in bronze is St John Nepomuk (in the middle of the bridge). It was cast in Nürnberg in 1683 from models by **Matthias Rauchmüller** and **Johann Brokoff**. Between the sixth and seventh piers of the

Sculptures on Charles Bridge *Plan*

Lesser Quarter bridge towers

St Wenceslas
by J. K. Böhm, 1858

SS Cosmas and Damian
by J. O. Mayer, 1709

**SS John of Matha,
Felix of Valois and Ivan**
and figure of a Turk
by F. M. Brokoff, 1714

St Vitus
by F. M. Brokoff, 1714
marble sculpture

St Adalbert
by F. M. Brokoff, 1709
copy 1973

St Philip Benitius
by M. B. Mandl, 1714

St Luitgard
by M. B. Braun, 1710

St Kajetan
by F. M. Brokoff, 1709

St Nicholas of Tolentine
by J. F. Kohl, 1706
copy 1969

St Augustine
by J. F. Kohl, 1708
copy 1974

**SS Vincent Ferrer
and Procopius**
by F. M. Brokoff, 1712

St Judas Thaddaeus
by J. O. Mayer, 1708

St Francis Seraphicus
by E. Max, 1855

St Antony of Padua
by J. O. Mayer, 1707

St John

SS Ludmila and Wenceslas
from workshop M. B. Braun
approx. 1730

St John Nepomuk
models by M. Rauchmüller and
J. Brokoff, 1683 bronze cast by W. H. Heroldt,
in Nuremberg

St Francis Borgia
by J. and F. M. Brokoff, 1710
restored 1937 by R. Vlach

**SS Wenceslas, Norbert
and Sigismund**
by J. Max, 1853

St Christopher
by E. Max, 1857

St John the Baptist
by J. Max, 1857

St Francis Xaver
by F. M. Brokoff, 1711
copy 1913

SS Cyrill and Methodius
and three allegorical
figures (Bohemia, Moravia,
Slovakia), by K. Dvořák, 1938

St Joseph
by J. Max, 1854

St Anne with Mary and Child Jesus
by M. W. Jäckel, 1707

Pietà
by E. Max, 1859
originally, 1695

Bronze crucifix
cast 1629 by J. Hilger
erected 1657 as first bridge sculpture
Hebrew inscription 1696
figures by E. Max, 1861

**SS Barbara, Margaret
and Elizabeth**
by F. M. Brokoff, 1707

**Mary with SS Dominic
and Thomas Aquinas**
by M. W. Jäckel, 1708; copy 1961

St Ivo
by M. B. Braun, 1711
copy 1908

Mary and St Bernard
by M. W. Jäckel, 1709; copy

St Luitgard

Old Town bridge tower

➜ N

© *Baedeker*

A bird's-eye view of Charles Bridge, for a change

bridge, a relief marks the spot from which St John Nepomuk was cast into the Vltava in 1393 on the orders of Wenceslas IV, because he had opposed the king in an ecclesiastical conflict. Canonized in 1729, he has been regarded since that time as Catholic Europe's »bridge saint«.

The Crucifixion Group has a Hebrew inscription; in 1696 a Jew was sentenced by the regional tribunal to make this contribution as a punishment for blasphemy.

Old Town Bridge Tower (Staremestká mostecká) forms the eastern entrance to Charles Bridge, and stands in fact on the first pier. Building started in 1357 and was completed at the beginning of the 15th century under King Wenceslas IV; the design was by the famous architect **Peter Parler** of the cathedral workshop. It is considered to be one of the finest Gothic towers in Central Europe. The **figural decoration** of Old Town Bridge Tower is one of the great accomplishments of Gothic sculpture in Bohemia (14th century). The tower was restored by Josef Mocker in the 19th century and given the roof it has today; its originally Gothic paintings were renovated by Peter Maixner.

Above the doorway arch on the east side are the emblems of all the lands ruled by the Luxembourg dynasty, and also the royal arms of Bohemia, the arms of the Roman emperor and the royal kingfisher, emblem of Wenceslas IV.

The first storey is adorned by the kings Charles IV and Wenceslas IV, enthroned; between them, elevated a little, stands the figure of St Vitus. Above, a shield beneath a non-heraldic lion displays the St Wenceslas eagle. At the very top are the Bohemian patron saints Adalbert and Sigismund.

Old Town Bridge Tower

🕐
Opening hours:
April–May, Oct
10am–7pm
June–Sept
10am–10pm
March
10am–6pm
Nov–Feb
10am–5pm

Malá Strana Bridge Towers On the west side Charles Bridge ends in the Malá Strana Bridge Towers, which are linked by an archway. The lower tower (dating from the last quarter of the 12th century) formed part of the fortifications of the earlier Judith Bridge; in 1591 it was given Renaissance gables and ornamentation on the outer walls. The taller tower was built in 1464 at the behest of King George of Poděbrady in place of an earlier Romanesque tower. Its late-Gothic architecture resembles that of Old Town Bridge Tower opposite, and some of its sculptural ornamentation replicates the style (Opening hours: April–Oct 10am–6pm).

Baedeker TIP

The Three Ostriches

Armenian Deodatus Damajan opened Prague's first coffee-house in this building in 1714. Today »U tí pštrosů« is a hotel and restaurant, and one of the best culinary addresses in the metropolis on the Vltava – the freshly made dumplings are hard to beat (Dražického náměstí 6, tel. 257 532 410).

The fine Renaissance house »**The Three Ostriches**« (U tří pštrosů) at the Malá Strana end of Charles Bridge was built in 1597; remnants of the façade painting by Daniel Alexius of Květná (1606) still survive. The upper storey, in early-Baroque style, is by master builder **Cril Geer** (1657); the notable beamed ceilings in the dining-rooms date from the 17th century.

★ Charles Square (Karlovo náměstí)

E 5/6

Location: Praha 1, Nové Město
Tram: 3, 4, 6, 14, 18, 22, 24

Metro: Karlovo náměstí

530m/580yd long and 150m/164yd wide, Charles Square is the largest square in Prague. Until 1848 the cattle market was held here. Today the square more resembles a park, with its green spaces and monuments of Czech scientists and writers. The pharmacy on the south side of the square is commonly known as Faust House; on the east side stands the Church of St Ignatius, at the northeast corner the tower of the former New Town Hall rises up to the sky. On Resslova, which leads to the Vltava and the ► Dancing House, two churches are well worth seeing: SS Cyril and Methodius and St Wenceslas on Na Zderaze.

Faust House (Faustův dům)

Legendary laboratory The Faust House, originally a late-Renaissance palace, was given a corner bastion when the fortifications were extended between 1606 and 1617, and remodelled in Baroque style in the 18th century. Under Rudolf II (1576–1611), the English alchemist Edward Kelley carried out gold-making experiments here. When another chemist set up his laboratory in the house in the 18th century, one Mladota of Solopysky (hence also: Mladota Palace), the legend arose that Dr Faustus had sold his soul to the devil, and was carried off to hell through the laboratory ceiling. Today – continuing an old tradition? – the polyclinic pharmacy is located here.

Church of St Ignatius

The imperial master builder **Carlo Lurago** created this Baroque sacral building (Kostel svatého Ignáce) between 1665 and 1668 as church of the former Jesuit college; today it houses a outpatients clinic. The grandiose doorway (1697–1699) with a statue of St Ignatius with an aureole (1671) on the tympanum is by **Paul Ignaz Bayer**. The other statues are by Tommaso Soldatti.

The interior of the hall church is especially worth seeing, with rich stucco work and figures of saints by Soldatti. The Baroque high altar of simulated marble (18th century) shows the *Glorification of St Ignatius of Loyola* (1688), a work by **Johann Georg Heintsch**. To him the church also owes its remarkable altar pictures. The painting *Christ Imprisoned* is by his teacher **Karel Škréta**; *St Liborius* is by **Ignaz Raab**. The Calvary group beneath the organ loft is the work of Johann Anton Quittainer.

Sumptuous Jesuit church

New Town Hall (Novoměstská radnice)

The originally Gothic building on the northeast corner of Charles Square was erected as the town hall in 1348. After Hradčany, Malá Strana, Staré Město and Nové Město were joined together as one administrative unit and the offices centralized in Staré Město (1784), this former town hall served as prison, court of law and registry office. Today the building is used for ceremonial and cultural purposes.

In the corner tower, erected between 1452 and 1456 and altered several times, is a chapel. At the beginning of the 16th century the façade looking towards the square was given a Renaissance look. In the 19th century, Empire elements were added; finally, in 1906, it was reconstructed in the original Renaissance style.

In earlier times Nové Město was inhabited predominantly by the poor. On 30 July 1419 the **first Prague defenestration** took place here: a crowd led by preacher Jan Želivský stormed the town hall, freed the Hussites imprisoned there and flung two Catholic councillors out of the window. This precipitated the Hussite Wars.

🕐 Opening hours:
May–Sept
Tue–Sun
10am–6pm
Further rooms open during exhibitions
Tue–Sun
10am–5.30pm

The neo-Renaissance Czech Technical University building (no. 14) was erected in 1867 from designs by V.I. Ullmann. Allegories of Work and Science from A. Popp's workshop flank the entrance; the sculptures of ancient geniuses above the second-floor windows are

Czech Technical University

The façade of New Town Hall was rebuilt in the 20th century.

by **Josef Václav Myslbek** (1879). Resslova branches off from Charles Square and has two further churches: SS Cyril and Methodius (Svatého Cyrila a Metoděje) and, diagonally opposite, St Wenceslas on Na Zderaze.

SS Cyril and Methodius
🕐 Opening hours:
May–Sept
Tue–Sun 10am–5pm
Oct–April until 4pm

The Church of SS Cyril and Methodius was originally dedicated to St Charles Borromäus. This Baroque building (no. 9) was built by Kilian Ignaz Dientzenhofer, and completed c1740; in 1935 it passed to the Greek Orthodox church. Stucco work by Michael Ignaz Palliardi adorns the interior.

In June 1942 the Czech resistance fighters who assassinated the »Deputy Reich Protector of Bohemia and Moravia«, Reinhard Heydrich, hid in the crypt after the attack. As a consequence, in gruesome reprisals, all male inhabitants of Lidice were shot by the German SS, the women and children were sent separately to concentration camps, and the village was razed to the ground. Not a single one of the resistance fighters survived the battle in and around the crypt (see the memorial plaque and exhibition).

St Wenceslas on Na Zderaze

Since 1926, St Wenceslas on Na Zderaze (Kostel svatého Václava na Zderaze) has belonged to the Czech Hussite Church. It was originally the parish church of Zderaze, which later became part of Nové Město. The 14th-century Gothic building still has traces of a Romanesque nave and church tower.

In the chancel are fragments of Gothic wall frescoes (Tree of Jesse), dating from around 1400. In 1586 and 1587 the church was provided with late-Gothic stellar vaulting by K. Mělnický. The wall frescoes depicting the legend of St Wenceslas (18th century) are attributed to Josef Hager.

Charles University (Karolinum)

E 4

Location: Praha 1, Staré Město, Železná   **Metro:** Můstek
9 (Pedestrian zone)

Charles IV founded the Karolinum, which was named after him, on 7 April 1348. It was the first university in Central Europe. The most notable collegiate structure is Rotlev House (1370), added under the patronage of Wenceslas IV in 1383, with its magnificent Gothic oriel windows that still survive today. The architecture of Charles University's other buildings ranges from Gothic to 20th-century.

As early as 1409 the Karolinum's history as a universal university – teachers and students came from all over Europe – seemed to be at an end as, urged on by Master Jan Hus, King Wenceslas curtailed Germans' rights. About 2000 students and many professors left the country. From this point, the reformer Hus held the post of rector (see the bronze statue by K. Lidický in the memorial courtyard), until in 1412 the Catholic faculty spoke out against him and he had to flee to southern Bohemia. After the Bohemian nobility's revolt had been put down the Jesuits took over the running of the university. In addition to the oriel windows, two pieces of ribbed vaulting in the former arcade and a few recently uncovered Gothic elements have survived from the original building. Baroque alterations to the site were undertaken in 1718 by **František Maximilian Kaňka**.

The heart of the Karolinum building is the 17th-century **aula**, which occupies two storeys and was extended (1946–1950) by Jaroslav Fragner.

The ►Estates Theatre is located just a few yards from the Karolinum.

Gothic oriel windows on the fruit market

St Gall St Gall's Church (Kostel svatého Havla) on Havelská, southwest of the Karolinum, was founded in 1232 at the same time as the southern German colony »Gallistadt«; it was one of four Staré Město parish churches completed by 1263. It was restructured in high Gothic style in 1353. Further alterations in the 18th century resulted in the apparently undulating façade and two towers.

The Baroque interior has valuable altar paintings, and on the left a Pietà carved in wood, probably by **Ferdinand Maximilian Brokoff**. In the right side chapel is the tomb of painter **Karel Škréta**. From 1363, the Austrian reform preacher Konrad of Waldhausen was active in St Gall, at the wish of Charles IV; he was a predecessor of the great Czech reformer Jan Hus.

Church of Our Lady Victorious

D 4

Location: Praha 1, Malá Strana, Karme-   **Tram:** 12, 22
litská

Not far from Maltézské náměstí (Maltese Square), at number 9 Karmelitská, stands the Church of Our Lady Victorious (Kostel Panny Marie Vítězné). It was built as a Carmelite monastery church in early Baroque style on the site of a Hussite church after the victory of imperial troops at the Battle of the White Mountain. The ground plan of the church is modelled on the Jesuit church »Il Gesù« in Rome. The altar by Franz Lauermann dates from1776. It is adorned by statues by **Peter Prachner** and a small silver Christ Child casket (1741) by Jan Pakeni. Three of the altar pictures are by **Peter Johann Brandl**. namely those of St Simon, St Joseph and SS Joachim and Anne. The main altar (1723) is from the workshop of Johann Ferdinand Schor. In the catacombs beneath the church, not open to visitors, are the mummified remains of Carmelites and their benefactors, well preserved thanks to the circulation of air.

⊙
Opening hours:
Mon–Fri
8.30am–6.30pm
Sat 7.30am–8pm
Sun 9am–9pm
In winter until 8pm

Prague's Infant Jesus On the right side wall of the church hangs the »Prague Infant Jesus«, still the object of profound veneration today; it is a 50cm/20in-tall wax figure from Spain, given to the monastery in 1628 by Princess Polyxena Lobkowicz. It is supposed to have protected the city in a variety of ways: against plague and pillage, for instance, during the Seven Years' War. Accordingly the Infant was not only deeply revered, but also showered with precious gifts: not least with a valuable gold and velvet dress by Maria Theresa. At that time there was an image of the Prague Infant Jesus in all Carmelite monasteries; today copies can be purchased in numerous shops – some nicely done, some nothing more than kitsch.

Vrtba Garden with its Baroque sculptures and Church of our Lady Victorious

Vrtba Palace and Garden

At number 18 Karmelitská, not far from ▶ Little Quarter Square, stands Vrtba Palace (Vrtbovský palác). The palace was converted in 1631 in late-Renaissance style. Its garden (Vrtbovská zahrada) is one of the most outstanding achievements of Baroque garden architecture in Central Europe. It was designed by **František Maximilian Kaňka**.

Wenzel Lorenz Reiner did the paintings for the Sala terrena; at the entrance to the former vineyard are statues of Bacchus and Ceres by **Matthias Bernhard Braun** (*c*1730). On the double steps, Baroque vases alternate with mythological sculptures. From the topmost terrace there is a spectacular view of St Nicholas Church (▶Little Quarter Square) and the city.

⊙
Opening hours:
Garden
April–Oct
daily 10am–6pm
www.vrtbovska.cz

Church of the Assumption of the Virgin Mary and Charlemagne

F 6

Location: Praha 1, Nové Město, Ke Karlovu 1

Metro: Vyšehrad, I. P. Pavlova
Tram: 6, 11

The Church of the Assumption of the Virgin Mary and Charlemagne (Kostel Nanebevzetí Panny Marie a Karla Velikého) is on Ke Karlo-

Octagon modelled on Aachen

vu, south of the Dvořák Museum located in Villa Amerika. Charles IV had this church with an octagonal groundplan built in 1358, on the model of the imperial chapel in Aachen. When it was dedicated to the Assumption of the Virgin Mary and Charlemagne in 1377, it had only a provisional roof. **Bonifaz Wohlmut** completed the stellar vaulting of the nave in 1575; it is considered one of Prague's most brilliant architectural achievements. Linked to it is the legend of the master builder who sold over his soul to the devil in order to be able to complete his work.

From 1720, **Kilian Ignaz Dientzenhofer** worked on the renovation of the church. Use of the former monastery church as a place of pilgrimage from the early 18th century, and the simultaneous installation of several chapels, very much diminished the originally Gothic character of the building. The Baroque cupolas were also a later addition.

City Gallery Prague

Internet: www.citygalleryprague.cz

The City Gallery Prague (Galerie hlavního města Prahy), with its permanent collections and regularly changing exhibitions, focuses mainly on **Czech art of the 19th and 20th centuries**. The exhibitions are presented at different locations in Prague. In **Troja Chateau** there is a permanent exhibition of 19th-century Bohemian art with reference to European developments and the nation's past. The work of sculptor František Bílek (1872–1941) is shown in **Bilkova vila** (Praha 6, Mickiewiczova 1). A representative of both Symbolism and Art Nouveau, Bílek himself designed the villa (1911). The **»House of the Golden Ring«** (U zlatého prstenu, Praha 1, Tynska 6) exhibits Czech art of the 20th century. Temporary exhibitions are put on in the »House of the Stone Bell« and in the town hall on ► Old Town Square.

✴ Convent of St Agnes (Anežský klášter)

E 3

Location: Praha 1, Staré Město,
U milosrdných 17
Bus: 207

Metro: Staroměstská
Tram: 5, 8, 14

The Convent of St Agnes is one of Prague's most significant historic buildings, and has been declared a national monument. It is worth visiting not only because it is a magnificent example of early Gothic architecture: in addition, the National Gallery's collection of medieval art is housed here.

The Convent of St Agnes was founded for the order of the Poor Clares (Franciscan nuns) in 1234 by Princess Agnes, sister of King Wenceslas I, modelled on the foundation of St Clare of Assisi. Agnes subsequently entered the order herself, and was the monastery's first abbess from 1235. At the same time the monastery of Minorite friars was founded, by 1240, with close links to the nunnery. In the years that followed, the churches of St Barbara (1250–1280) and St Francis (c1250), and the Franciscan convent were built, in the Cistercian Gothic style current in Burgundy. The Church of the Holy Saviour (1275–1280) is considered the most important example of early Bohemian Gothic. Investigations have shown that the church was probably the burial place of the Přemyslid dynasty (capital sculptures of Přemyslid rulers).

DON'T MISS

- Master Theoderich: renowned for »beautiful Madonnas« (first wing)
- Master of Hohenfurth: panel paintings (whole room dedicated to him)
- Master of Třebon (Wittingau): altar paintings with nine wing panels (whole room)
- Albrecht Altdorfer: *Martyrdom of St Florian* (last room)

The presbytery and St Barbara's Church date from the 14th century; Baroque alterations to the church were undertaken in 1689. In the presbytery, archaeological researchers have uncovered the graves of King Wenceslas I, the convent's founder St Agnes (†1282) and further Přemyslids.

The exhibition of medieval art in Bohemia and Central Europe (13th–16th centuries) is very well presented. Most of the sculptures and panel paintings come from Bohemian churches. Artists not known by name are designated according to their work, and the place it was found. The Madonna is the most frequently recurring motif in medieval Bohemian art.

Národní galerie/ collection
🕐 Opening hours: Tue–Sun 10am–6pm
www.ngprague.cz

The first part of the chronologically arranged exhibition is displayed in the monastery: it shows the development of panel painting and sculpture up to the middle of the 14th century. Following some early Gothic figures of the Madonna, a whole room is dedicated to the cycle produced by the **Master of Hohenfurth** (Mistr Vyšebrodského oltáře). There the altar of the former Cistercian foundation is displayed; it dates from c1330–1350, and consists of nine panels. The cycle of scenes from the life of Christ, created by the Master of Hohenfurth with at least two further assistants, represents a new conception of spatiality through composition and three-dimensionality of figures and landscape, and a differentiated narrative style. This was influenced by Italian Trecento painting, especially that of Siena. Up to that time a style influenced by Anglo-French paintings had predominated in Bohemia. Next comes the room with works by **Master Theoderich**. The only artist here who is known by name is considered to represent the soft style of Bohemian Gothic painting.

1200–1378

*Whether for the lovely Madonnas or the medieval portraits,
St Agnes' Convent is definitely worth a visit.*

He created wall paintings and 128 panel paintings for Charles IV at
►Karlštejn Castle, of which six are on display (St Elizabeth, St Vitus,
St Jerome, St Matthew, Pope Gregory, St Luke; mid-14th century). In
this instance, too, Italian painting of the time influenced the style.
The votive picture of Prague archbishop Johann Očko of Vlašim
(c1370), with portrait-like pictures of Charles IV and Wenceslas IV,
transcends the soft style.

1378–1437 The next room is devoted to the fragmentary cycle of the **Master of
Tebo (Wittengau)**. The three panels of the winged altar, painted on
both sides (only opened on feast days), show on the open side Christ
on the Mount of Olives, the Entombment and Christ's Resurrection;
on the reverse is a cycle of pictures of saints, also from the Master of
Třeboň's workshop (he himself painted only the heads).

There follow paintings and sculpture which demonstrate the development of late-Gothic art in Bohemia, with particular emphasis on
the soft style. This style was most widely employed in the early 15th
century and is represented, for instance, in the childlike Madonna by
Český Krumlov (c1400) and in the Madonna from the Franciscan
monastery in Plzeň. The **Master of the Rajhrad Altarpiece** (Mistr
Rajhradského oltáře; early 15th century) initiated a new development
in Bohemian painting with the almost caricature-like contortion of
his crucifixion figures.

While Bohemia and especially Prague counted as important independent European centres of art in the 14th century, in the 15th century the influence of Central Europe increased. The works of the **Master of the Litomice Altar** (Litoměřice was responsible for decorating the upper part of the walls in the Wenceslas Chapel in St Vitus Cathedral with the saint's legend) show this clearly, as does the artist's *Madonna and Child* with the monogram I W; he was one of the most important pupils of Lucas Cranach the Elder.

The exhibition ends with the works of the Master of the *Lamentation of Christ* from Žebrák and the altar shrine carved in wood by Master I.P. (*c*1520); the influence of Albrecht Dürer is discernible. These works, together with Albrecht Altdorfer's *Martyrdom of St Florian*, are in the last exhibition room.

✳ Dancing House ·
Ginger & Fred (Tančicí dům)

Location: Praha 1, Nové Město, Rašínovo nábřeží 80/corner of Resslova

Metro: Karlovo náměstí

Among the few examples of contemporary architecture in Prague is the »Dancing House« of 1996, an office block on the Vltava affectionately referred to by natives of the city as »Ginger & Fred« – after Ginger Rogers and Fred Astaire, the star couple of the American musical. Its two glass and concrete towers were for a long time considered controversial, but now, along with the castle or Old Town Square, they have become part of the Prague sightseeing programme. Yugoslav architect **Vlado Milunič** – who for years lived in a house alongside the empty plot, as did Václav Havel – found financial backing for his idea in a Dutch insurance company, and a collaborator in the Californian architect **Frank O. Gehry**, who brought greater incisiveness to the plans.

The straight tower accentuates the street corner and behaves rather like a standing leg, while its glass counterpart snuggles up against it. The fluid movement recalls the Baroque style so prevalent in the city. The projecting

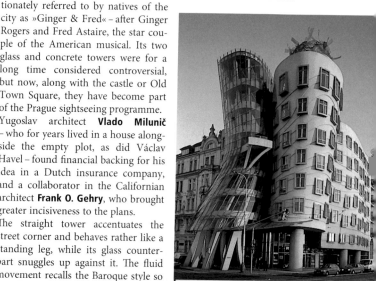

Popularly known as »Ginger & Fred«

windows and undulating surface of the façade guard against monotony, at the same time ensuring integration into the adjoining rows of houses. The airy stilts convey lightness, and set the ground floor back from the street. The building is literally crowned by a punched metal ball, the so-called »Head of Medusa«, that echoes the globe on Havel's house next door, and the neo-Gothic onion towers and oriel windows in the neighbourhood. Spectacular as the building looks from outside, the internal arrangement conforms conventionally to its function as office block.

Emmaus Monastery (Emauzy)

E 6

Location: Praha 1, Nové Město, Vyšehradská

Metro: Karlovo náměstí
Tram: 3, 4, 7, 10, 14, 16, 17, 18, 21, 24

⊙ Opening hours: Mon–Fri 9am–4pm

Emmaus Monastery (Monastery of the Slavs, Klášter na Slovanech) was closed in 1949. The monastery and its Church of Our Lady were returned to the Benedictine order only in 1990.

Charles IV founded the monastery in 1347 (with papal approval) for Benedictines of the Slav rite – Croatians, Serbs, Czechs and Russians. The language used to celebrate Mass was Old Church Slavonic, through which the church sought to extend its sphere in the relatively unexploited east. In the 14th century the monastery was an important cultural and educational centre; until 1546 it housed the Glagolithic part of the so-called Rheims Gospel Book, on which the kings of France swore their coronation oath.

In 1945 the building burnt down as a result of a US air attack. Only in 1967 was the restoration of the Gothic monastery church completed; the original towers were replaced by two modern intertwining concrete spires that stretch heavenwards like a pair of wings.

! **Baedeker TIP**

Rock for an Ave Maria
The monastery church, which was damaged heavily in world War II, was renovated without any extravagant decorations and the Gothic roof was replaced with a modern one. Inside there are rough cement walls and undressed brick. Since the church looks like an empty New York factory it is appealing to the rock bands who are allowed to perform here now.

Gothic cloisters The frescoes in the Gothic cloisters have been restored several times. They are among the most significant surviving works from the early Prague school of painting; as in late medieval Bibles of the Poor, important salvation events from the New Testament and scenes from the Old Testament are depicted in a total of 26 wall panels (dated c1360). Unfortunately however, they are not especially well preserved.

Emmaus Monastery's Church of Our Lady was built in Gothic style between 1348 and 1372. It consists of three large aisles, equal in size. It underwent Baroque alterations in the 17th century, and then neo-Gothic remodelling. The concave spires of 1967 are the work of architect **František M. Černý**; they represent a compromise between Baroque towers and a pointed Gothic pediment.

Church of Our Lady
🕐
Opening hours:
Mon–Fri 9am–4pm

Diagonally opposite Emmaus Monastery is the Church of St John of Nepomuk on the Rock (Kostel svatého Jana Nepomuckého na Skalce, Vyšehradská 18). The central building with two towers and double flight of steps, built in around 1730 by **Kilian Ignaz Dientzenhofer**, is one of the most beautiful late-Baroque churches.
The fresco by Karel Kovář (1748) shows St John of Nepomuk's ascent into heaven. Johann Brokoff carved the wooden statue of the saint on the main altar; there is a bronze realization of the wooden model on ▶Charles Bridge. The church is open during services.

St John of Nepomuk on the Rock

Going south, Vyšehradská becomes Na slupi, on which the entrance to the Botanical Garden (Botanická zahrada) is located. Laid out by the Florentine apothecary Angelo in the reign of Charles IV, the garden boasts a 600-year history, a contains a multitude of native and exotic plants to match. The university garden founded in Smíchov in 1775 was moved here in 1897. Open: April, Sept, Oct, daily 9am–6pm, May–Aug until 7pm; Nov–March until 5pm.

Botanical Garden
🕐

Estates Theatre (Stavovské divadlo)

E 4

Location: Praha 1, Staré Město, Železná 11

Metro: Můstek

Count Anton of Nostitz-Rieneck had this, the first theatre in the Vltava valley, built in Classicist style (1781–1783) from a design by Anton Haffenecker. East front and interior fittings are by architect Achill Wolf (1881). At the end of the 18th century the Nostitz Theatre was run by the Bohemian nobility as an »Estates Theatre«, from the mid-19th century as a »German regional theatre«. In 1945 it was re-named Tyl Theatre after the Czech dramatist and actor Josef Kajetán Tyl (1808–1856). In November 1991, after a seven-year renovation period, it was re-opened by the president of the republic, Václav Havel, as Estates Theatre, with a young *Don Giovanni* by Czech-Swedish director David Radok. Today, the small theatre has become part of the Czech National Theatre.
Three operas by Antonio Vivaldi, two operas by Gluck, and works by Jommelli, Rutini and Boroni were premiered at Prague's Estates Theatre. On 29 October 1787 the first performance of Mozart's opera *Don Giovanni* took place here, and was a resounding success. The

www.stavovske divadlo.cz

Resplendent since the 18th century

event was recorded in literary form by Eduard Mörike, among others, in his work *Mozart's Journey to Prague*. In the years 1813–1816 composer Carl Maria von Weber (1786–1826) led the theatre orchestra; at a later date, Gustav Mahler and Carl Muck ran the theatre.

The ▶Charles University, the oldest university in Central Europe, is next door at number 9 Železná.

Grand Priory Square (Velkopřevorské náměstí)

D 4

Location: Praha 1, Malá Strana   **Tram:** 12, 22, 23

Grand Priory Square is given its character by the two high Baroque palaces facing one another: that of the Grand Prior, and Buquoyský Palace. North of Grand Priory Palace stands the Church of Our Lady Below the Chain. Further along Prokopská in a southerly direction is Nostitz Palace, on the south side of Maltese Square (Maltézské náměstí).

Grand Priory Palace

Today the Grand Priory Palace of the sovereign order of Maltese Knights (Palác maltézského velkopřevora) in Malá Strana is once again the seat of the order, jointly with its former convent in number

4 Lázeňská, and residence of the Maltese Grand Prior. The impressive Baroque rooms have wooden dado panelling, elaborate Baroque stoves and beautiful inlaid floors.

Commissioned by Grand Prior Gundaker Poppo Count Dietrichstein, the Italian architect **Bartolomeo Scotti** constructed the double-winged corner palace between 1724 and 1728 by adapting the original Renaissance building and adding ornamental cornices, oriel windows, and a new doorway for the order. The vases and lamp-bearing statues in the stairwell are from the workshop of Matthias Bernhard Braun.

Buquoyský Palace

Standing opposite Grand Priory Palace, Buquoyský Palace (no. 486) today houses the French embassy. Commissioned by Marie Josefa von Thun (of the Valdštejn family), it was built (1719) according to plans by **Giovanni Santini-Aichl**, probably in collaboration with **František Maximilian Kaňka**. In 1735 it was extended. The ornamental moulding was done by **Matthias Bernhard Braun**. After the Buquoy family acquired the palace, the interior was decorated in neo-Baroque style. In the years 1889–1896, J. Schulz gave a neo-Renaissance look to the stairwell and rear wing; the two tapestries (16th and 18th century) in the large hall of the rear wing are worth seeing. Further alterations were made in 1904. The old, informal garden of the palace extends as far as ►Kampa Island.

Our Lady Below the Chain

To the north of Grand Priory Palace is the Church of Our Lady Below the Chain (Kostel Panny Marie pod Řetězem, Lázeňská). It is one of the oldest Malá Strana churches, and was founded in 1169 with the former Maltese order monastery as the administrative headquarters of the order's Bohemian province. Remains of the Romanesque basilica, which burnt down in 1420, can be seen in the right-hand wall of the forecourt. The two massive towers were completed in 1389. In the 17th-century **Carlo Lurago** gave the presbytery its Baroque look, still evident today.

Among the most notable features of the Baroque interior are the high altar painting (*The Assumption of Our Lady*) and a painting of St Barbara, both by Karel Škréta. The pulpit is by Johann Georg Bendl.

Nostický Palace

The four-winged Nostický Palace on Maltese Square (no. 1, southwest of Grand Priory Square) – today the seat of the Dutch embassy and various departments of the ministry of culture – fills the south side of the square. It was built in Baroque style, 1658–1660, for Jo-

Impressive interior of Nostický Palace, grand Dutch embassy quarters

hann Hertwig of Nostitz (probably from plans by **Francesco Caratti**). It was enriched in 1720 by projecting dormer windows and statues of emperors from the Brokoff workshops (now copies), and in 1765 by the Rococo columned entrance by Anton Hafenecker. It is worth taking a look at the courtyard, and at the ceiling frescoes with mythological motifs (by Wenceslas B. Ambrozzi, *c*1757). The palace houses the **Dobrovský Library** (formerly Nostický Library; more than 15,000 volumes).

★ Hradčany Square (Hradčanské náměstí)

C 4

Location: Praha 1, Hradčany   **Metro:** Hradčanská, Malostranská
Tram: 22, 23

The town of Hradčany, founded as Prague's third town in about 1320, was not a royal free town; it was governed by the burgrave of Prague Castle. Initially occupying only the space around Hradčany Square, Charles IV expanded it and enclosed it within a ring of walls. Hradčany Square, with the Baroque plague column by **Ferdinand Maximilian Brokoff** (1725) and a notable iron lamppost from the 19th-century era of gas lighting, forms the approach to ▶ Prague Castle and was the centre of the earlier town of Hradčany. The Bohemian kings' coronation procession, starting in ▶ Vyšehrad, crossed the square, and it was on Hradčany Square that the leaders of the unsuccessful Estates' revolt against the Habsburg Ferdinand I were executed in 1547. Today it still has the extent and groundplan of a medieval marketplace, although it never served this purpose. After the fire of 1541 the square was entirely rebuilt. Old burgher houses were demolished in order to make way for aristocrats' and cathedral canons' palaces.

No. 10, called the Saxon-Lauenburg residence, was the residence of the master builder of St Vitus Cathedral, **Peter Parler**, in 1372; he also owned Hrzán Palace on ►Loretánská. In the 18th century façade of this house and that of the adjoining number 9 were given a shared facing.

Parler House

In the centre of Hradčany Square stands the Marian plague column, erected in gratitude for the end of the epidemic in 1726. It was designed by **Ferdinand Maximilian Brokoff** (1688–1731). The figures on two levels at the foot of the column represent the saints: John Nepomuk, Elizabeth, Peter, Paul, Norbert, Florian, Charles Borromäus on the lower level; above them are Wenceslas, Vitus and Adalbert. The column is crowned by the figure of Maria Immaculata (Virgin of the Immaculate Conception; a popular Baroque motif), which was made after Brokoff's death, probably in his workshop.

Plague column

Archbishop's Palace (Arcibiskupský palác)

The Archbishop's Palace on the north side of the square originated as a Renaissance house; Ferdinand I purchased it from royal secretary Florian of Gryspek and conferred it on the first post-Hussite Catholic archbishop. In the years 1562–1564 it was altered, using plans by H. Tirol; in around 1600 it was enlarged; and between 1675 and 1684 it was given a Baroque look by the French architect **Jean Baptiste Mathey**, and a grandiose main portal (1676). **Johann Joseph Wirch** was responsible for its present Rococo appearance with the façade clad in marble facing (1763–1764). Two corner projections counterbalance the central projection, which is further accentuated by a shallow gable. The family coat of arms of Prince-Archbishop Anton Peter Count of Přichowitz crowns the sculptures by Ignaz Michael Platzner, of which Faith and Hope were replaced in 1888 by new works by T. Seidan.

Wirch was also responsible for the late-Baroque interior. Nine tapestries by A. Desportes, made in the Parisian Atelier Neilson, address the theme of »Ancient and Modern India«. There is a wealth of woodcarving and stucco ornamentation, as well as two reliquary busts of apostles Peter and Paul in the chapel, the collection of glass and porcelain is also noteworthy.

A passageway from the left doorway of the Archbishop's Palace leads to ►Šternberský Palace with its collection of early European art.

Changing guards on Hradčany Square, a real tourist spectacle! In the background, the archbishop's palace.

Martinický Palace

On the northwest side of Hradčany Square stands Martinický Palace, now occupied by the capital's chief architect. Exhibitions, concerts and lectures on literature are held in the palace rooms.

The Renaissance building was erected at the end of the 16th century as a modest edifice with four wings for **Andreas Teyfl**; in 1624 it was taken over by Jaroslav Bořita z Martinic, one of those governors who went down in history because of the second Prague defenestration. Bořita Martinic added an upper storey with a Renaissance gable and heraldic arms.

The east front is decorated by figural Renaissance sgraffiti with scenes from the life of Samson (from 15th-century German woodcuts) and from the life of Hercules (c1634).

Similar sgraffiti from the 16th and the first half of the 17th century have also been found on the front of the palace facing the square, with biblical scenes (incl. Joseph's flight from Potiphar's wife).

Inside, take a look at the Renaissance beam ceilings and the palace chapel with its richly ornamented Renaissance vaulting.

Toskánský Palace

This two-storey, four-winged palace (no. 5) on the narrow west side of the square was built between 1689 and 1691 by the French architect **Jean Baptiste Mathey** for Michael Oswald Thun-Hohenstein. From 1718 to 1918 it was owned by the dukes of Tuscany; today it belongs to the Czech Republic's ministry for foreign affairs.

The building's proportions appear well balanced against the cool aloofness of its surroundings. The early-Baroque front is ornamented with two pillared entrances and the dukes of Tuscany's heraldic arms on the wide space over the balconies; the tympanum carries six Baroque statues of the liberal arts by **Johann Brokoff**, father of Ferdinand Maximilian Brokoff, one of Prague's outstanding Baroque sculptors. The corner figure of St Michael fighting the dragon is by Ottavio Mosto (1693).

Schwarzenberg Palace (Schwarzenberský palác)

Opening hours:
Tue–Sun
10am–6pm

The former Schwarzenberg Palace, which now houses the Military History Museum, is one of the dominant features in the Hradčany skyline, along with the castle and Archbishop's Palace. Schwarzenberg Palace is a prime example of northern Renaissance style, with its richly adorned gables, projecting lunette sills based on the Lombardian model, refined diamond sgraffito décor modelled on north Italian (especially Venetian) graphic art, and representations of ancient gods and allegorical figures in the interior. Occupying the south corner of the square, the palace was created by the conversion of two Renaissance palaces. Alterations were undertaken in Empire style

(1800–1810) by F. Pavíček for Archbishop Salm – hence the initial »S« over the doorway.

The right-hand part of the building, constructed between 1545 and 1563 by Agostino Gali, houses the **Military History Museum**. The museum shows the development of the art of war from ancient times to the end of World War I in 1918. A main focus is the Napoleonic wars.

Tempera frescoes (c1580) by an unknown artist adorn the ceiling of the main hall on the second floor. They depict personifications and allegories from Homer's famous epics (the judgement of Paris, the abduction of Helen, scenes from the Trojan war and the flight of Aeneas from the burning city of Troy). In the neighbouring room the Phaeton myth is shown. Two further rooms are decorated by paintings of Chronos and Persephone, and Jupiter and Juno.

The steep approach to Schwarzenberg Palace

In the inner courtyard, 16th–20th-century guns for use on land and at sea are displayed. The collections include prehistoric weaponry and all European army weapons known to military history. There is also a large display of army uniforms for all ranks from various countries, a collection of medals and awards, military flags, banners, maps and plans of significant battles.

◄ ✳ Josefov

Location: Praha 1, Staré Město, Maiselova etc.
Bus: 207

Metro: Staroměstská
Tram: 17, 18

Enclosed in the heart of Staré Město is Josefov, the former Jewish town, one of the oldest and most important Jewish communities in the whole of the west. The number of people living and working in this decidedly small district amounted at times to more than 7000. Several pogroms in different centuries decimated the population time

District brimming with history

and again, and laid waste the district. It was called Josefov in memory of Emperor Joseph II, who, at the end of the 18th century, was the first to elevate the Jewish ghetto, which had existed for 600 years, to a district of Prague with rights on a par with other districts.

! *Baedeker* TIP

The eternal temptress
Not exactly part of the Judaic programme: the small Galerie La Femme shows the diversity with which Prague's painters approach the erotic, from Romanticism to Cubism. Whether blue-stockinged or emerging from the bath, these are stimulating perspectives. Bílkova 2, daily 11am–7pm; www.glf.cz.

The **Jewish Museum** (www.jewish-museum.cz, Židovské muzeum), founded in 1906 and under state guardianship from 1950 to 1994, belongs to Prague's Jewish community.

The museum holds not only of items from the former Jewish town. During their surge of destruction, the Nazi authorities wanted to make out of the limited inventory of the Jewish Museum as it was in 1939 an »Exotic Museum of an Extinct Race«. In the course of the German occupation the collection was extended to almost 200,000 items. On the initiative of Prague's Jewish community, valuable material from Bohemian, Moravian and other European synagogues was brought together to provide unique documentation.

⏲ Opening hours:
April–Oct
9am–6pm
Nov–March
9am–4.30pm
except Sat and
Jewish holidays

The Maisel Synagogue, the Spanish Synagogue (in which concerts are given during the summer), the Pinkas Synagogue, the Old Jewish Cemetery, the Klaus Synagogue and the ceremonial hall all belong to the Jewish Museum. The Old-New Synagogue does not.

Maisel Synagogue (Maiselova synagóga)

Mordecai Markus Maisel, Primate of Prague's Jewish town under Emperor Rudolf II, founded the synagogue that bears his name as a family house of prayer; the master builders were **Joseph Wahl** and **Juda Goldschmied**. After a fire in 1689 the building was renovated in Baroque style; from 1893 to 1905 Alfred Grotte modified it according to neo-Gothic notions. Only the general outline of a nave and two aisles and the women's gallery remained.

The Jewish Museum shows the **history of the Jews in Bohemia and Moravia** from the 10th to the 18th century. The main points of emphasis are the beginnings of Jewish settlements in Bohemia and Moravia and the position of Jews in the Middle Ages, as well as the Renaissance era – which links in neatly with the founding of Maisel Synagogue.

✶ Spanish Synagogue (Španělská synagóga)

The Spanish Synagogue occupies the site of the oldest synagogue in Prague (12th century), the so-called Old School (Stará škola), which was destroyed. The synagogue's name goes back to a group of Jews who fled to Prague from the Spanish Inquisition. In the following centuries the synagogue was burnt down several times, and built up again on each occasion.

The Spanish Synagogue was given its present form between 1882 and 1893 by **Ignaz Ullmann**; it is a central-plan building in Moorish style with impressive cupola and open galleries on three sides. The interior was designed with Granada's Alhambra in mind: oriental-type stucco work was introduced (1882/1883). Here, the second section of the history of the Jews in Bohemia and Moravia is displayed – from the Enlightenment to the present day.

Reminiscent of the Alhambra

Pinkas Synagogue (Pinkasova synagóga)

The Pinkas Synagogue arose on the south side of the Old Jewish Cemetery in a house which the leading family of the Jewish community, the Horovitz family, had bought from Rabbi Pinkas in the 14th century. In 1535 Salman Munka Horovitz had a synagogue built in late-Gothic style; the reticulated vaulting dates from this time. Juda Goldschmied de Herz converted the synagogue in 1625 in late-Renaissance style, and extended it to include a women's gallery, vestibule and meeting-room.

The Pinkas Synagogue and the Old-New Synagogue are the oldest and, in terms of their architecture, the most important in Prague. Archaeological excavations have confirmed that the Pinkas Synagogue dates from the 11th or 12th century, and that there was once a ritual bath here.

In the years 1950–1958 the **Holocaust Memorial** was erected in the synagogue, bearing the names of all 77,297 victims. The building was closed at the end of the 1960s, the inscriptions on the walls having suffered from the effects of ground water. During the course of renovation work, an old well and a ritual bath were discovered. In the 1990s the names of the victims were once more inscribed on the synagogue walls.

In the permanent display are children's drawings, exercise books, diaries, letters and lyric poetry from the Nazi concentration camp ►Terezín (Theresienstadt).

✶ Old Jewish Cemetery (Starý židovský hřbitov)

Crowded gravestones The Old Jewish Cemetery and Old-New Synagogue are amongst the most significant historic remnants of the former Jewish town and, according to many, number among the »ten most interesting sights in the world«. The cemetery dates back to the beginning of the 15th century; burials took place until 1787. There are still approximately 12,000 gravestones beneath the ash trees.

1900sq m/0.5ac of ground were sacrificed to a sanitation programme in 1903. The limited space was too small for the large number of graves, and fresh earth had to be piled onto the existing graves in order to create plots for new graves. According to Jewish law, graves may never be given up, so in some places there are up to nine layers, one on top of the other. This has resulted in the impressive array of gravestones; their accumulation and age give the Old Jewish Cemetery its distinctive appearance.

The Hebrew inscriptions on the gravestones provide personal details – the name of the deceased and father's name (for married women, also the husband's name) – as well as date of death and of the funeral. The good works of the deceased are listed not only in prose, but also in verse. Reliefs on the gravestones often give a visual image of the deceased person's name (stag, bear, carp, cockerel etc.), his profession (physician's instruments, tailor's scissors etc.), and some-

Jewish law decrees that graves be maintained for ever.

Josefov Map

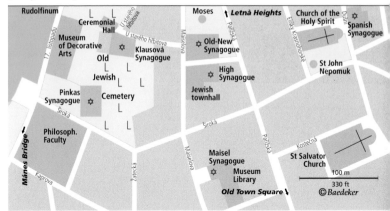

times other symbols, such as blessing hands or pitchers (for members of priestly families), grapes (for the tribes of Israel), crowns, pine-cones or other motifs.

The oldest gravestone marks the resting-place of scholar and poet Avigdor Karo († 1439), who experienced the pogrom of 1389 and wrote an elegy upon it. The most recent grave, of Moses Beck, dates from 1787; since that time there have been no more burials here.

A sarcophagus in late-Renaissance style with chiselled lions and writing-tablets framed by arcades marks the **grave of the learned Chief Rabbi Jehuda Löw ben Bezalel** († 1609).

Further identified tombs include those of the Primate of Prague's Jewish town, Mordecai Markus Maisel († 1601), historian and astronomer David Gans († 1613), scholar Joseph Schlomo Delmedigo († 1655) and book-collector and scholar David Oppenheim († 1736).

One of the richest and loveliest is the gravestone of Heudele Bassevi († 1628), wife of Wallenstein's financier, the first Prague Jew to be elevated to the aristocracy.

The pebbles on the graves are laid there by relatives or friends. This custom dates back to the people of Israel's wandering through the desert under Moses: at that time it was customary to cover the dead with stones, for protection against wild animals, because there was no

 DON'T MISS

- Mosaics inspired by the Alhambra in Granada (Spanish Synagogue)
- The names of 77,297 victims of the Holocaust etched into the wall with red ink (Pinkas Synagogue)
- The grave of Rabbi Löw, creator of Golem, with allegorical lion, bears and roses (Old Jewish Cemetery)
- *Death of a Jew*, cycle of 15 pictures of the observances of the burial fraternity (Old Jewish Cemetery, ceremonial hall)
- Anniversary lights, showing when to pray for the dead: 3 June, Franz Kafka (Old-New Synagogue)

GOLEM, GRAVES AND SCHOLARS: THE PRAGUE GHETTO

Little has survived of the Prague district once inhabited by Jews – only a town hall, six synagogues and part of the old Jewish cemetery. Everything else was demolished at the beginning of the last century, to make way for a new city district.

At that point the crooked alleyways disappeared, where houses with such expressive names as »The Cold Hostelry«, »The Mousehole« and »No Time« had been crammed together. But the story of the ghetto has been kept alive – and not only by the small community of scarcely 1000 Jews who today once more celebrate religious services in Old-New Synagogue and run the Jewish museum.

The old cemetery, with approximately 12,000 crumbling funeral stelae dating from 1439–1787, is enormously fascinating. Here the legendary Jehuda Löw ben Bezalel is buried, that great **Rabbi Löw** of whom it is said that he created the gigantic **Golem** out of clay at the end of the 16th century. It was God's will that this soulless matter (»Golem« in Hebrew) should assist the rabbi and defend the persecuted

The Jewish cemetery in Žižkov became a burial ground when there was no more room in Josefov. Although the gravestones here are not so old, and not packed so tightly next to or even on top of one another, here, too, it seems that time came to a standstill at some point.

Jews. In order to bring the creature to life, the rabbi placed in its mouth a parchment scroll bearing the ineffable name of God. Now the dumb creature worked week by week for the scholar, except on the Sabbath, when no Jewish believer may work. The inevitable happened: on one holy Sabbath the rabbi forgot to remove the scroll in order to let Golem rest. The giant was torn between his duty to work and his existence according to the will of God, which forbade him to work on this day, and he raged frantically. With a mighty crash he smashed the furniture of the rabbi, who was just leading the community in the synagogue, singing the 92nd psalm. The people rushed out of the synagogue, but it was impossible to stop Golem. In order to avert the ultimate catastrophe, the rabbi threw himself upon Golem and pulled the sacred scroll away. Then he removed him – to this day, nobody knows quite where he took him – and in some attic or other Golem must have turned to dust or clay. (But beware: from time to time, on dark nights, Golem is reportedly seen on the streets of Prague!) Afterwards the rabbi had the community sing the 92nd psalm once more, and that has remained a tradition in Prague's synagogues to this day.

Rabbi Löw, as conceived by Ladislav Šaloun

Jews from all over the world seek out Josefov and the Jewish cemetery.

Scapegoats

Just as Golem could not protect the Jews in the long term, so also they received little help from other sources over the centuries. A good 100 years after the Jews first settled in Malá Strana in 995, the first pogrom was instigated by fanatical Crusaders. In the twelfth century the Jews had to move from Malá Strana to the other side of the Vltava, where their settlement was enclosed by a wall, as laid down by the Third Lateran Council (1179). For centuries their history was marked by exclusion of this sort. It was never difficult for Christians to find a reason for a pogrom: for instance, Jews were blamed for the plague – after all, they succumbed to the disease far less frequently. People did not realize that their periodic relative exemption from this illness, which is spread by rat fleas, was attributable to Jewish ritual cleansing customs; they lived far more hygienically than did the Christians.

So-called privileges

With very few exceptions, the so-called Christian benefactors who granted the Jewish ghetto short periods of security and self-determination did so only to enrich themselves: Rudolf II (1576–1611), for instance, annulled all the privileges he had granted the Jews in previous decades, at the very moment when the Jewish merchant Mordecai Markus Maisel died; Rudolf had been financially dependent on him. Moreover, the so-called privileges which the Jews enjoyed from time to time were usually only rights or permissions which other groups took for granted, such as the right to »protection against arbitrary persecution«, or permission to convey the dead without tax from one

Torah scrolls contain the Jewish laws; this one is in Klaus Synagogue.

province to another. The Habsburg Joseph II (1765–1790), after whom the Jewish ghetto was renamed Josefov in 1861, is the only one of whom it can be said that he supported the Jews without considering his own advantage. Thanks to Joseph's enlightened attitude Josefov was recognized as a city district with equal rights, and exclusion of Jews was temporarily suspended. However, in the first two decades of the 19th century the former Jewish ghetto was almost entirely demolished – condemned, because the buildings had been packed closer and closer together during the centuries of enforced settlement, and the quarter was therefore grim and largely run down. The violent end of the Jewish community, repeatedly persecuted by pogroms, pillage and expulsions (e.g. under Ferdinand I in the 16th century, and under Maria Theresa in the 18th century), came

with the genocidal madness of the Nazis. 90% of Bohemia and Moravia's Jews lost their lives between 1939 and 1945. Their names are inscribed in the Holocaust memorial to the 77,927 Czech Jews in Pinkas Synagogue.

Sightseeing

The few Jews who still live in Prague see that their cultural memorials, made into a museum, now number among the city's main tourist attractions. On a quiet day out of season visitors to the synagogue and old cemetery area will find an enthralling magic in the ancient weathered gravestones, which have survived for centuries, though part or all may have sunk into the ground. Yet when masses of snapshot-seeking tourists crowd the paths of the old cemetery at the height of the season, one or other of the Jewish community may yearn for Golem, who would know how to restore peace.

other possibility amidst the desert sand. The faithful throw little messages onto the tomb of Chief Rabbi Jehuda Löw, invoking his help – it is said he can work miracles.

Ceremonial hall Beside the exit from the Old Jewish Cemetery is the neo-Romanesque ceremonial hall with its small tower, built in 1911/1912 according to a design by J. Gerstl. In earlier times the ceremonial hall was used for mourning rites, which could last up to seven days. Now, the second part of the exhibition of Jewish Customs and Traditions is shown here, including the practices of the Prague burial fraternity. The 15-part cycle dedicated to the fraternity's observances is by an unknown artist; it is dated 1780.

Klaus Synagogue (Klausova synagóga)

The Klaus Synagogue is located directly next to the exit from the Old Jewish Cemetery and ceremonial hall. Built in 1694 in Baroque style and remodelled on the outside in 1884, the Klaus Synagogue houses a permanent exhibition displaying Jewish traditions and habits, the significance of the synagogue and Jewish festivals.

? DID YOU KNOW ...?

■ where the name of the Klaus Synagogue originated? It comes from Latin »clausum« (closure) and has nothing to do with the forename Klaus.

Rabbi Jehuda Löw ben Bezalel taught in the Klaus Synagogue as one of the most important Jewish philosophers of the 16th century. The prestige of the Klaus Synagogue in Prague's Jewish ghetto was attributable to its size and to the fact that it was reserved for the burial fraternity.

✱ Old-New Synagogue (Old-New School, Staronová synagóga)

Opposite the High Synagogue stands the Old-New Synagogue. The name actually derives from the Hebrew »altnai«, meaning »on condition that«. Behind this name lies a legend: for the building of Prague's synagogue, angels brought stones from the ruin of the temple in Jerusalem, but only on condition that these stones would be taken back to Jerusalem when the Messiah came to rebuild his temple. It is the only synagogue in Europe of this age that still serves as such.

The oldest part of the building is the early-Gothic south hall, originally principal chamber of the house of prayer; in the 13th century it was extended by a double-aisled hall in Cistercian Gothic style. Its five-ribbed vaulting is unique in Bohemian architecture. The women's galleries were completed in the 17th and 18th centuries – only men may pray in the main hall. The large flag was a present from Charles IV, who conferred the »lofty banner« on the Jewish com-

🕐 Opening hours:
April–Oct
Sun–Thu
9.30am–6pm
Fri 9.30am–5pm
Nov–March
Sun–Thu
9.30am–5pm
Fri 9.30am–2pm

munity in 1358 as a sign of their privileges; today's flag is from the reign of Charles VI (1716). This red flag with the six-pointed Star of David and hat was the official banner of Prague's Jews, and it occurs on the capital's historic coat of arms, as third emblem from the right beside the Bohemian lion. This makes Prague the only city in the world with a Jewish emblem in its heraldic arms. On the east side of the synagogue in a Torah shrine lies the Pentateuch parchment roll (the first five books of the Old Testament). In the centre is the raised pulpit, separated by lattice-work (15th century). The synagogue was renovated as early as 1618, according to Hebrew inscriptions on the walls; further extensive reconstructions followed in 1883 and 1966.

> ## ! Baedeker TIP
>
> ### Fascinating Golem
> Anyone interested in the Golem legend is well served with literature. It has been a topic of both Czech and German writing, for instance in the work of Gustav Meyrink (1868–1932) in his novel *Golem*, as well as in one of the stories in *The Powder Tower* (*On Golem's Track*) by reporter Egon Erwin Kisch (1885–1948).

Legend has it that in the attic of the Old-New Synagogue lie the remains of **Golem**, the most famous mythical figure of Prague, created by Rabbi Löw in 1580 – or in 5340 according to Jewish dating – in order to protect Prague's Jews from persecution.

In the little park beside the Old-New Synagogue stands a statue of Moses by František Bílek (1872–1941).

Opposite the Old-New Synagogue, at no. 18 Maiselova on the corner of Pařížská, stands the former Jewish Town Hall (Židovská radnice). This is the seat of Prague's Jewish community and the council of Jew-   **Jewish Town Hall**

Old-New Synagogue and former Jewish Town Hall. The hands on the gable clock run in the opposite direction – like Hebrew script.

ish communities in the Czech Republic, and is not open to the public. Mordecai Markus Maisel, court banker and mayor of the Jewish town under Emperor Rudolf II, donated this town hall to the Jewish community in around 1580. Building was undertaken in 1586 in Renaissance style; it was converted in Baroque style (1765) by Josef Schlesinger.

The south extension dates from the first decade of the 20th century. The north gable beneath the wooden clock-tower has a clock with Hebrew numbers. The hands run anti-clockwise; Hebrew script likewise runs from right to left.

High Synagogue Like the Jewish Town Hall, its once affiliated High Synagogue (Vysoká synagóga) at number 4 Červená is not open to the public.

The synagogue was built in 1568 by Pankraz Roder, also on a square ground plan; in the 19th century it was separated from the town hall and provided with its own stairway and street access. The interior chamber was constructed on the first floor – hence »High« Synagogue. It was extended in the 17th century and re-designed in neo-Renaissance style in the 19th century. There is a contrast between this chamber with its magnificent stellar vaulting – a prime example of Jewish sacral building – and the synagogue's modest exterior.

Church of the Holy Saviour Church of the Holy Saviour (Kostel svatého Salvátora) in Salvátorská (accessible from Pařížská) was originally a Lutheran church; today it serves the Bohemian Brothers. It was built from 1611 to 1614 from designs by Swiss-born J. Christoph in Renaissance style; bought by the Pauline order (hermits of St Francis of Paola) in the mid-17th century, it was given a Baroque look, and in 1720 it was provided with a tower. Protestants from all over Europe contributed to the construction costs.

Jungmann Square (Jungmannovo náměstí)

E 5

Location: Praha 1, Staré Město **Metro:** Můstek
Tram: 3, 9, 14, 24

On Jungmann Square stands the Jungmann monument (Jungmannův pomník), created by Ludvík Šimek in 1878. The writer, philosopher and linguistic researcher **Josef Jungmann** (1773–1847) was an important representative of the »rebirth« of Czech national sentiment during the Romantic era; he compiled an extensive Czech-German dictionary and wrote a history of Czech literature.

Our Lady of the Snows The Church of Our Lady of the Snows (Kostel Panny Marie Sněžné) was commissioned in 1347 by Charles IV as a coronation and monastery church; it was intended to surpass St Vitus Cathedral (▶

Prague Castle) in height. By 1397 only the 30m/98ft-high chancel was complete; on the north side was a fine Gothic doorway with numerous sculptures of saints. The building fell into decay from the 15th century; in 1611 the vaulting fell in, and the Franciscans replaced it with a Renaissance ceiling. The Baroque high altar (1625–1651) is the largest in any of Prague's churches. Above the left side altar hangs a painting by **Wenzel Lorenz Reiner**, *The Annunciation*.

The church played an important part in the Hussite movement. Jan Želivský preached here to the city's poor against the papal church, the aristocracy and the wealthy bourgeoisie. In 1419 Želivský stormed the town hall in Nové Město with the most radical of his supporters and flung the Catholic councillors out of the window. This so-called **first Prague defenestration** precipitated the Hussite Wars. Even after the murder of Želivský (in 1422), who lies buried here, the Church of Our Lady of the Snows continued to be a Hussite centre.

To the south of the Church of Our Lady of the Snows lies the green oasis of the Franciscan monastery garden (Františkánská zahrada). Passages link this public space to ► Wenceslas Square and to the streets Jungmannova, Palackého and Vodičkova.

Franciscan garden

Kampa (Kampa)

D 4/5

Location: Praha 1, Malá Strana, Kampa   **Metro:** Malostranská
Tram: 12, 22, 23

Separated from Malá Strana by the idyllic Čertovka arm of the Vltava (formerly also a dangerous stretch of river, hence the name »Devil's Stream«), the river island of Kampa forms the green strip on the Vltava's left bank, from Legií Bridge to Mánes Bridge. The west section of ► Charles Bridge passes over the island; some of the little houses on the island have their foundations supported on the arches of the original Judith Bridge. North of Charles Bridge, the Čertovka flows through two rows of houses, often referred to as »Prague's Venice« (Pražské Benátky).

The cultivation of this initially boggy land to create several gardens did not begin until the 15th century. After this, the Čertovka

> ## Baedeker TIP
>
> ### Canoe, ahoy!
>
> River-rafting fans can plunge straight into dramatic rapids right here in Prague. At the weekend, rubber dinghies congregate in the foaming waters around the dams. Canoeists will need to muster all their skills to paddle along the Devil's Stream (Čertovka). Mastering the straits of Devil's Mill (also known as Grand Priory Mill) is excellent training for winning Olympic gold, as Prague's crack canoeists have already demonstrated. The watersports club is on the island.

was used to power several mills; some of the mill-wheels are on show near Charles Bridge and the bridge leading to Grand Priory Square. The large wheel of Grand Priory Mill (late 16th century) has recently been restored.

There are potters' markets on Kampa Island, and it is a pleasant place to stroll. It offers delightful views of the Vltava and Shooters' Island, of Charles Bridge and Staré Město, and of the waterfront gardens of some of the Malá Strana palaces, where a large park has been created through the amalgamation of previously separate palace gardens.

Close to Charles Bridge is the late-Gothic statue of Roland, reconstructed by L. Simek in 1884. It once marked the border between Malá Strana, administered according to Magdeburg law, and Staré Město, where Nuremberg law prevailed.

Karlova

E 4

Location: Praha 1, Staré Město   **Metro:** Staroměstská, Můstek
Tram: 17, 18

On the route of the historic coronation procession

Karlova is part of the historic coronation route from ► Old Town Square to ► Charles Bridge. The thoroughfare's showpiece is the house at number 3, **»The Golden Well«**. Remains of masonry in the basement show that there was once a Romanesque building on this spot. The Renaissance façade seen today is embellished with a magnificent Baroque stucco relief from 1701 by Johann Ulrich Mayer, showing the saints Wenceslas, Rochus, Sebastian, Ignatius of Loyola, Franciscus Xaverius and Rosalia. There is an inviting wine tavern on the ground floor. The German astronomer Johannes Kepler lived at no. 4 from 1607-1612. he had been invited to come to Prague by Tycho Brahe in 1600 to be his assistant and took over his position when Brahe died in 1601. An ultramodern interior and the story of Prague's earliest coffee-house distinguish the Renaissance house at number 18, **»The Golden Serpent«**. Here dwelt the Armenian Deodatus Damajan, who sold coffee in Staré Město's narrow streets, and then opened Prague's first café in **»The Three Ostriches«** (► Charles Bridge) in Malá Strana. **Palais Pötting** (no. 8), whose patron is recalled by his coat-of-arms impaled with those of his wife on the doorway of the Baroque façade, houses the State Conservatory's experimental theatre, the »Disk«.

Prague's first cinema was opened in 1907 by Viktor Ponrepo or, as the case may be, Dismas Šlambor in **»The Blue Pike«** (no. 20). Several shops on Karlova offer Bohemian glass, pillow lace and other arts and crafts, while excellent antiquarian bookshops, for instance **Palais Colloredo-Mansfeld** (no. 2) and **»The Stone Mermaid«** (no. 14), invite passers-by to browse through rare publications.

✱ Karlštejn Castle (Hrad Karlštejn)

Location: 40km/25m southwest of
Prague

Internet: www.hradkarlstejn.cz

North of the little wine-growing community of Karlštejn (population 1200) towers the mighty Hrad Karlštejn (formerly Karlův Týn), the most famous of Bohemia's medieval castles.

From the car park outside the village it is an approximately 2km/1.5mi walk up to the terraced fortifications, which soar up from a wooded hill surrounded by limestone cliffs (319m/1050ft) above the slopes of a tributary valley of the river Berounka (Beraun). The castle is classified as a national monument of culture and is preserved with great care. It was built during the relatively short period between 1348 and 1357, in the reign of Emperor Charles IV, to house in safety the treasures of the Holy Roman Empire of the German Nation, the Bohemian royal insignia, numerous relics and important state documents. The designs were in all likelihood provided by the French architect **Matthias of Arras**.

Severely damaged by Hussite attacks in 1422, it was repaired a few years later; it was restored with some alterations in the second half of the 16th century, and restored once again – also with various alterations – by Friedrich Schmidt and Josef Mocker (1887–1899).

The Burgrave Courtyard (Purkrabský dvůr) can be entered from the north through two tower buildings, approximately 100m/110yd

🕐
Opening hours:
Tue–Sun
March, Nov, Dec
9am–3pm
April, Oct until 4pm
May, June, Sept
until 5pm
July, Aug until 6pm

**Burgrave
Courtyard**

Karlštejn Castle Plan

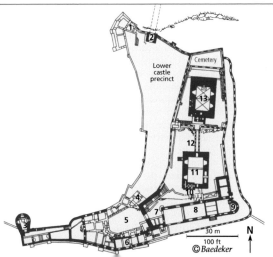

Lower
castle
precinct

Cemetery

1 First gate (late 15th century)
present-day entrance

2 Old castle gate

3 Well tower

4 Second gate
(to Burgrave courtyard)

5 Burgrave courtyard

6 Burgrave house

7 Castle courtyard

8 Imperial Palace

9 St Nicholas Chapel

10 St Katherine's Chapel

11 Tower of Our Lady
Chapter Church of Our Lady

12 Wooden passage-way

13 Large tower with
Chapel of the Cross

30 m
100 ft
© *Baedeker*
N

Bohemia's most famous Gothic fortress:
built as reliquary, and repository for royal insignia

Accessible only with
guided tour! ▶
apart. Here the guided tour begins; visitors have to join a tour to
view the castle.The four-floored **Burgrave's House** (Purkrabství) is
on the south side of the courtyard; parts of it date back to the 15th
century.

Well Tower
At the extreme west end of the castle site stand some former farm
buildings and the large Well Tower (Studniční věž) with a 90m/
295ft-deep well and large scoop wheel.

Imperial Palace
To the east of the Burgrave Courtyard, through a large gate, lies the
narrow Castle Courtyard (Hradní nádvoří). On the right is the Imperial Palace (Císařský palác), with steps going up on the extreme
right-hand side. An antechamber leads into the **Feudal Lords' Assembly Hall**. The double-aisled hall has a coffered ceiling supported by
four upright wooden beams.
On the second floor, Charles IV's study, his bedchamber with an altar picture by **Tommaso da Modena**, and the Imperial Chamber with
precious wood-panelling are all that remains of the original imperial
apartments. The half-timbered top floor, originally the female do-
main, was replaced by wooden battlements when the castle was restored. Adjacent to the east side of the Imperial Palace stands **St
Nicholas Chapel**.

Marian Tower
Opposite the Imperial Palace stands the Marian Tower (Mariánská
věž). On the second floor (access via stairs in the wall) is the **Chapter
Church of St Mary**, with its painted beamed ceiling and wall frescoes
that date back in part to the 14th century; they depict scenes from
the Apocalypse and portray Charles IV.

In the southwest corner of the Marian Tower is the vaulted **Chapel of St Katherine**; Charles IV had the original painted decoration replaced by plates of semi-precious stones set in the walls. Over the entrance is a painting of Emperor Charles IV and his wife Anna. In the altar niche an original picture of the Madonna has been preserved.

On the uppermost level of the castle's rock foundation stands the enormous 37m/121ft-high **Great Tower** (Velká věž), which is linked to the Marian Tower by a wooden bridge – formerly a drawbridge. The **Chapel of the Holy Cross** (Kaple svatého Kříže) on the second floor was dedicated in 1360. A gilded iron screen divides it into two

> ! **Baedeker TIP**
>
> **The highlight of the guided tour**
> Viewing of the most important attraction, the Chapel of the Holy Cross, is possible only from July to November, and only by prior arrangement, but there are rich rewards for the effort. Since the number of visitors is limited it is worth booking from Prague in good time. (Státní památkový ústav středních Čech, Sabinova 5, Praha 3, tel. 274 008 154 – 156, rezervace@stc.npu.cz)

parts. Its markedly extensive vault is entirely gilded and covered with glass stars, creating the illusion of a canopy of the heavens. Above the candle rail on the walls (for 1330 candles) are more than 2200 semi-precious stones inlaid in gilded plasterwork and 128 painted wooden panels (1348–1367) by the Gothic **Master Theoderic** (largely now copies); today six of these panels are to be found in ►St Agnes Convent. The panels served to enclose reliquaries.
Also by Master Theodericare the paintings in the window embrasures. The imperial crown jewels (now in Vienna's Hofburg treasury), and later also the Bohemian royal insignia (now in the coronation chamber of St Vitus Cathedral at ► Prague Castle) were once kept in a niche behind the altar.
Every year a solemn memorial Mass is celebrated in the castle in the early evening of 29 November, the anniversary of Charles IV's death.

Klementinum

E 4

Location: Praha 1, Staré Město, Křižovnická, Platnéská, Karlova
Bus: 207

Metro: Staroměstská
Tram: 17, 18

The former Jesuit college between Knights of the Cross Square and Mariánské Square is now the seat of the State Library of the Czech Republic. It contains more than 5 million volumes, 6000 manuscripts – including the Codex Vyšehradiensis – and more than 4000 incunabula.

🕐
Opening hours:
May–Oct Mon–Fri
2pm–7pm
Sat, Sun
10am–7pm
March, April
Nov Dec
Mon–Fri 2pm–6pm
Sat, Sun
11am–6pm

When Ferdinand I became ruler of Bohemia and Hungary in 1526 by right of his wife, he wished to reconvert the lands he had inherited to Catholicism, but without the use of excessively rigourous methods; in 1556 he invited the Jesuits to Prague. They took over the monastery and church of St Clement from the Dominicans who had been there since 1232. An entire Staré Město district with more than 30 burgher houses, three churches and several gardens was demolished. Under the leadership of master builder **Francesco Caratti** and later **František Maximilian Kaňka**, the demolished buildings were replaced from 1578 with the buildings of the Klementinum. It was the largest building complex in the city after ▶ Prague Castle. In 1622 Charles University (▶the Karolinum) was joined to it.

The site of the Klementinum includes five inner courtyards separated by various wings of the buildings, the churches of St Clement and the Holy Saviour (▶Knights of the Cross Square), the Italian Chapel – belonging to the Italian community – and an observatory (1751). The main façade of the collegiate building opposite the Church of St Francis goes back to the mid-17th century, and is decorated by richly structured stucco work in the form of shells, laurel, grimacing demons and busts of Roman emperors.

Inside, it is worth taking a look at the Jesuits' **library** (»Barokní sál«) on the first floor, built from designs by František Maximilian Kaňka

Klementinum library: considered one of the loveliest Baroque spaces in Prague, with its gallery running right round.

and ornamented with ceiling frescoes by Johann Hiebl, which show the muses and biblical themes. In the centre, the painted cupola canopy grabs the attention, with the illusion of depth so dear to Baroque sensibility.

Also worth seeing is the Mozart room with Rococo painting and bookshelves from the same era. The former Chapel of Mirrors was built in 1724 by František Maximilian Kaňka, and embellished with a ceiling fresco (pictures of the Virgin Mary) by Hiebel. Today it is used for chamber music concerts and exhibitions. The Mathematical Room with its collection of globes and table clocks is also interesting. In the southwest court the *Prague Student* statue commemorates the students' part in defending Charles Bridge against invading Swedes at the end of the Thirty Years' War (1648).

★ St Clement's Church

The Baroque Church of St Clement (Kostel svatého Klimenta) is part of the Klementinum site and is linked by an ironwork screen to the Italian Chapel. The church was built between 1711 and 1715. The sculptures in it number among the great treasures of Bohemian Baroque. **Matthias Bernhard Braun** created the eight sculptures of evangelists and fathers of the church, and also the wood carvings on the side altars, pulpit and confessional box. The altar picture is by Peter Brandl, and portrays St Linhart. Today, St Clement's serves the Greek Catholic community.

★ Knights of the Cross Square

(Křižovnické náměstí)

Location: Praha 1, Staré Město, Křižovnické náměstí   **Tram:** 17, 18

One of the loveliest squares in Prague

The traffic rushing across it nothwithstanding, the architectural layout of Knights of the Cross Square makes it one of the loveliest squares in Prague. It was laid out in the 16th century at the head of ► Charles Bridge, and the traditional Bohemian coronation procession crossed it. On the east side is the Church of the Holy Saviour, on the north is the Church of St Francis Seraphinus, which belongs to the Order of the Knights of the Cross.

The Knights of the Cross with the Red Star was a military order which developed from a fraternity caring for the sick during the era of the Crusades, and expanded particularly in Silesia, Bohemia and Moravia.

Church of the Holy Saviour

On the east side of Knights of the Cross Square stands the Church of the Holy Saviour (Kostel svatého Salvátora), the Jesuit church originally included in the ► Klementinum complex. It was built between

Knights of the Cross Square with churches of St Francis and St Salvator

Opening hours:
Tue
6.30pm–8.30pm
Thu 7.30pm–10pm
Sun
1.30pm–3.30pm
7.30pm–9.30pm

1578 and 1601 in Renaissance style. **Carlo Lurago** and **Francesco Caratti** added the projecting Baroque doorway (1638–1659), for which **Johann Georg Bendl** provided the vases and statues of saints (1659). The statue of Christ on the tympanum is flanked by two evangelists on either side. The figures on the balustrade represent the four Fathers of the Church, framed in by two of the order's saints. In the central niche stands a figure of the Madonna. The towers, from a design by **František Maximilian Kaňka**, were not completed until 1714. The ceiling fresco by **Karel Kovář** shows the four continents known at the time (1748).

Church of the Knights of the Cross

The Baroque Church of the Knights of the Cross (also: Church of St Francis Seraphinus, Kostel sv Františka Serafinského) was built between 1679 and 1689, from designs by **Jean Baptiste Mathey**, on the foundations of an early Gothic church, the remains of which still exist below ground level. The church commissioned by the Order of the Knights of the Cross was intended to equal, if not surpass, the architecture of the Church of the Holy Saviour that stood at the head of Charles Bridge and was a good 80 years older. This aim was indeed achieved, thanks not least to the high drum cupola which can be seen from afar.

The niches in the façade are ornamented with figures of saints from the workshop of **Matthias Wenceslas Jäckel** in French pre-classical style. The angels at the top, now replaced by copies, are by Jäckel himself. The statues of the Mother of God and St John Nepomuk in front of the entrance are by **Jan Antonín Quittainer**; some features

anticipate the Rococo style. To the side of the church is the **Vintners' Column by Johann Georg Bendl** with a statue of St Wenceslas (1676).
In the richly ornamented **interior** the large cupola fresco of the Last Judgement by **Wenzel Lorenz Reiner** (1722) is especially noteworthy. The altar painting by Johann Christoph Liïka shows St Francis receiving the stigmata; the same artist was responsible for the cupola paintings of nativity scenes.

Between Knights of the Cross Square and Old Town Bridge Tower (► Charles Bridge) stands a cast-iron monument to Charles IV, which was unveiled in 1848 to mark the 500th anniversary of Prague University.

Charles IV monument

✷ Letná Gardens (Letenské sady)

Location: Praha 6, Hradčany, Na baště sv Tomáše, Praha 7, Holešovice, Kostelní   **Tram:** 1, 8, 12, 17, 18, 22, 26

Northeast of ►Prague Castle, above the left bank of the Vltava, are the Letná heights. It was here that the coronation of Otokar II took place in 1261. In 1858 the plateau passed to the city authorities, who made it into a park.
Steps lead up from Svatopluk Čech Bridge to the viewing platform of the fortress-like base of the Stalin monument that was dismantled in 1962 (30m/99ft high, and weighing 14,000 tons). The sculpture, once the largest in the world, had a short life-span: one year after its unveiling, Stalin was condemned and the gigantic monument was blown up. In its place now stands an enormous metronome by **David Černý**, and there is a fine view of Prague, ► Petřín hill and St Vitus Cathedral (►Prague Castle).

Ample car parking between Exhibition Grounds and Castle

❓ DID YOU KNOW …?

■ what fate awaited the sculptor of the monumental Stalin memorial? The model – designed as a life-sized statue by Otokar Švec – was executed as a figure the size of a six-storeyed house. In the face of such monumentality, excruciating nightmares finally drove the artist to suicide.

Hanavský Pavilion got its name from the foundries of Count Hanavský where the iron pavilion was made for the 1891 exhibition from a design by Z. E. Fiala; in 1898 it was moved to Letná plateau, and made into a restaurant with a panoramic view.

Hanavský Pavilion

The second pavilion was made for the **Brussels Expo** of 1958. Czechoslavakia's pavilion was re-erected here after the Expo was over. The prize-winning pavilion, in which there is a restaurant, now offers little more than a good view of the historic city centre.

Expo Pavillon

★ Lesser Quarter Square

(Malostranské náměstí)

D 4

Location: Praha 1, Malá Strana   **Metro:** Malostranská
Tram: 12, 22, 23

Lesser Quarter Square has been the centre of city life ever since Malá Strana was founded. It began as a market below Prague Castle. Nowadays it is divided into two smaller squares by the buildings around St Nicholas Church. It contains notable buildings such as Malá Strana Town Hall and the late-Baroque Kaiserstein Palace on the east side, as well as the Rococo »Stone Table« house next to the Church of St Nicholas.

Each square used to have a well. The upper one was replaced in 1715 by a **plague column** with a Holy Trinity sculptural group and the Bohemian patron saint by Johann Ulrich Mayer and Ferdinand Geiger. The lower one was replaced in 1858 by a memorial to Austrian field marshal Josef Václav Radecký, exhibited today in the National Museum's Lapidarium (stone collection) in ►Stromovka Park.

Kaiserstein Palace
Kaiserstein Palace (U Petzoldů, no. 23) was reconstructed in the 1980s; it now belongs to the chamber of commerce. Its predecessors were two 15th-century Gothic houses which were amalgamated in 1630 and redesigned in 1700 for Helfried Kaiserstein. The tympanum is adorned by allegories of the four seasons by Ottavio Mosto; the Kaiserstein coat-of-arms can be seen above the central first-floor window. At the beginning of the 20th century the famous opera diva

Lesser Quarter Square Map

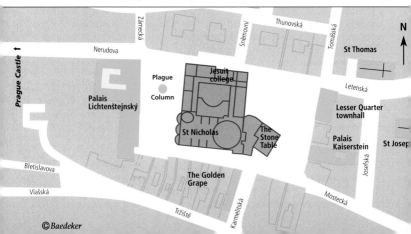

© Baedeker

Baroque and Rococo façades characterize Lesser Quarter Square.

Ema Destinnová (»Kittlová«, 1878–1930), partner of legendary tenor Enrico Caruso, lived in the palace; the »Destinnová« room is a reminder of her.

The house at number 4 (U zlatého hroznu) on the corner of Lesser Quarter Square and Karmelitská has been renovated to a high standard and is open to the public. It owes its Baroque appearance to radical alterations undertaken in the years 1707–1710.

The Golden Grape

The imposing Lichtenstein Palace is a focal point of the upper square, which was named Italian Square in the 17th century, and, since 1847, also St Stephen's Square. In 1591 Jan z Lobkowicz bought up five burgher houses and made them into one. In 1621 they became the property of Charles of Lichtenstein. The classicist façade dates from 1791. Today Lichtenstein Palace houses the Prague Academy of Music.

Lichtenstein Palace

Malá Strana Town Hall (Malostranská radnice)

The former Malá Strana Town Hall acquired its municipal function at the end of the 15th century. The interior was altered in 1660, the exterior in the 19th century. It was here that the important negotiations concerning the Bohemian edict of religious toleration took place in 1575, amongst others.

The building was given its current appearance during the late Renaissance (1617–1622); today it is used for cultural events. The doorway with the fine armorial bearings of the city was added in 1660.

In the course of building work undertaken in the town hall's cellar vaults, valuable pre-1600 texts were discovered, including the »Lesser Quarter Hymnal« (1572), which is now preserved in the State Library.

✱ ✱ St Nicholas (Chrám svatého Mikuláše)

🕐 Opening hours:
daily 9am–4pm

The former Jesuit church was erected on the site of a Gothic church of the same name. Three generations of Prague's best Baroque architects were commissioned to build it. The great nave with side chapels, galleries and vaulting was the work of **Christoph Dientzenhofer**, carried out between 1704 and 1711.

Conveying the typically Baroque sense of life and vitality, the two-storey façade completed in 1710 is regarded as the greatest achievement of Bohemian Baroque. The coat-of-arms of the Count of Kolovrat above the main doorway and the statues of the fathers of the church on the balustrade are from the workshop of Johann Friedrich Kohl. The chancel with its 75m/246ft-high dome was built by **Kilian Ignaz Dientzenhofer** (1737–1752). Construction of the church was completed by **Anselmo Lurago** with the erection of the 79m/260ft bell-tower (1756).

! Baedeker TIP

Big Brother is listening

During the Socialist era the bell-tower was used as a listening post by secret police. They tapped the embassies in the area with radio transmitters, and kept diplomats' windows under surveillance with binoculars. Now anyone can climb the so-called »earpiece« to enjoy the charming views of the Malá Strana rooftops. Views from the window were shot from this perspective for Oscar-winning film *Kolja*. Daily 10am–5pm.

The sumptuous **interior** of the church is regarded as a prime example of high Baroque. The overwhelming overall impression derives from the coloured stucco marble, rich sculptural ornamentation and outstanding frescoes. The large ceiling fresco above the nave was painted in 1760/1761 by **Johann Lukas Kracker**; it shows scenes from the life of St Nicholas. The dome fresco depicts the glorification of the saint and the Last Judgement (1752/1753), and is by **Franz Xaver Palko**, who also painted the wall frescoes in the chancel in collaboration with Joseph Hager.

The sculptures in nave and choir, and the figure of St Nicholas on the main altar, are by **Ignaz Franz Platzer the Elder**; the mighty organ (1745) was made by Thomas Schwarz. The simulated marble pulpit ornamented with gold is the work of Richard and Peter Prachner (1765); it is decorated in Rococo style with allegories of Faith, Hope and Charity, and with the *Beheading of John the Baptist*. The side altars in the transept have paintings by Johann Lukas Kracker, the *Visitation of the Virgin Mary* and *Death of St Joseph*, both dating from 1760. The altar pictures and ceiling paintings in the side chapels, by Ignaz Raab, Franz Xaver Palko and others, are also worth seeing.

The 150 sq m/1614 sq ft **ceiling painting** by Kracker is one of the largest of its kind in Europe. The Nicholas figure of the painted scenes is the 4th-century bishop of Myra in Asia Minor, who was seen in the Middle Ages as patron saint of municipal authorities and guardian of justice.

St Nicholas, surrounded by angels, dominates the action; he holds his episcopal staff in his left hand, while his right hand is raised in blessing. In another scene a priest is seen distributing little bottles with miracle-working oil presented as a gift by the saint. Then St Nicholas gives money to a man whom poverty is forcing to sell his daughter. The painting on the right-hand side of the vault refers to a 14th-century martial conflict, in which St Nicholas's intervention saved three Romans from execution. On the left-hand side a coastal landscape is used to suggest that St Nicholas was also venerated as protector of seafarers and merchants. Pictures of coasts and seaports had a great appeal at the time.

On the north side of the church are the cloisters of the former **Jesuit order** (13th/14th century), partially redesigned in Baroque style in the 17th century.

St Thomas (Kostel svatého Tomáše)

On the northeast side of the square, at the point where Letenská branches off, stands the Church of St Thomas. The church, whose Gothic origins can still be clearly discerned in the buttresses on the outside walls of the presbytery, was founded in 1285 for the order of Augustinian Hermits, and completed by 1379, together with the adjacent former Augustinian monastery (now an old people's home) and St Thomas Brewery.

The restructuring in high Baroque style (1727–1731) was undertaken by **Kilian Ignaz Dientzenhofer**. In a niche above the Renaissance doorway by **Campione de Bossi** (1617) stand statues of St Augustine and St Thomas, created by **Hieronymus Kohl** in 1684.

The lavish interior, not open to visitors, contains paintings and statues by famous Bohemian artists. **Wenzel Lorenz Reiner** painted the ceiling fresco in the nave in 1730, with scenes from the life of St Augustine. The pictures from the St Thomas legend in the chancel and

the dome are also by Reiner. **Karel Škréta** designed the main altar in 1731; the figures of saints are by Johann Anton Quittainer, Ferdinand Maximilian Brokoff and Ignaz Müller. Further works by Karel Škréta adorn the altars in the transept (*St Thomas*, 1671) and the chancel (*Assumption of the Virgin Mary*, 1644).

Lobkowicz Palace (Lobkovický palác)

C 4

Location: Praha 1, Malá Strana, Vlašská 19   **Tram:** 12, 22, 23

Today, Lobkowicz Palace is the home of the German embassy. The early Baroque building was erected at the beginning of the 18th century by Giovanni Battista Alliprandi; in 1769 it was redesigned by Michael Ignaz Palliardi and the side wings were raised. From 1753 the palace belonged to the Lobkowicz family, whose coat-of-arms appear on the gable. The finely structured façade with its impressive doorway is adorned by a tympanum complete with heraldry and symbols, and an attica with numerous statues. A ceiling fresco in the stairwell shows the triumph of peace over war; it is attributed to Johann Jakob Steinfels, as are more of the skilful paintings in the interior (*c*1720). The garden side is embellished by a projecting cylindrical building and the Sala terrena, a pilastered hall with three round-arch arcades opening onto the memorial courtyard. From the three-winged memorial courtyard at the back there is a way through a wrought-iron gate (with sculptures of the abduction of Proserpina and Oreithyia) to the garden terraces, established at the time of building and adapted at the end of the 18th century to a less formal English landscaping style.

> ! **Baedeker TIP**
>
> **View**
>
> Opposite Lobkowicz Palace stands the family hotel »Dům U Velke Botý«. The view alone would be recommendation enough for this 17th-century establishment; the individually and tastefully decorated and furnished rooms are another reason to pay it a visit (Vlašská 30, tel. 57 53 32 34, fax 57 53 13 60, www.volweb.cz/rippl).

In October 1989 historic scenes were played out in the building, when more than 4500 GDR citizens wanting to flee their country sought admission here. Their refusal to give up forced the authorities eventually to let them travel to the Federal Republic, but they had to leave their beloved Trabants behind. These events are commemorated by the **bronze Trabant** *Quo Vadis?* in the courtyard (1989) by **Adam Černý**.

← *St Thomas ceiling fresco with scenes from St Augustine's life*

Schoenborn Palace Vlašská runs down along the foot of ►Petřín hill, and turns into the street called Tržiště. Here stands the spaciously laid out Schoenborn Palace (Schönbornský palác, no. 15) with its relatively unadorned and yet imposing façade. Today the palace is the home of the American embassy – it is not easy to gain access here, any more than to Lobkowicz Palace. **Giovanni Santini-Aichl** provided the four-winged building with gables and dormer windows, and the passage through to the courtyard with four giant statues, in about 1715. By the mid-17th century Schoenborn Palace garden was already famous. Its terraces rise from a checkerboard parterre to an arcaded gloriette (formerly a wine-press).

Loretánská ulička

C 4

Location: Praha 1, Hradčany   **Tram:** 22, 23

Loretánská ulička is an alley running east-west between ►Hradčany Square in front of Prague Castle and ►Loreta Square in Malá Strana. Of historic interest is the dwelling at number 1, which until 1784 served as Hradčany Town Hall; it was built at the beginning of the 17th century by K. Oemichen of Oberheim, following the promotion of Hradčany district to a royal town in 1598. Remains of the imperial coat-of-arms on the sgrafitto façade and the Hradčany coat-of-arms over the doorway bear witness to this glittering era.

Hrzán Palace Hrzán Palace (at number 9) also warrants a special mention; it was originally a Gothic house owned by master builder Peter Parler. In the mid-16th century the building was remodelled in Renaissance style, and in the late 18th century it was given its late-Baroque façade. At the beginning of the 20th century Ferdinand Engelmüller's (1867–1924) school of painting was located here, as commemorated by a bust in the courtyard. Refashioned for the last time in the mid-1950s, the palace is used today for official governmental and ceremonial purposes.

! *Baedeker* TIP

New world

North of the Loreta shrine, a road leads off to the »new world« (Nový Svět), a unique and poetic corner of Hradčany, which is becoming increasingly populated by artists and students. In around 1600, the astronomer Johannes Kepler lived in the house known as »The Golden Horn«.

Loreta Square (Loretánské námestí)

C 4

Location: Praha 1, Hradčany, Loretánské   **Tram:** 22, 23
námestí

From ► Hradčany Square in front of ► Prague Castle, ► Loretánska   **Replica of the**
ulička leads to Loreta Square, which along with ► Knights of the   **home of the**
Cross Square and a few others is surely one of the most impressive   **Virgin Mary**
squares in Prague. The southwest side of Loreta Square is entirely occupied by the front of Černín Palace, 150m/492ft long, with 30
pilasters; on the east side, descending steeply to the north, is the area
of the Loreta, shrine and place of pilgrimage.

✴ Loreta

The Loreta is the best-known pilgrimage destination in Bohemia.   🕐
The Loreto cult – part of the cult of the Virgin Mary – spread from   Opening hours:
Italy to Central Europe as early as the 15th century. It originated in   Tue–Sun
the biblical story of the house of the Holy Family in Nazareth, where   9am–12.15pm
the archangel Gabriel announced the birth of Christ to the Virgin   1pm–4.30pm
Mary. From the 13th century, a legend spread according to which
the holy house (Casa Santa) was transported to Italy in order to pro-   www.loreta.cz
tect it from infidels; this legend found great favour among Catholics
in the Baroque era. During the Counter-Reformation, some 50 such
places of pilgrimage were established in Bohemia on the model of
the medieval Casa Santa Loreta shrine in an attempt to increase the
popularity of Catholicism.

Different architectural styles have left their mark on the Loreta. The   **History of the**
Casa Santa was completed in 1631; the cloisters of 1634 were given a   **building**
second storey after 1740. The façade is dated post-1721 and is based
on designs by **Christoph and Kilian Ignaz Dientzenhofer**. In erecting
the main façade, the architects were charged with the task of creating
a uniform front for the complex of buildings dating from different
eras, and one which would offer an appropriate architectural re-
sponse to the monumental Černín Palace on the opposite side of the
square.
Patrons of the façade were Count Philipp of Lobkowicz, Duke of Sa-
gan, and his wife Eleonore Carolina; their impaled arms were inset
over the main doorway by **Johann Friedrich Kohl**. In addition, the
sculptor created the statue group of St Felix of Cantalice, St John Nepomuk, and probably also SS Francis and Anthony over the main
portal (1721).
For the somewhat older, early-Baroque bell tower, which dominates
the façade, the Prague clockmaker P. Naumann in 1694 set up
chimes with 27 bells (total weight approx. 1540kg/1.5 tons), which
the wealthy merchant Eberhard of Glauchau had purchased in 1694

from the Amsterdam bell and gun-barrel foundry of Claude Fremy. In summer the bells ring out the Czech Marian hymn *Tisíckrát pozdravujeme Tebe* (»We greet thee a thousand times«) every hour.

Casa Santa In the middle of the cloisters, with their upward extension of arcades, stands Casa Santa, the architectural and spiritual centre of the pilgrimage complex; the patron was Countess Benigna Katharina of Lobkowicz (1626). The chapel's master builder was **Giovanni Battista Orsi** from Como; he completed it in 1631. The original painting on the façade was replaced from 1664 by sculptures and stucco reliefs modelled on those in Italy, with scenes from the life of the Virgin Mary, Old Testament prophets and pagan sibyls. They are the work of G. Agosto, G. B. Colombo and Giovanni Battista Cometa (1664). On the chapel's east wall, the Casa Santa legend is depicted.

The interior is adorned with picture cycles from the Virgin Mary's life painted by Malá Strana artist František Kunz in 1695, as well as a silver altar and a Madonna carved out of lime-wood. This is encased in a silver wreath of winged angels attributed to Prague goldsmith Markus Hrbek. Casa Santa's silver adornments have a combined weight of more than 50kg/110lb.

Casa Santa is an imitation of the Virgin Mary's dwelling.

17th-century Annunciation relief adorns Casa Santa.

Fountains

In the courtyard, on either side of Casa Santa, are two fountains by Johann Michael Brüderle (1739–1740). Completed after Brüderle's death by Richard J. Prachner, they have now been replaced by copies. One shows the Assumption of the Virgin Mary; the other, the Resurrection of Christ.

Cloister

The ground level of the cloisters, begun in 1634, has vault frescoes by Felix Anton Scheffler (1750; restored 1882), with symbolic renderings of the Lauretanian litany. Against the arcade walls are several altars with pictures of saints by unknown artists of the late-Baroque era.

The **Loreta Treasury** is in the upper west passage of the cloisters. Mass vestments and liturgical items can be viewed here, and also precious monstrances, from the 16th to the 18th century. These include: the Small Pearl Monstrance, adorned with 266 diamonds and a ruby in addition to pearls (1680); the Ring Monstrance of 1748 made of silver-gilt (492 diamonds, 186 rubies, a sapphire, 24 pearls, and emeralds, amethysts and garnets); and the famous sunburst Diamond Monstrance (more than 6200 diamonds from the estate of Ludmilla Eva Franziska Kolovrat), made in Vienna by court jewellers Matthias Stegner and Johann Künischbauer in 1699.

Chapels

There are seven cloister chapels. Of particular note are the chapels of St Francis Seraphinus (1717) and St Anthony of Padua (1710–1712), both by **Christoph Dientzenhofer**. The former has a main altar by **Matthias Wenzel Jäckel** with a picture of the saint from the workshop of Prague's great Baroque painter, Peter Johann Brandl. Jäckel was a key contributor to the sculpture in the Anthony of Padua chapel. He made the altar, for which Sebastian Zeiler provided the paintings. On the east side of Loreta in the middle of the cloisters is the Church of the Nativity of Our Lord (Kostel Narození Páně). Begun by Christoph Dientzenhofer in 1717, work was continued by his son Kilian Ignaz and completed in 1735 by Georg Aichbauer. The light interior is dominated by a high altar with Nativity altarpiece by **Johann Georg Heintsch**. The ceiling fresco *Christ in the Temple* (1735–1736) by **Wenzel Lorenz Reiner** is painted in delicate colours, and shows the influence of Venetian illusionism on the artist. The ceiling frescoes *Adoration of the Shepherds* and *Adoration of the Magi* (1742) are the work of Johann Adam Schöpf, who headed the Prague painters' guild in 1740/41.

Černín Palace (Čzernínský palác)

Palace »a l'italiana« The monumental Černín Palace stands on the southwest corner of Loreta Square. Its 150m/492ft-long frontage with high diamond-patterned ashlar plinth and 29 colossal pilasters was commissioned in 1669 modelled on Palladian architecture by Count Humprecht Jan Černín of Chudenice, imperial ambassador to Venice. His son, Hermann Černín, completed the building in 1697. Italian builders and stonemasons were employed throughout, the most important being **Francesco Caratti**. **František Maximilian Kaňka** carried out alterations on the palace after 1720. The adjacent formal gardens on the north side and the magnificent stairway with ceiling fresco (*Fall of the Titans*, 1718) by **Wenzel Lorenz Reiner** date from the same period. During the French occupation of Prague in 1741/1742 the building suffered grave damage; it was repaired by **Anselmo Lurago** between 1744 and 1749. Three new front doorways were added; the orangery in the garden was remodelled in Rococo style. In the mid-18th century **Ignaz Franz Platzer** created several sculptures for the palace. In 1851 the building was turned into a barracks, but at the beginning of the 1930s it was restored. Now it is the seat of the Ministry of Foreign Affairs.

> **❓ DID YOU KNOW …?**
>
> ■ the joke that went round the Ministry of Foreign Affairs during Socialist times? »How many people work in this huge building? Half of them!«

Capuchin Monastery With the plain design typical of Capuchin architecture, this is the first Capuchin monastery in Bohemia (Kapucínský klášter, 1600–1602) and occupies the north side of Loreta Square, set down on a rather lower level. A covered bridge-passage links the building with the Loreta Monastery opposite. Adjoining the monastery is a simple church of Our Lady which was once adorned with 14 Gothic panel paintings of unknown origin (now in the National Gallery).

Mánes Exhibition Hall

D 5

Location: Praha 1, Nové Město, Masarykovo nábřeží

Metro: Karlovo náměstí
Tram: 17, 21

The Mánes Exhibition Hall (also known as the Mánes Gallery; no. 20) was built between 1923 and 1930 in Constructivist style from designs by **Otakar Novotný** for the Mánes (►Famous People) Artists' Society founded in 1898, on the site of the former Šítka mills. The exhibition hall's severe Functionalism contrasts sharply with the surrounding Art Nouveau and Classicist buildings, and with the water tower alongside it. The Mánes Artists' Society played an uncompromisingly modern role – just like the architecture of the time – which was of decisive importance in the opening up of Czech art to modernity. Today the building hosts temporary exhibitions of contemporary art, and is also the seat of the Artists' Association.

No frills

Beside the Mánes Gallery stands a 15th-century Renaissance tower (Šítkovská věž), which has suffered from fires and bombardment and been restored several times; it contrasts nicely with the modern building. The Baroque roof dates from the end of the 18th century. The water tower is named after mill owner Jan Šítka (born 1451); since the late 15th century it has supplied the wells and fountains of upper Nové Město with water.

Šítka water tower

Žofín (also called Slav Island, Slovanský ostrov) came into existence in the 18th century through natural silting. From the 1830s the island developed into the centre of Prague's political and social life. Concerts, balls and congresses took place here – the latter especially in the revolution year of 1848. Famous composers such as Hector Berlioz and Franz Liszt performed their works here. The renovated neo-Renaissance building on the island dates from 1884. In that year the Rudolfinum opened, and a good 25 years later the Municipal House; cultural life came increasingly to be centred on those two buildings.

Žofín

Mariánské Square (Mariánské náměstí)

E 4

Location: Praha 1, Staré Město

Metro: Staroměstská

Brimming with monuments and sculptures, Mariánské Square (Mariánské náměstí) is also home to Prague's largest public library. After alterations were made at the beginning of the twentieth century only the south and west sides of the square were retained in their original form.

The impressive stairwell of Palais Clam-Gallas

Clam-Gallas Palace
(Clam-Gallasův palác)

Today the former Clam-Gallas Palace houses the city archives (entrance from Husova třída, the road running south from Mariánské Square). The magnificent Baroque palace was built in 1707 according to plans by Viennese architect **Johann Bernhard Fischer von Erlach**; its patron was Johann Wenzel, Count von Gallas. Stone giants guard the doorway on Husova třída, which intersects with▶Karlova, one of the sections of the Prague »coronation procession« route.

When the palace was renovated at the end of the 1980s it surprisingly transpired that the heads of the 3m/10ft-tall figures had been replaced by copies at the beginning of the 20th century. The doorway giants, parapet figures and fountain statue in the first courtyard are the work of **Matthias Bernhard Braun**. Carlo Carlone created the stairwell frescoes (1727–1730). He was also responsible for ceiling paintings in two rooms on the second floor (*Olympus*, *Coronation of Art and Science*), and in the library (*Luna, Helios and Stars*). In the southeast corner of the square, close to the wall of the Clam-Gallas courtyard, stands the fountain statue *Vltava* by Václav Prachner (1812). The west side of Mariánské Square is bordered by the extensive complex of the former Jesuit college, the ▶ Klementinum.

On the east side of Mariánské Square stands the **New Town Hall** (Nová radnice), built in late Art Nouveau style between 1909 and 1912. Since 1945 this building has housed the chancellery of the mayor of Prague, the large meeting chamber, and municipal offices. The two statues on the outer ends of the façade are by Ladislav

Šaloun; they depict the Iron Knight and Chief Rabbi Löw (►Josefov). The allegorical relief at the entrance to the town hall and the figures *Auditing* and *Book-keeping* are by Stanislav Sucharda; the groups *Frugality*, *Strength* and *Perseverance* on the balcony were designed by J. Mařatka.

Municipal House (Representační dům)

E / F 4

Location: Praha 1, Staré Město, Náměstí Republiky 5
Tram: 5, 8, 14, 26

Metro: Náměstí Republiky
Internet: www.obecni-dum.cz

The Municipal House (Obecní dům) was built (1906–1911) from designs by Antonín Balšánek and Osvald Polívka on the historic site where the Royal Court had been established in 1380 and abandoned in 1547. Officially it is the »Ceremonial House of the City of Prague« (Representační dům hlavního města Prahy). It is considered the city's finest Art Nouveau building, with a restaurant steeped in tradition, a café, a wine tavern, exhibition rooms, offices and Prague's largest concert hall, the Smetana Hall (Smetanova síň, complete with organ), and is a typical example of Czech Secession architecture of the late 19th and early 20th centuries, with its predilection for ornamentation, geometrical forms and elaborate detail, plant motifs and the ever-recurring theme of youth.

A whole generation of artists contributed to the exterior and interior design. The façade ornamentation, the balcony pillar supports and the ceiling mouldings in the Smetana Hall are by **Karel Novák**; **Ladislav Šaloun** designed the allegories *Humiliation* and *Resurgence of the Nation* on the front, as well as *Bohemian Dances* and *Vyšehrad* on the Smetana Hall podium. The symbolic wall frescoes of the fine arts in Primator Hall were done by **Alfons Mucha**; in Rieger Hall there are paintings by **Max Švabinský**; and in Palacký Hall stands a bust by Josef Václav Myslbek. Allegorical ornamentation also adorns Grégr Hall, while Sladkovský Hall was provided with landscape paintings by J. Ullmann.

✶ Powder Gate (Prašná brána)

This 65m/213ft late-Gothic tower, through which the southern trade route into Prague passed, was modelled on Old Town Bridge Tower (►Charles Bridge) and formed part of the Staré Město fortifications. Building of this gate started in 1475; there was an earlier fortified gate here, built in the 13th century. Master builder M. Rejsek erected the tower for King Vladislav Jagiello. Vladislav lived initially in the adjacent royal court, no longer in existence; when he moved his residence back to ► Prague Castle the importance of the Powder Gate

🕐
Opening hours:
April–Oct
daily 10am–6pm

lessened. The present name arose in the 18th century when the gate served as gunpowder store.

When the city was besieged in 1757 by Frederick the Great of Prussia, the sculptural ornamentation was severely damaged. Josef Mocker undertook neo-Gothic renovations in 1875 and provided the tower with a roof and a circular gallery. The sculptures include portraits of Bohemian kings and patron saints. Inside, the exhibition »Royal Court«, spread over three floors, illustrates life in medieval Prague. The climb up 186 stone steps is rewarded by a very fine view of the city.

Hibernian House The Hibernian House (U hybernů) stands opposite the Municipal House and was originally a late-Baroque church, built in the years 1652–1659 by the monastery of Irish Franciscans (Hibernians) who had been there since 1629. The east and north wings of the monastery were added in the 18th century.

After the dissolution of the monastery in 1786, and the closure of the church four years later, J. Zobel converted the church into a Customs House with Classicist façade (1808–1811), using plans by **Georg Fischer**; the sculptural ornamentation is by Franz Xaver Lederer (1811). In the early 1940s the interior of the Hibernian House was redesigned for exhibitions and cultural events. The building is currently being renovated; its future use will be decided when work has been completed.

★ Museum of Decorative Arts

E 4

Location: Praha 1, Staré Město, 17. listopadu 2
Bus: 207

Metro: Staroměstská
Tram: 17, 18

🕐 Opening hours:
Mon–Sun
10am–6pm
Tue until 7pm
www.upm.cz

The Museum of Decorative Arts (Uměleckoprůmyslové muzeum) on the west edge of the Old Jewish Cemetery (►Josefov) was founded in 1884. The din-de-siècle house was built under the supervision of architect **Josef Schulz** in neo-Renaissance style, 1897–1901 and is itself a work of art.

It houses a world-famous collection of glass, porcelain and ceramics, as well as furniture (16th–19th century) and gold artefacts (15th–19th century). Further exhibition areas include textiles, measuring instruments, clocks, book-bindings, working drawings, small bronzes and coins in their historical development (going back in some cases to the 8th century AD). On occasion there are also very carefully prepared temporary exhibitions. Audio guides are available in Czech and English.

The specialist art history and decorative arts library is open to the public; it includes a collection of 15th-century manuscripts.

Na příkopě (On the Moat)

Location: Praha 1, Staré Město (Pedestrian zone)

Metro: Můstek, Náměstí Republiky

The street »Na příkopě« (On the Moat) is considered the liveliest in the city. It links the lower end of ► Wenceslas Square to the Square of the Republic (Náměstí Republiky). Na příkopě, Wenceslas Square and Národní třída with their side-streets and lanes form the so-called »**Golden Cross**«, Prague's centre of business and commerce, with administrative and office buildings, banks, arcades, shops, hotels, restaurants and cafés.

Once there really was a moat between the fortifications of Staré Město and Nové Město, flowing along what is now the Na příkopě pedestrian zone, but it was filled in as long ago as 1760.

Looking from Wenceslas Square, Staré Město spreads out on the left, Nové Město on the right. On the corner of Na příkopě and Na můstku is the distinctive administrative building belonging to the machine factory »**ČKD Praha**« , opened in 1983. A large clock from a previous building on the site crowns the gable of the modern steel construction, which also houses several places of refreshment open to the public, including a café on the fifth floor with a fine view of Staré Město.

U černé růže, a popular shopping centre, Na příkopě

AMADEUS, YENTL AND JACKIE CHAN

Who would have thought it: all three of them came from Prague. At least, you could say so – if the place where these three famous films were made is counted as their birthplace. For Amadeus does not walk the streets of Vienna in Miloš Forman's box-office hit, as the film-makers would have the audience believe. Instead, the cinematic Mozart was nowhere other than in the romantic, winding alleyways and majestic palaces of Prague.

It was there, in the Archbishop's Palace in Prague Castle and not at Vienna's imperial court, that the ambitious master of court music, **Antonio Salieri**, met **Mozart** for the first time, and was at once torn in two by simultaneous worship and hatred of his genius. He, who had laboured all his life and finally become Emperor Joseph II's court musician, and

had to struggle for every little tune – which were still not up to much – had to see a young musical genius fooling around and taking the court, his court, by storm. Tom Hulce is the playful, childish Amadeus, who drives his rival (F. Murray Abraham) insane with his overwhelming music. Miloš Forman, the Czech emigrant who had made famous Hollywood films such

Josef Vilsmaier filmed the comet-like rise of the »Comedian Harmonists«. Their appearances were widely acclaimed until the Nazis seized power. Although the action is set in Berlin, many scenes were shot in Prague.

as *One Flew Over the Cuckoo's Nest* (1975) and *Hair* (1979), could hardly have chosen a better setting for his music and picture spectacular: instead of dismantling neon advertisements and street signs in Vienna, building stage-sets and restructuring façades in order to achieve something like an 18th-century ambience, the director chose the »unspoilt« old city of Prague. Here he could film without time-consuming alterations, for instance in the picturesque Nerudova, on the romantic castle site, in the Estates Theatre and by Charles Bridge, in front of Wallenstein Palace and in St Giles' Church (Kostel sv Jiljí), where Amadeus marries Constance (Elizabeth Berridge).

Ideal conditions

Film directors are not drawn to Prague just by the atmosphere of the city. On a hill on the outskirts of the city are the famous Czech **Barrandov**

Film Studios (www.barrandov.cz), which not only have excellent technical equipment, rare animation skills, special effects, and several hundred well-trained staff, but also look back on long years of experience. The studios were founded in 1931 by Václav and Miloš Havel, the father and uncle of the former Czech president, and named after the French geologist Joachim Barrande, who worked in the 19th century on trilobites found near Prague. The studios had their first success as early as 1934: the film *Ecstasy* by **Gustav Machatý** won awards in Venice for direction and camera work. Yet experimentation and freedom for innovative directors were not allowed to last long: when Hitler marched into Prague on 16 March 1939, the Barrandov Studios were put under the Third Reich's propaganda minister Joseph Goebbels. As the bombardment of Germany increased, German

Numerous scenes have been filmed on Charles Bridge.

film production was moved almost entirely to Prague. Shortly after the end of the war, film activists brought the film studios under state control; the pressure of Communist doctrine on the arts did not impinge on film-makers until 1948. Little of more than national significance was achieved in the 1950s, but in the 1960s there was a discernible upward trend: directors who were not party members produced films of humorous social criticism, which made an impression through the originality of their protagonists and their success in conveying the general unease of the time. The arrival of Soviet troops during the Prague Spring of 1968 put a sudden end to this so-called New Wave.

After the box-office hit in the early 1980s of the monumental *Amadeus*, made in Prague, there were several more large-scale projects: in 1983, for instance, *Yentl* was made in the city, with Barbra Streisand in the lead.

Hollywood in the East

After the »Velvet Revolution« the Barrandov Studios, privatized once more, were quick to join up with the international film scene. *Kafka* received an unusual treatment as a spooky thriller with Jeremy Irons (1991), catching Prague's mystery in sinister black-and-white. In *Mission Impossible* (1995) Tom Cruise showed that anything is possible in Prague: the murder of secret agents beneath Charles Bridge, Old Town Square under water. Director Joseph Vilsmaier has produced a major series of films here since the 1980s. After the war epic *Stalingrad* and the sentimental *No-One Weeps for Me*, he made *Comedian Harmonists* in the Prague ghetto (1997). Ben Becker and Katja Riemann marry in front of the camera in Jubilee Synagogue (on Jeruzalémská). The marriage feast takes place in the wrought-iron Hanavský Pavilion, an Art Nouveau gift

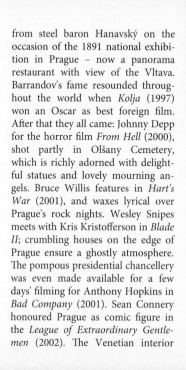

Tom Hulce plays Wolfgang Amadeus Mozart – a musical genius plays the fool.

from steel baron Hanavský on the occasion of the 1891 national exhibition in Prague – now a panorama restaurant with view of the Vltava. Barrandov's fame resounded throughout the world when *Kolja* (1997) won an Oscar as best foreign film. After that they all came: Johnny Depp for the horror film *From Hell* (2000), shot partly in Olšany Cemetery, which is richly adorned with delightful statues and lovely mourning angels. Bruce Willis features in *Hart's War* (2001), and waxes lyrical over Prague's rock nights. Wesley Snipes meets with Kris Kristofferson in *Blade II*; crumbling houses on the edge of Prague ensure a ghostly atmosphere. The pompous presidential chancellery was even made available for a few days' filming for Anthony Hopkins in *Bad Company* (2001). Sean Connery honoured Prague as comic figure in the *League of Extraordinary Gentlemen* (2002). The Venetian interior was recreated in convincingly genuine style in Prague. While this was going on, karate champion Jackie Chan blew up a few disused factory buildings on the edge of Prague for *Shanghai Knights*. The flood of the century (August 2002) yielded gruesome film motifs for the vampire shocker *Underworld*. And 007 himself has paid the Golden City a visit: the most recent James Bond movie *Casino Royale* (2006), with Daniel Craig in the lead role, was made partly in the Barrandov and Modrany studios in Prague, in Strahov Monastery library and outside the National Museum.

Opposite, on the corner with Wenceslas Square, stands **House Koruna**, built in 1911 from a design by Antonín Pfeiffer. The three lower storeys are dominated by shop windows. A spacious passage links the two streets, and was the model for subsequent buildings in the vicinity.

Nearby stands **Sylva-Taroucca Palace** (no. 10), a jewel of Bohemian late-Baroque housing a museum as well as a fast-food restaurant. **Anselmo Lurago** built the Baroque palace for the nobleman Ottavio Piccolomini between 1743 and 1751 from plans by Kilian Ignaz Dientzenhofer. Under the influence of French Classicism, two courtyards, a garden with a riding-school and a gateway with pillars were created. Distinctive characteristics of Dientzenhofer's late style are discernible on the façade: alongside the triangular gable which crowns the three central axes of the nine-axis façade, two smaller gables arch over the middle axis of the two outer segments. Here Dientzenhofer allowed a measure of Rococo influence. The rich decorative structure of the façade with mythological sculpture and the ornamentation of the Rococo steps are by **Ignaz Franz Platzer the Elder**; the interior stucco is by Carlo Bassi. The frescoes on the stairwell vaulting (Helios' chariot and allegories of the four seasons) are by Václav Bernard Ambrozzi.

! **Baedeker** TIP

Coming to terms with the past...
...the Czech way. In the Museum of Communism in Savarin Palace (no. 10), visitors can go on a guided tour of the country's recent history. While the Czechs themselves have until now not been particularly interested in the reappraisal of the history of Czechoslovakia, American business-man Glenn Spicker's museum enjoys great popularity with tourists from throughout the world. Daily 9am–9pm, www. www.muzeum-komunismu.cz.

The neighbouring neo-Romanesque house »The Black Rose« (U černé růže) once belonged to the University of Prague. German followers of the great reformer Jan Hus met here from 1411. Disciples of the »Black Rose« (such as Draendorf and Turnow) made a major contribution to the spread of Hussite beliefs in Germany.

The only Empire-style church in Prague, the **Church of the Holy Cross** (Kostel svatého Kříže), was built in 1819–1821 by J. Fischer for the Piarist teaching order. The Piarist convent's former school buildings are on Panská.

The house at number 20 on Na příkopě is in Bohemian Renaissance style, decorated with allegorical mosaics from designs by Mikoláš Aleš and reliefs from the workshops of Celda Klouček and Stanislav Sucharda.

The Baroque palace, Příchovských, was built in 1695–1700 by Count Jean B. Vernier de Rougemont. It was known as the »German House« from 1875 to 1945 because Prague's German population met there; after World War II it was renamed »**Slav House**« (Slovanský dům). Late 19th-century alterations gave it a Classicist appearance; today the renovated building houses a shopping centre with restaurants, cafés, garden and a multiplex cinema (www.slovansky-dum.cz).

House number 24 on Na příkopě is the **Palace of the Czech State Bank**, built between 1894 and 1896; today a trade finance bank. In days gone by there were famous hotels here: the »Blue Star« and the »Black Horse«, where European celebrities (including Liszt and Chopin) lodged in the 19th century. It was in the Blue Star that the Treaty of Prague between Austria and Prussia was signed in 1866.

National Gallery (Národní galerie)

The National Gallery developed out of the earliest Prague gallery, accessible to the public from 1804. It is the second oldest in Europe, after the Louvre in Paris. The collections are spread around various locations in the city.

► Veletržní Palace (19th and 20th-century art)

► St Agnes Convent (medieval Bohemian and Central European art, 13th–16th century)

► St George's Convent at ► Prague Castle (Bohemian art, reign of Rudolf II to Baroque era)

► Sternberg Palace (early European art)

► Zbraslav Castle (Asian art)

► Goltz-Kinský Palace on ► Old Town Square (drawings and graphic art, medieval to modern)

► Wallenstein Riding School in Valdštejnská, belonging to ► Wallenstein Palace: temporary National Gallery exhibitions ► House at the Black Madonna (permanent exhibition of Czech Cubism; currently closed).

> **? DID YOU KNOW ...?**
>
> ■ how extensive the Czech National Gallery collections are? The gallery owns some 14,362 paintings, 7575 sculptures, 242,634 items of graphic art, 60,972 drawings, 12,114 oriental exhibits and 51 modern-media items.

National Museum (Národní muzeum)

F 5

Location: Praha 1, Nové Město, Václavské náměstí 68
Tram: 11

Metro: Muzeum
Internet: www.nm.cz

🕐
Opening hours:
May–Sept
daily 10am–6pm
Oct–April
daily 9am–5pm
closed first Tue in
the month

The National Museum was founded in 1818. In this year a Bohemian Enlightenment group – among them, Count Kašpar Maria Šternberk, Josef Dobrovský and František Palacký – called for a museum to be founded; it was made up initially of various »private collections» and was located in Sternberg Palace on ► Hradčany Square.

National Museum Plan

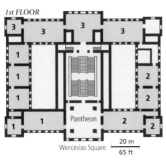

1st FLOOR

Pantheon

Wenceslas Square

20 m
65 ft

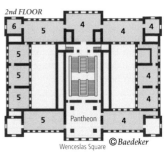

2nd FLOOR

Pantheon

Wenceslas Square

© *Baedeker*

1 Ancient history and archaeology
2 Mineralogy

3 Temporary exhibitions
4 Zoology

5 Palaentology
6 Anthropology

Not until the end of the 19th century did the collections acquire a building of their own.

The National Museum is the oldest museum in the Czech Republic and has more than 13 million items in its collections. It comprises the Ethnography Museum, the Náprstek Museum with collections from Asian, African and American cultures, and the Museum of Physical Education and Sport (► Tyrš House), all of which are located in their own buildings.

The main building with newly gilded cupola occupies the upper end of ► Wenceslas Square. It was built (1885–1890) in neo-Renaissance style from designs by **Josef Schulz**. The lofty rectangular building is approached by a double ramp and a triple flight of steps. Corinthian columns and pilasters structure the façade vertically. The central projection and tower with four-sided segmental cupola emphasize the centre of the building; the corner projections are each superelevated by smaller octagonal cupolas.

The interior has an impressive six-armed staircase with an arcaded gallery. A pantheon extending over two floors is devoted to the most important Czechs, whose statues and busts are displayed here; they include Josef Václav Myslek, Ladislav Šaloun and Karel Dvořák. In the arches beneath the cupola are allegories of science, art, inspiration and might.

Collections   The National Museum houses the Science Museum, the Historical Museum and the National Museum Library (more than 3.6 million volumes).

The extensive mineralogical collection is displayed in old showcases. On display, too, are base forms of precious and semi-precious stones, and meteorites. The zoological exhibits include the more than 20m/

66ft-long skeleton of a finwhale. The palaeontological display traces the development of flora and fauna through the different geological eras.

The historico-archaeological department focuses in detail on the Bronze Age and Ice Age; it has finds from Bohemia, Moravia and Slovakia, as well as reconstructions. A pleasant curiosity is the exhibition of 19th and 20th-century orders and medals.

National Technical Museum

E 3

Location: Praha 7, Holešovice, Kostelní 42

Tram: 1, 8, 25, 26

The National Technical Museum (Národní technické muzeum) has a lot to offer the visitor to Prague. Situated on the north slope of Letná plateau (► Letná Gardens), the museum conveys a vivid picture of the development of cinematography, radio and television technology, transport and mining. The 600m/1970ft-long reproduction coal-mine is particularly worth seeing.

Re-opening 2008 after renovation

www.ntm.cz

In the large hall are automobiles, aeroplanes and engines, as well as Emperor Franz Joseph's court train (two coaches) in which the Austrian heir to the throne, Franz Ferdinand, and his wife travelled to Sarajevo on 28 June 1914, where the disastrous assassination took place that led after the July crisis to the outbreak of World War I.

National Theatre (Národní divadlo)

D/E 5

Location: Praha 1, Nové Město, Národní třída 2

Metro: Národní třída
Tram: 6, 9, 17, 18, 21, 22, 23

The Czech National Theatre was built (1868–1881) by **Josef Zítek** in neo-Renaissance style, modelled on the Nostitz Theatre; it burnt down shortly after the first performance. **Josef Schulz**, a pupil of Zítek, had the theatre rebuilt within the space of only two years, using money donated by the general public in a wave of national sympathy. On 18 November 1883 the first season began with the festive premiere of Smetana's national opera *Libuše*, which was composed for the occasion.

The theatre was founded during an epoch of national resurgence, and embodied »all the yearnings and leanings of a people returning to European culture and consciousness, full of energy, action and enthusiasm after long slumbers«. The foundation stone had been hewn from Říp mountain, from where founding father Čech took possession of Bohemia.

NATIONAL THEATRE

✶ ✶ The National Theatre is a manifestation of Czech national pride. It was financed largely by donations. 13 years after the foundation stone was laid, it was opened with much pomp and ceremony in 1881. Two months later the building burnt down. The curtain rose for the second time, two years later, on Bedřich Smetana's opera *Libuše*.

① Minerva
The goddess Minerva's gladiator team on Prague's National Theatre is called the Triga (team of three) – the Quadriga is in Berlin. Bohuslav Schnirch created the bronze triumphal chariot with the goddess of victory.

② Façade
The projecting portal gives strong emphasis to the front of the building; it has a towering loggia with pillars. The side of the building is on the waterfront; here there was an entrance for coaches.

③ Foyer
Mikoláš Aleš provided the cartoons for the 14 lunette frescoes on the theme of *My Homeland*. They show, in neo-Romantic spirit, mythical figures and important landmarks in Czech history. The ceiling fresco by František Ženíšek glorifies the decline and rebirth of the Golden Age of art. The bronze busts of Czech composers should also be seen in the spirit of glorification of the arts.

④ Auditorium
The ceiling paintings by František Ženíšek symbolize the fine arts. The semicircular auditorium has four levels above the stalls, and a total of 1700 seats.

The sumptuous ambience of the National Theatre continues into the foyer. Patrons linger here in style before the performance and between the acts.

A few days before the official opening, a fire swept through the National Theatre, caused by work being done on the roof. As little as six weeks later, enough money had been donated for rebuilding to begin.

Further along Národní třída, in the direction of Jungmann Square, is **St Ursula** the Baroque Church of St Ursula (Kostel svaté Voršily, no. 8), with its very striking, richly structured façade. It was built (1702–1704) as part of the Ursuline convent, from designs by **Marc Antonio Canevale**. In 1747 **Ignaz Franz Platzer the Elder** created the John Nepomuk group of statues in front of the church. The lavish Baroque interior is remarkable above all for the ceiling frescoes by Johann Jakob Steinfels *Holy Trinity*, 1707) and the altar picture by Peter Johann Brandl (*Assumption of the Virgin Mary*).

✳ Nerudova

C/D 4

Location: Praha 1, Malá Strana   **Metro:** Malostranská
Tram: 12, 22

Nerudova, once the main approach leading steeply up to ► Prague Castle, begins at ► Lesser Quarter Square. Formerly known by the German name of »Spornergasse«, it is one of the loveliest of Prague's cobbled streets, with predominantly late-Baroque townhouses. In the **»House of the Two Suns«** (U dvou slunců; no. 47) lived the writer Jan Neruda, 1845–1857; a memorial plaque on the early-Baroque façade commemorates this fact.

The Morzin Palace (Morzinský palác; no. 5) is one of the finest Baro-   **Morzin Palace** que palaces in Malá Strana. For this building – now the seat of the Romanian embassy – three houses were amalgamated in 1714, merging the Baroque architecture of **Giovanni (Johann Blasius) Santini-Aichl** with the sculpture of **Ferdinand Maximilian Brokoff**. Heraldic figures of Moors, emblems of the aristocratic Morzin (Moor) family, support the balcony; over the doorway are allegories of day and night. The house front opposite is adorned by a Baroque sign of a red eagle carried by two cherubs. Three little criss-cross violins form the pretty house-sign of no. 12, inhabited by Prague's violin-maker Edlinger family, 1667–1748; now it is an inviting wine tavern. The originally Gothic, subsequently Renais-

! *Baedeker* TIP

Tales of the Little Quarter
In the 19th century, Nerudova provided the setting for Czech writer Jan Neruda's stories. The *Tales of the Little Quarter* give an affectionate picture of everyday life in the 19th century, replete with petit-bourgeois superstitions, scandals and gossip. A good read!

sance-style **Valkoun House** (Valkounský dům; no. 14) also owes its late-Baroque appearance to **Giovanni Santini-Aichl**. It is worth taking a look at further house-signs, such as that on the Renaissance **»Golden Bowl«** (U zlaté číše; no. 16), and the Baroque **»House of St John Nepomuk«** (U svatého Jana Nepomuckého; no. 18).

MEDIEVAL SIGNS

When a stranger walked through the streets of Prague in the High Middle Ages, looking for the house of a friend, he had to contend with problems very different from the complicated unfolding of a newly patented city map, or the exasperating search for a street name in an overfilled square on the map. The medieval stranger had to make do without city map, without house numbers, and even without street names.

At a time when even family names were still unknown it would have been odd to introduce modern means of orientation, quite apart from the fact that few streets were clearly demarcated, and the direction streets took could quickly change. Hereditary family names only became necessary when trade blossomed in the twelfth century and large cities evolved in which a precise distinction needed to be made between people, especially in matters of law. At the same time people started to want an unmistakable way of identifying their house,

which would outlast a change in ownership. This prompted the individual and imaginative creation of so-called house-signs, visual representations in stone, wood or metal, which were fixed like a coat-of-arms above the entrance to a house in order to identify it. Initially the signs were mostly drawn from items in the vicinity of the house, »By the Chestnut Tree«, or »By the Bridge«, or from the owner's profession, trade or craft. There were signs like »At the Mill« and »At the Salthouse«, as well as symbolic depictions of the professions such as a key for a locksmith, scissors for a tailor, or the famous »Three Little Violins« in Nerudova for a violin-maker.

Imaginative names

Symbols of all sorts fulfilled a very important function in the Middle Ages, since communication through writing was impractical in an illiterate society. Familiarity with the meaning

In Nerudova, many house-signs tell the story of earlier inhabitants. They recount whole legends, or denote guilds, or patron saints; sometimes their meaning has been forgotten.

of signs and symbols was therefore much more widespread than it is now. Whereas a visitor of today would be likely to enter **»The Golden Goblet«** in the cheerful expectation of quenching his thirst, the medieval stranger would have known at once that here he would find a goldsmith. And whereas a loosely folded towel would now call to mind a laundry, or perhaps for the fanciful a sauna, this sign in fact indicated the house of a barber. In addition, biblical representations were very popular. A careful observer will still find house-signs like **»The Golden Angel«** or »The House at the Black Madonna« in Celetná. Depictions of animals also served as house-signs, such as **»The Three Little Bears«** or **»The Green Frog«**, as did plants, such as **»The Three Red Roses«**, or celestial bodies, such as **»The Two Suns«**. Importance was attached also to the magic qualities of the numbers three, seven, and so on.

Present-day matter-of-factness

Present-day house numbers, anything but imaginative – let alone magical – were introduced in 1770 under Empress Maria Theresa, who imitated French models in this matter. Gradually the significance of certain signs and symbols faded into oblivion, so that people are now uncertain about

house-signs like **»The Golden Serpent«**. It is known, however, that some family and even street names derive from certain house-signs. The opposite can also be the case, as with the house **»U tří pštrosů« (At the Three Ostriches)** by Charles Bridge, whose owner was called Pštros (ostrich).

Two numbers

Yet Prague still displays a further idiosyncrasy: the walls of the houses regularly boast not one but two numbers. The less showy number on a blue background always indicates the normal numbering, whereas the one on a red background represents the property registration number. Beneath it the city district is indicated. Just as the medieval stranger would have been driven to despair by this complicated system, so also our present-day visitor would be horrified if he was directed to look for the house of **»The Golden Vulture«** with no explanation. It's easier with numbers, but today the house-signs remain a pleasant reminder of the past.

Norbert Vinzenz Kolovrat was patron of the Baroque **Thun-Hohenstein Palace**, no. 20, which was built between 1710 and 1725, again from plans by **Giovanni Santini-Aichl**. Immigrant son of an Italian stonemason, he belonged from 1700 to the leading high Baroque artists in Bohemia; the radical blending of Gothic and Baroque elements is characteristic of his style. Today the palace is the seat of the Italian embassy. Linked to Slavata Palace on Thunovská, it has a fine doorway with two heraldic spread eagles (Kolovrat family coat-of-arms), and the Roman divinities Jupiter and Juno.

In the direction of ►Prague Castle stands the Church of St Kajetan, built from plans by Jean Baptiste Mathey and probably also by Santini (1691–1717); it is also known by the German name of the Theatinerkirche. The neighbouring house, the **»Ass at the Cradle«** (Osel u kolébky) is the setting for Neruda's story *A Week in a Quiet House*. The old Malá Strana pharmacy, restored in 1980, in the **»House of the Golden Lion«** (U zlatého lva; no. 32) today houses a museum of pharmacy in the Bohemian royal lands. The Baroque **Bretfeld Palace** (no. 33) is also called »Summer and Winter«; illustrious guests once lodged here, including Wolfgang Amadeus Mozart and Giacomo Casanova. The earliest Malá Strana pharmacy was located in the **»House of the Golden Horseshoe«** (U zlaté podkovy; no. 34). The Baroque townhouse at number 49 (U bílé labutě) has a house-sign consisting of an elaborate white swan. From here, it is just a short distance up the »Ke Hradu« steps to Prague Castle.

★ ★ Old Town Square (Staroměstské náměstí)

Location: Praha 1, Staré Město, Staroměstské náměstí	**Metro:** Staroměstská
Bus: 207	**Tram:** 17, 18

Old Town Square is second only to ►Prague castle in its significance in the history of Prague. The 9000sq m/2.2ac square, with the monumental memorial to reformer **Jan Hus** in the centre, began in the 11th and 12th centuries as a central marketplace for merchants. Over the centuries the square has witnessed historic moments, both tragic and glorious. It was one of the stop-off points for the traditional Bohemian kings' coronation procession, from ► Vyšehrad to ► Prague castle, but it was also a place of execution.

In 1621 the leaders of the Estates' revolt were executed on Old Town Square; a bronze plaque on the Old Town Hall records the names of the 27 put to death.

In more recent history, the citizens of Prague demonstrated here for an independent Czechoslovakia in 1918, and in 1945 an exultant

Old Town Square with Gothic Týn Church is at the very heart of Prague. →

crowd welcomed the victorious Red Army. Old Town Square was also the scene of the violent end of the Prague Spring in 1968, when Warsaw Pact troops marched in. In 1988, on the 20th anniversary of the Prague Spring, thousands took part in a protest march through Staré Město, demonstrating against the continuing Soviet occupation and the suppression of the reform movement, and in favour of liberty and civil rights.

Development

Late 1987 saw the completion of large-scale restoration of Old Town Square and its magnificent buildings, which include the Old Town Hall, Týn Church and school, Goltz-Kinský Palace and the Church of St Nicholas (Staré Město). Most of the façades around the square are now coloured in pastel tones.
A brass plate charts in Latin and Czech the path of the meridian once used to calculate time in Prague.

Jan Hus Memorial

The colossal memorial to Jan Hus dominates the centre of the square. It was commissioned in 1903 and unveiled in 1915, on the 500th anniversary of his death. **Ladislav Šaloun** (1870–1946) designed the sculpture, which shows the reformer amidst the persecuted and exiled. The monument also symbolizes Czech national renewal, partly because of its fleeting resemblance to the traditional Column of Our Lady, symbol of Habsburg Catholicism and therefore also of subjection.

✷ ✷ Old Town Hall (Staroměstská radnice)

⊙
Opening hours:
April–Oct
Mon 11am–6pm
Tue–Sun
9am–6pm
Nov–March
until 5pm

The former town hall is used today for cultural and social events (e.g. weddings), but has retained its name. The history of the Old Town Hall – parts of which date from the 11th century – is a history of individual burgher houses and perpetual building activity.
In 1338 King John of Luxembourg granted the Staré Město inhabitants leave to build a town hall as their own administrative centre. The core was the **Stein corner house**, which was extended by a square tower in 1364. The oriel chapel on the northeast side of the tower was dedicated in 1381; seriously damaged in 1945, it was subsequently restored in part. The mayor of Prague announced in 2007 that plans are being made to complete the restorations soon.
A casket is embedded in the wall with earth from Dukla Pass, where Czechs and Russians repelled the German troops in 1944. On the east side hangs a bronze **memorial** to the leaders of the Czech-Protestant revolt who were executed in 1621, and set into the paving are two crossed white swords with thorn wreath, the date of the execution and 27 small crosses. A bust by Karel Lidický commemorates the Hussite preacher Jan Želivský who was executed in 1422.
The Astronomical Clock on the south side of the tower was built in the 15th century; by 1480 the Gothic doorway on the south front had been completed as main entrance.

In addition, the **Kříž House** was bought in around 1360. The lettering »Praga Caput Regni« (»Prague, capital of the kingdom«) above the Renaissance window dates from 1520. The third building, the Mikeš House, was added in 1458 (remodelled in neo-Renaissance style, 1878).

The »**Cock House**« (»U kohouta«) became part of the town hall complex in 1830; a Romanesque room has survived in the cellar. The Renaissance ceilings and wall paintings on the first floor are also notable.

Building acquisition and activity did not cease until the end of the 19th century. The town hall was seriously damaged on the penultimate day of World War II, when last remaining units of German armed forces fired on the tower:

! *Baedeker* TIP

You may now photograph the bride

The registry office is also located in the Old Town Hall. The garlanded carriages, gleaming vintage cars and wedding ceremonies with confetti pouring out of the old lead windows are sure to put the happy couple in the right mood – and they are also serve as favourite motifs for all camera-wielding visitors to Prague with an eye for a romantic scene. Tourist weddings are possible, if desired: passport and birth certificate are enough. It doesn't always have to be Las Vegas... Tel. 221 097 469.

the neo-Gothic extensions (east and north wings) and the city archives were destroyed. Today there is a small park on this spot.

The south wing was entirely restored in the years 1978–1981. The council chamber on the second floor is still preserved in its original Gothic form (1470). In the large meeting hall are two paintings by Czech historical painter Václav Brožik: *Jan Hus before the Council of Constance*; and *The Election of George of Poděbrady as King of Bohemia*. Paintings by Cyril Bouda (1901–1984) adorn the room where weddings are celebrated. The City of Prague Gallery is located in the cloisters. From the third floor there is access by lift or stairs to the 69m/226ft **town hall tower**. Don't miss the panoramic view of Prague's Old Town from the viewing gallery!

✱ Astronomical Clock (Orloj)

On this clock it was possible to see the movements of the heavens throughout the whole year with the number of months, days and hours. Rising and setting of the stars, the longest and the shortest days, the equinoctia, the feast days for the whole year, the length of day and night, new and full moon and the quarters, the three different striking hours according to the whole and the half clock.

This is how the painter, copper engraver and art publisher Merian described the horologium clockface on the south side of the town hall tower in 1650. Scarcely anything has changed in 500 years. The original construction of the clock is said to date from 1410, and in 1490 Master Hanuš of Charles University made additions to it. The story goes that the councillors had Hanuš blinded in order to prevent him from making anything of the sort for any other city. Shortly be-

The clock on Old Town Hall draws large crowds of visitors to Staré Město, eager to see the spectacle that awaits them when the full hour strikes.

fore his death the blind man climbed the tower and stopped the clock mechanism before the Apostles' procession had begun. The clock stood still until 1551 – but here the legend ends: between 1552 and 1572, Jan Táborský restored the mechanism.

The Astronomical Clock comprises three parts: **Apostles' procession**, clockface and calendar-wheel. The main attraction is the Apostles' procession with 19th-century figures that takes place on the hour: with one arm Death pulls the passing-bell, with the other he lifts up the hourglass. The windows open, and Christ and the twelve Apostles move across. As the windows close, a cockerel flutters and crows in the niche and the hour chimes. A Turk shaking his head beside the clock, a miser gazing at his moneybags, and a vain man looking at his reflection in the mirror complement the allegory.

The clockface is divided into two circles. The upper one shows the movement of sun and moon, and the time. The lower circle is subdivided into 24 segments and shows Bohemian time (from sunrise to sunset) in Arabic numerals. The historical painter Josef Mánes (1820–1871) painted the scenes for the **calendar-wheel**. There are twelve round zodiac pictures, grouped around Prague's coat-of-arms, and scenes from rustic life for each of the months. The originals are in the stairwell of the ►Prague City Museum.

Minute House Adjoining to the southwest is the »Minute House« (U minuty) with figural sgraffiti of biblical and mythological scenes. The house was built in around 1600; most of the sgraffiti were added in 1615, some later. The figure of a lion on the corner goes back to the 18th century. Through the arcades there is a passage to the smaller square of Malé náměstí.

»Na Kamenci« on the south side of Old Town Square is an originally Romanesque building with Gothic extensions; its late-Gothic doorway dates from the 16th century, the early Baroque façade from the 17th century. Next door to it is the early Baroque **»House of the Blue Star«**(U modré hvězdy; no. 25), which has served wine since the 16th century. The **»Golden Unicorn«** (U zlatého jednorožce; no. 20) outgrew its Romanesque form in the 14th century and was extended in late-Gothic style in 1496; the late-Baroque façade dates from the 18th century. A memorial plaque on the house commemorates the famous composer Bedřich Smetana, who founded his first music school here. The last of the magnificent Baroque houses on the south side of the square is the neo-Renaissance **Štorchv dm** (no. 16). Originally there was a Gothic building here (14th/15th century); it was replaced in 1897 by today's building, according to plans by Friedrich Ohmann. The façade painting of St Wenceslas on horseback is by Mikoláš Aleš.

Na Kamenci

»Death« and the »Turk« – allegorical representations of transience and desire

Týn School (Týnská škola)

This originally Gothic building, with ribbed vaulting in the arcade on the east side, was extended in the mid-16th century in Venetian Renaissance style, and adorned with double gable. For four centuries, from the beginning of the 15th century, it housed the Týn parish school; in the mid-15th century the great master builder Matthias Rejsek of Prostějov taught here. Through the third arch from the left there is access to Týn Church.

✷ Church of Our Lady Before Týn (Kostel Panny Marie před Týnem)

The Gothic Týn Church on Old Town Square is considered to be the emblem of Prague's Old Town. It is obscured a little by the school in front of it. Nevertheless, its two towers dominate the eastern side of the square. It was constructed with three aisles in 1365 to replace a Romanesque church. The chancel was completed in 1380; King George of Poděbrady had the façade with its high gabled roof built in 1460. At the time of the Hussite reform movement Týn Church was the Bohemian Utraquist centre in Prague.

A golden chalice was placed on the gable by King George of Poděbrady beside his statue to commemorate his coronation; it was replaced by a Madonna, for whose halo the chalice gold was used, after the Protestants' defeat at the Battle of the ▸ White Mountain (1620).

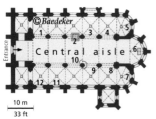

Týn Church Plan

1 St Adalbert altar
2 Late-Gothic baldachin
3 St Joseph altar
4 Annunciation altar
5 Calvary group
6 High altar
7 Gothic corbels, pewter font
8 St Barbara altar
9 Marble grave of Tycho Brahe
10 Renaissance altar
11 Gothic Madonna
12 St Wenceslas altar

The 80m/262ft towers, topped with delicate pinnacles, were built in 1463–1466 (north tower) and 1506–1511 (south tower). Noteworthy, too, is the north doorway with Gothic baldachin and tympanum from Peter Parler's workshop (*Christ's Passion*, copy).

The interior seems a little gloomy in spite of the high Gothic chancel. The **high altar** at the end of the central aisle is very striking, with its splendid paintings *The Assumption* and *The Trinity* by Karel Škréta (1649). In the chapel to the north of the choir is a 15th-century Gothic **Calvary group**; the end of the south aisle is adorned by Gothic corbels from the Parler workshop, busts of an unknown royal couple, and **Cyril and Methodius** in marble by Emanuel Max (1847). Moreover, there is a lovely Gothic pewter font here, dated 1414.

The altar painting of St Adalbert on the first central column of the north aisle is also by Škréta, who also created the paintings for the Annunciation altar and St Barbara altar after 1660, and the picture for the St Joseph altar (1664). A **late-Gothic tabernacle** (1493) by Master Matthias Rejsek of Prostějov overarches the neo-Gothic St Luke's altar (19th century); the altar painting is by Josef Hellich. In the southern chancel pier is thered marble **tomb of Danish astronomer Tycho Brahe** (►Famous People), who was active at the court of Rudolf II. The two Latin sayings above the picture mean: »To be rather than to seem«; and »Not power, not riches, only art is eternal«. The court astronomer is shown in full armour; the artist responsible for the tomb is not known.

The Gothic Madonna in the second chapel of the south aisle was created in about 1400. The relief of the baptism of Christ was made for the Renaissance altar at the beginning of the 17th century, the St Wenceslas altar picture at the end of the 17th century (A. Stevens).

Next to Týn School stands »The Stone Bell« (U kamenného zvonu). The front of this house, with soaring Gothic windows, was covered by a neo-Gothic façade of 1899 until restoration work was undertaken in the 1960s. The history of the house began in the second half of the 13th century; the name »At the Stone Bell« is first recorded in a document of 1417. The probable patron was Queen Elisabeth, wife of John of Luxembourg. Alterations were made at the end of the 15th century, and further alterations ensured that from 1685 little remained to indicate the grand design of what was once a royal residence. After extensive reconstruction work, the building was restored in 1987 to its old Gothic shape.

The Stone Bell

The **Prague City Gallery** puts on exhibitions (Tue–Sun 10am–6pm), concerts and lectures in »The Stone Bell«.

Goltz-Kinský Palace
(Palác Goltz-Kinských)

In the former Goltz-Kinský Palace (no. 12), directly next door to »The Stone Bell«, is the National Gallery's graphic art collection (Grafická sbírka Národní galerie) with more than 320,000 exhibits dating from medieval to modern times. Among the outstanding items are works of the Italian Renaissance (Veronese, Zuccaro), Flemish masters of the 16th and 17th centuries (Bruegel the Elder, Samuel van Hoogstraten) and examples of Mannerism from Rudolf's time (Hans of Aachen, Bartholomäus Spranger). Bohemian artists of the Baroque period and the 19th century are well represented.

Národní galerie
Opening hours:
Tue–Sun
10am–6pm
www.ngprague.cz

The late-Baroque building with impressive Rococo elements was erected on the foundations of an earlier Romanesque and subsequent early Gothic house (remains in the basement of the west wing). The designs for the palace commissioned in 1755 by Count Jan Arnost Goltz are by **Kilian Ignaz Dientzenhofer**; his successor **Anselmo Lura-**

For St Nicholas, too, a Dientzenhofer was responsible.

go completed the building in 1765. After only three years the palace passed to Prince Rudolf Kinských.

The almost Classicist frontage on the square, with rich stucco work by G. Campione de Bossi and pilastered projections, has two triangular gables. A balcony supported by two pillared doorways runs across the wide façade. Four standing and four lying mythological sculptures by **Ignaz Franz Platzer the Elder** adorn the tympanum. The finely structured window surrounds are in Rococo style, with typical rock motif. The three side wings in Empire style were added later.

Church of St Nicholas, Staré Město (Kostel svatého Mikuláše)

The church of the former Benedictine monastery (▶Emmaus Monastery) belongs today to the Czech Hussite church.

The magnificent, light sacral building on the northwest corner of Old Town Square was built in Baroque style, 1732–1735, according to plans by **Kilian Ignaz Dientzenhofer**, with a monumental south front, a long nave with side chapels and a cupola.

The sculptured ornamentation is by **Anton Braun**, the rich stucco work by Bernardo Spinetti, the ceiling paintings (lives of St Nicholas and St Benedict) by Peter Asam the Elder, who also painted the frescoes in the presbytery and side chapels. The crystal chandelier in the nave was provided in the late 19th century by the Harrachov glassworks. The statue of St Nicholas on the side façade is by B. Šimonovský, and was added in 1906.

Since both monastery and church were secularized in 1787, the high altar, the pews and many of the paintings that were originally here are now in other churches.

! *Baedeker* TIP

Kafka's Prague
A bronze plaque commemorates the Prague writer's birthplace, west of St Nicholas Church on »náměstí Franze Kafky« (no. 5). Opposite St Nicholas stood his school, and Kafka's parents had a haberdashery shop in Kinský Palace. No other writer has such close ties with the city: traces of him can also be found in many other spots in Prague.

Palace Gardens (Palácové zahrady)

D 4

Location: Praha 1, Malá Strana, Valdštejnská

Metro: Malostranská
Tram: 12, 22, 23

The Palace Gardens beneath Prague Castle can be accessed from Valdštejnská 12–14, from Ledeburg Palace (Valdštejnské náměstí 3) and via the Garden on the Ramparts.

By the beginning of the 16th century the southern slope beneath Prague Castle, for the most part vineyards and orchards, no longer had a part to play in defending the area. Various aristocratic families acquired the plots of land, some with buildings on them, in order to create Italianate Renaissance gardens. After the 1648 siege of Malá Strana the ruined gardens were restored in Baroque style; this resulted in symmetrically placed monumental steps and balustraded terraces, with loggias, pavilions and galleries, which afford a wonderful view of Malá Strana.

The gardens are separated from one another by walls; steep steps lead up and down; at the top they are interconnected.

⏲ Opening hours:
April daily
9am–6pm
May daily
10am–7pm
June, July until 9pm
Aug until 8pm
Sept 10am–7pm
Oct 10am–6pm
www.palacove
zahrady.cz

Giovanni Battista Alliprandi or František Maximilian Kaňka are the putative architects of **Ledeburg Garden** (Ledeburská zahrada) to the west, as they are of the palace of the same name on Valdštejnské náměstí. It is accessed by way of steps over the wall opposite the Sala terrena. Here stands a statue of Hercules fighting Cerberus. The garden's steep steps – geometrically constructed around a central axis – lead up to a pentagonal pavilion. To the east of Ledeburg Garden is the Small Pálffy Garden.

The present layout of the **Large Pálffy Garden** dates back to 1751 and was created for Maria Anna of Fürstenberg. Steps lead to the lower terrace with a fountain. The central flight of steps lead up to the higher viewing terrace.

Steeply rising terraces beneath Prague Castle

To the east of the Large Pálffy Garden is the **Kolovrat Garden**. It has not been exploited in the same manner as the other gardens; after two houses were demolished in 1858 it was made into a terraced orchard.

The **Small Fürstenberg Garden** is only partially accessible since the Small Fürstenberg Palace at the foot of the garden belongs to the Czech senate. It was laid out in the years 1784–1788, from plans designed by architect Michael Ignaz Palliardi. The centrally constructed steps lead from a gloriette at the bottom up past a loggia to a pavilion with viewing terrace. From this point a path continues to Prague Castle's Garden on the Ramparts.

✶ Petřín

C/D 4/5

Location: Praha 1, Malá Strana   **Tram:** 6, 9, 12, 22, 23
Funicular: Lanovka

The 318m/1050ft Petřín hill forms a large park, a very pleasant place for relaxing walks. From the 12th to the 19th century there were vineyards on the hill. The Kinský Garden was laid out in the southern part of the park between 1825 and 1830, with a little pleasure palace.

A 2km/1.2mi scenic walk begins in the garden of ► Strahov Monastery, and leads via the seminary garden to Kinský Garden. Alternatively it is possible to reach the top of Petřín hill using the funicular railway, the lower station being located just off Újezd. Close to the midway stop an old vintner house has been converted into an inn called »Nebozízek« (1984– 1985), named after the vineyard first mentioned in documents of 1433. There is a marvellous view of Prague from here. Petřín is an eastern foothill of the ► White Mountain; on it are Petřín lookout tower (»Prague's Eiffel Tower«), the Church of St Lawrence, the Štefánik Observatory, the Mirror Maze and »Hunger Wall«.

St Lawrence   The originally Romanesque Church of St Lawrence (Kostel svatého Vavřince), first mentioned in 1135, was converted in Baroque style by **Ignaz Palliardi** between 1735 and 1770, when it was given a dome and two towers. On the main altar a painting by J.C. Monnos (1693) shows the martyrdom of the saint.

The legend of the founding of St Adalbert's Church on a heathen ritual site in 991 is depicted in the sacristy ceiling fresco (1735). The German name of Petřín – Laurenziberg – derives from the patron saint of the church, which since 1994 has belonged to the Old Catholic Church.

Close to the Church of St Lawrence stands a pavilion with the diorama *Battle of the Prague Students against the Swedes on Charles Bridge in the Year 1648* by Karl and Adolf Liebscher and Vojtěch Bartoněk (1898).

Beside it, a miniature wooden construction from the former Charles Gate in ►Vyšehrad houses the **Mirror Maze** (Bludiště), built at the same time as the lookout tower. Open: April, Sept daily 10am–7pm, May daily 10am–10pm, June–Aug daily 10am–8pm, Oct daily 10am–6pm, Nov–March only Sat, Sun 10am–5pm

> ! **Baedeker** TIP
>
> **Prague's Eiffel Tower**
> The 60m/197ft iron tower with 299 steps was built on the occasion of the Industrial Exhibition in Prague in 1891, a copy of the Eiffel Tower in Paris; until 1990 it was used for telecommunications. From the upper gallery (384m/1260ft above sea level) there is a panoramic view of the city and surrounding central Bohemian region. Open: Aug daily 10am–7pm, May–Sept daily until 10pm, Oct daily until 6pm, Nov–March Sat, Sun 10am–5pm.

Petřín hill in Malá Strana: tempting for a refreshing walk, or just idling

Štefánik Observatory In the summer of 1928 the first part of the Štefánik Observatory (Hvězdárna hlavního města Prahy) was opened to the public. Today the Astronomical Institute of the Czech Academy of Science is located here. Like the planetarium (▶Stromovka Park), the observatory puts on a range of astronomy events.

There are regular guided tours and exhibitions, and regular Wednesday evening astronomy programmes for the general public, in addition to introductory courses on astronomy and space travel, school courses and geographical lectures. Among the modern pieces of equipment are a 40cm/16in mirror telescope (by Carl Zeiss, Jena), the earliest large (»King«) telescope and the original »comet seeker« light telescope.

Stargazers can indulge in their hobby here every evening except Monday. Opening hours vary from month to month: enquiries at tel. 257 32 05 40, www.observatory.cz.

Hunger Wall From the peak of Petřín hill, the fortified city wall erected between 1360 and 1362 under Charles IV runs down to the foot of the hill. Legend has it that the ruler had it built by the poor to allow them to earn their daily crust. Hence the name »Hunger Wall«.

Kinský Square At the foot of Petřín hill lies Kinský Square (Náměstí Kinských), until 1991 Soviet Tank Square (Náměstí sovětských tankistů). It received this name from tank no. 23, left here as a memorial to the liberation of Prague by General Leljuschenko's tanks on 9 May 1945. On the initiative of Adam Černý, the tank was symbolically painted pink in 1991, before the decision was taken to remove it.

Spartakiáda Stadium Approximately 500m/550yd southwest of the lookout tower there are several sports fields. The oldest and largest is the Spartakiáda Stadium (Spartadiádní Stadion), which was built in 1926 for the Sokol gymnastics festival. During the era of Communist rule the stadium was enlarged several times, as the scene of Spartakiádas – the huge talent-spotting sports events organized in the former Communist/Socialist countries.

Poděbrady Palace (Palác Jiřího z Poděbrady)

E 4

Location: Praha 1, Staré Město, Řetězová 3

Metro: Můstek
Tram: 17, 18

Opening hours: May–Oct daily 10am–6pm

One of the best-preserved Romanesque houses in Prague stands on Řetězová. The house of the lords of Kunštát and Poděbrady (Dům pánů z Kunštátu a z Poděbrady) was built at the end of the 12th or beginning of the 13th century. The cross-vaulting in the cellar has survived from the early Romanesque building. A lord Boczko of

Kunštát is documented as owner in 1406, uncle of George of Poděbrady (1420–1471) who was regent of the kingdom of Bohemia in the mid-15th century. Often described in history books as the »Hussite king«, after his election (1458) King Poděbrady moved to the royal court, demolished in 1902, on what is now the Square of the Republic. Since that time Poděbrady Palace has had several non-aristocratic owners, and in 1970 the restored building was made accessible to the general public. On the occasion of the 525th anniversary of George of Poděbrady's election as Bohemian king, a memorial room was opened. In the cellar the Prague Conservation Centre displays archaeological finds pertaining to the earlier history of Prague, including 9th-century ceramics, 14th-century tiles, Hussite army weapons and craft tools of the Gothic era.

Prague Castle (Praský hrad)

C/D 4

Location: Above the Vltava, to the northwest
Tram: 22, 23

Metro: Malostranská, Hradčanská
Internet: www.hrad.cz

Along with ► Charles Bridgeand ► Josefov, Prague Castle (Pražský hrad, in Hradčany) is one of the city's main attractions. Since 1918 it has been the official seat of the president of the republic.

Prague Castle was founded in the late 9th century by the Přemyslids as a three-part wooden stronghold surrounded by an embankment. St Wenceslas had a Romanesque rotunda built in honour of St Vitus on the spot where the Wenceslas Chapel stands today.

In addition to the prince, from 973 the bishop of the newly founded diocese of Prague resided in the castle. Under Břetislav I, in 1042, it was enclosed by a wall 2m/6.6ft thick; at the east and west ends, towers were built, and later on a gate was added on the south side. After 1135, Sobieslav I expanded the castle into an imperial palace in Romanesque style. The 30m/100ft »Black Tower« served as prison. Work began on the central part of the former royal palace under Otokar II. After the end of the Hussite Wars, alterations were made under the Jagiellonian rulers and under King Vladislav (from 1471) and King Ludvík II (from 1516). In these phases the first Renaissance elements came into existence, combined with late Gothic. Both Ferdinand I (emperor from 1556), who brought artists from Italy, the Netherlands and Germany to Prague, and Rudolf II enriched the castle and its immediate surroundings with magnificent Renaissance buildings. A great fire in 1541 necessitated further renovations. In 1614 Emperor Matthias commissioned the first secular Baroque building in Prague, the free-standing gate-tower to the west. In the 18th century, at Maria Theresa's behest, this tower was incorporated into the building that framed the newly laid out first courtyard. This

Opening hours:
April–Oct
daily 9am–6pm
Nov–March
daily 9am–4pm

Don't miss the changing of the guard!

alteration made Prague Castle into an architectural whole, a distinctive feature anchored in the cityscape of Prague. After the coup d'etat of 1918 and the liberation of 1945, Prague Castle was adapted for ceremonial and cultural purposes.

First Courtyard (První nádvoří)

Changing of the guard
Access to the first and most recent of the three castle courtyards, also known as the Memorial Courtyard, is by way of ► Hradčany Square (Hradčanské náměstí), through a portcullis on which the *Battling Titans* (1786; copies since 1912) by **Ignaz Franz Platzer the Elder** are enthroned. The castle guards stand here, and the hourly changing of the guard attracts inquisitive crowds.

The First Courtyard was constructed between 1756 and 1774 under Maria Theresa, from plans by Vienna's chief court architect **Nikolaus Pacassi**. Anselmo Lurago was in charge of the work. The plasterwork trophies above the cornices are further copies of works by Platzer. The most recent alterations were undertaken in the 1920s by Slovenian architect **Josip Plečnik**. He was commissioned by Tomáš G. Masaryk to renovate – in a simple yet distinguished manner – everything in the castle that could symbolize the independence of the state, and to lessen the threatening aspect of this seat of power.

Matthias Gate
Emperor Matthias had the Matthias Gate (Matyášova brána) built by **Giovanni Maria Philippi** in 1614 as a free-standing west entrance to Prague Castle. In 1760 the tower was combined with the newly

erected castle frontage by **Pacassi**. Flights of steps, also by Pacassi (1765/1766), lead up from the gate to the castle's ceremonial rooms: the Throne Room, a room with paintings by Václav Brožík, the Mirror Room, the Music Room and the Reception Room. The residence of the president of the Czech Republic is also in this wing.

The flag-poles in front of the Matthias Gate are pine trunks from Czech frontier forests – Josip Plečnik's idea.

Second Courtyard (Druhé nádvoří)

Entry to the Second Courtyard is through Matthias Gate. Over time the architecture was adapted in Renaissance and late-Baroque style, and the façades by **Pacassi** were made to match those in the First Courtyard.

In the centre is a Baroque fountain, built by **Francesco della Torre** in 1686 and adorned with figures by **Hieronymus Kohl**. The wrought-iron grille covering the draw-well dates from 1702. An attempt was made in 1967 to lighten the severity of this courtyard by introducing a modern lion fountain (V. Makovský) and glittering granite paving (J. Fragner). On the north front of the Second Courtyard the Plečnik Hall was created (1927–1931) by restructuring older parts of the building; together with the so-called Stair Hall it became the entrance hall for the Spanish Hall and Rudolf Gallery.

DON'T MISS

- The changing of the guard every hour on the hour and at midday with fanfare and flag ritual (First Courtyard, Matthias Gate)
- Giuseppe Arcimboldo's portrait of Emperor Rudolf II in fruit and veg (Rudolf Gallery, Second Courtyard)
- Vladislav Hall: reticulated vaulting, Prague Gothic's most beautiful hall (Royal Palace)
- »Bull Staircase«: modern architecture from the 1920s by Josip Plenik (Third Courtyard)
- Kafka's little house at number 22 Golden Lane (third courtyard)

From the Second Courtyard the Powder Bridge (spanning the Stag Moat) leads to a terrace walk (Mariánské hradby) which goes past the **Royal Garden** (accessible only in spring) and the former Ball-Game House to the ►Belvedere.

In 1965 the former Imperial Stables in the north wing and the ground floor of the west wing were converted to form the **Castle Gallery** (Hradní galerie). In six rooms, 107 paintings and three sculptures are displayed from the former **Rudolf Gallery** and the Castle Gallery of Ferdinand II, which was formed later and subsequently broken up. Outstanding works in this collection of European and Czech art include: the portrait of Emperor Matthias by **Hans of Aachen** (c1612); **Titian's** *Young Woman at her Toilet*; **Tintoretto's** *Adulteress before Jesus*; **Veronese's** *St Katherine with the Angel*; and **Rubens'** *Assembly of the Gods at Olympus* (c1602). For Rudolf II, **Arcimboldo** painted the emperor in the form of the ancient god Ver-

tumnus (1590). In addition there are pictures by Bohemian Baroque artists (Jan Kupecký, Peter Johann Brandl) and sculptures by **Adriaen de Vries** (*Adoration of the Magi*) and Matthias Braun.
In the gallery rooms, remains have been discovered of a 9th-century Church of Our Lady, the earliest sacral building in Prague Castle.

Chapel of the Holy Cross
In the south corner of the Second Courtyard is the Chapel of the Holy Cross (Kaple svatého Kříže). Since 1961 it has served as treasury for St Vitus Cathedral. Here precious liturgical items are stored, such as Mass vestments, monstrances and relics; also St Wenceslas' coat of mail and St Stephen's sword.
The Chapel of the Holy Cross was built between 1756 and 1763 under the supervision of **Anselmo Lurago**. In the mid-19th century alterations were made (1852–1858) in an attempt to lighten the Classicist severity. **Emanuel Max** designed the statue of St John Nepomuk inside the chapel in 1854, and also the statues of SS Peter and Paul in the recesses. The sculptures on high altar and side altars are from the workshop of **Franz Ignaz Platzer**; the central crucifixion painting on the high altar is by Franz Xaver Balko.

Third Courtyard (Třetí nádvoří)

The Third Courtyard was once the centre of castle life. This is where the main route of the old Slav settlement began.
The northern border of the Third Courtyard is St Vitus Cathedral. On the south side of the cathedral the walls of a Romanesque bish-

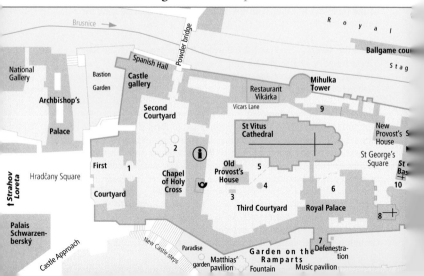

Prague Castle Map

op's chapel can be seen, excavated 1920–1928. Between 1750 and 1770 the older buildings of the royal estate (the former Renaissance palace of Rudolf II, the early Baroque queens' palace and Maximilian II's palace) were given a uniform façade by **Nikolaus Pacassi**. Beneath the balcony with lamp-bearing statues by **Ignaz Platzer** is the entrance to the president of the republic's chancellery.

The Mrákotín granite obelisk on the south side of the former provost's lodging by **Josip Plečnik** (1928) commemorates the victims of the First World War.

The equestrian statue of St George (a copy; the original is in St George's Convent) is by the sculptors **Georg and Martin of Klausenburg** (1373). Tomáš Jaroš restored the early Gothic sculpture after the castle fire of 1541. The pedestal in place today is by Josip Plečnik (1928). From the south wing of the Royal Palace the so-called »Bull Staircase« (Býčí schodiště) by Plečnik links the Third Courtyard to Paradise Garden. The stairs and pathway are inspired by Greek and Egyptian mythology.

! **Baedeker TIP**

Shakespeare at the castle

There is a balcony for Juliet, and Romeo stands in the courtyard. Summer theatre takes over the medieval castle and the ruler's official residence to present Shakespeare dramas in chivalric setting: Verona's lovers and *A Midsummer-Night's Dream* play against the backdrop of Prague Castle. And this time it is a puppet who asks whether to be or not to be – *Hamlet* is staged with marionettes, and the figures and costumes for the production received an American Theatre Award. Late July–mid-Sept daily from 8.30pm. Information: www.shakespeare.cz.

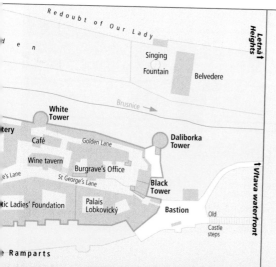

1 Matthias Gate
2 Fountain
3 Obelisk
4 St George
5 Romanesque remains
6 Palace courtyard
7 Bohemian chancellery
8 All Saints Chapel
9 Mladota House
   (Old deanery)
10 Chapel of St John
    Nepomuk

N

50 m
165 ft

Old Provost's Lodging Adjoining the west side of St Vitus Cathedral is the former provost's lodging (Staré proboštství). Originally a Romanesque bishop's palace, it was given its present Baroque form during 17th-century alterations. The statue of St Wenceslas is by **Johann Georg Bendl** (1662).

✶ ✶ St Vitus Cathedral (Chrám svatého Víta)

Prague Castle's most magnificent building St Vitus Cathedral is the metropolitan church of the archbishopric of Prague. It occupies the site of a rotunda which Duke Wenceslas dedicated to St Vitus in 925.

135 years later Duke Spytihněv II donated a Romanesque basilica with double chancel. Charles IV began building the Gothic cathedral in 1344. The east end was designed by French master builder **Matthias of Arras**, influenced by the older Gothic style of southern France (cathedrals of Narbonne and Toulouse). He was responsible for the chancel, 47m/154ft long and 39m/128ft high, of which only the lower parts were completed at the time of his death (1352). **Peter Parler** succeeded Matthias of Arras and enriched the cathedral with the upward-soaring forms of German Gothic. Thereafter **Parler's sons Wenzel and Johann** took over (1399–1420); the entire chancel with ambulatory chapels and the foundations of the main tower are

A must for visitors to Prague: the castle with St Vitus Cathedral

of this period. After the Hussite Wars **Bonifaz Wohlmut** and **Hans of Tyrol** gave this 99m/325ft tower a Renaissance cupola with a parapet; in 1770 it was given its Baroque bulbiform roof (design by Nikolaus Pacassi).

It was not until the early 20th century that St Vitus Cathedral was finally completed. From 1872 on, **Josef Mocker** oversaw work on the cathedral; drawing on Peter Parler's plans he began with the neo-Gothic west part of the main portal, which was completed under Kamil Hilbert in 1929.

St Vitus Cathedral is not only the grandest church in Prague and Prague Castle's most magnificent building; with its external length of 124m/407ft, its transept width of 60m/197ft and height of 33m/108ft in the central aisle, it is also the largest church in Prague. The south tower with its Gothic, Baroque and Renaissance elements – accessible in the summer months – is architecturally unique. In addition to three Renaissance bells, it has the largest bell in Bohemia: the Sigismund bell, cast in bronze (1549).

The usual entrance to the cathedral is the west doorway. The upper part of the south doorway, also called the »**Golden Gate**« (»Zlatá brána«), has 14th-century glass mosaics (restored) showing the *Last Judgement*. At the top, Christ passing judgement on the world is depicted in a mandorla, flanked by Mary and John. Below him are the country's six patron saints, in two groups of three: Procopius, Sigismund and Vitus; Adalbert, Ludmila and Wenceslas. Below them are portraits of Charles IV and Elisabeth of Pomerania. At the side the apostles can be seen, and beneath them the righteous and the damned.

Above is a 40,000-piece glass tracery window by **Max Švabinský** (1934), also depicting the Last Judgement.

Exterior

Between the pillared arcades and chancel windows runs the **triforium gallery**. In the outer triforium are busts of the cathedral's master builders, the family of Charles IV, and other contemporaries. The portrait gallery, emanating for the most part from the Parler workshop, is of great art-historical significance: although the emperor still occupies the central position, the portrayal of master builders alongside spiritual and secular rulers attests to a novel self-assurance on the part of the late-Gothic artist; and the individualized facial characteristics of the subjects anticipate the Renaissance.

There is no access to the triforium itself; indeed, it has never been exposed to the gaze of ordinary church visitors.

Interior

Opposite the south doorway is the two-storey organ loft by **Bonifaz Wohlmut** (1557–1561). After the cathedral was completed, the organ loft was moved from its original position inside the west façade to its current position in the north transept. The mighty organ (1757) has 6500 pipes.

Organ loft

ST VITUS CATHEDRAL

✶✶ Although the foundation stone was laid in 1344, the cathedral was not completed until the beginning of the 20th century. The architectural highlights are attributable above all to the cathedral's master builder, Peter Parler from Schwäbisch-Gmund, who was commissioned to undertake the work at the age of 23.

🕐 Open:
April–Oct, daily 9am–6pm
Nov–March, daily 9am–4pm

① Rose window
A great rose window, more than 10m/33ft in diameter, dominates the west front.

② Wood reliefs
In the chancel ambulatory is an interesting two-part wood relief by Kaspar Bechteler. It shows the *Flight of the Winter King, Friedrich of the Palatinate* from Prague after his defeat at the Battle of the White Mountain. The panorama of the pre-1635 city on the Vltava is well worth seeing for the many interesting details it reveals.

③ Grave of Count Leopold Schlick
The marble memorial to Field-Marshall Count Leopold Schlick was made by František Maximilian Kaňka from a design by architect Josef Emanuel Fischer von Erlach.

The Gothic gargoyles that deflect rain water have the form of monsters and devils. They are supposed to protect the cathedral from evil powers which, according to ancient superstition, flee from their own likeness.

④ St Wenceslas Chapel
The Wenceslas Chapel is the highlight of the cathedral. A stellar vault by Peter Parler crowns the square construction. Here, the saint's mortal remains are preserved. The decoration of the chapel is noteworthy. The walls have been inlaid with more than 1300 precious stones. Above is a Passion cycle; a further cycle presents 31 scenes from the life of St Wenceslas and is attributed to the master of the Litomice altar.

⑤ Golden Gate
The cathedral entrance is adorned with mosaics of the Last Judgement; in the centre Christ is enthroned in a mandorla.

⑥ South entrance porch
The Golden Gate's three pointed arches open into the south entrance porch, which is one of the loveliest spaces in the whole cathedral. Peter Parler removed all weight from the Gothic ribbed vaulting so that it seems to float free.

Art Nouveau artist Alfons Mucha created the »Cyril and Methodius« window in the third chapel.

Because of its size and the quality of its ornamentation, looking into St Vitus Cathedral chancel is still impressive.

Amalia, daughter of Maria Theresa. Rudolf II (1552–1612) rests in the Renaissance pewter coffin; in the granite sarcophagus lie the children of Charles IV.

The Royal Crypt was redesigned in the years 1928–1935.

The exit from the crypt leads back to the nave, just in front of the chancel.

By the first pillar opposite Wenceslas Chapel is the Baroque memorial to Field Marshal Count Schlick († 1723); it was made in 1723 by **Matthias Braun** from a design by **Joseph Emanuel Fischer von Erlach**, and is reminiscent of Bernini's Roman works. The obelisk is flanked by Minerva (Wisdom) and Mars (Valour). Putti hold the crowned armorial emblem, and Fama makes known the dead man's reputation. The bust of the deceased shows a countenance rapt in thought.

Tomb of Count Schlick

The loveliest of the ambulatory chapels is the Gothic Chapel of St Wenceslas, which extends as far as the south transept. **Peter Parler** built the chapel (1358–1367) on a square groundplan with star-ribbed vaulting; it took the place of the originally Romanesque rotunda in which St Wenceslas was buried. The chapel contains the reliquary shrine of Duke Wenceslas, patron saint of Bohemia, murdered in 935 by his brother Boleslav I in Stará Boleslav. Although legend has it that as he was murdered Wenceslas clung to the lion's

Chapel of St Wenceslas

head door-ring now mounted here, the door-ring has in fact been dated to the turn of the 12th/13th century, so cannot have given support to the saint at the moment of death.

The chapel walls are inlaid around the lower part with 1300 semi-precious Bohemian stones. The outstanding ornamentation can be matched in the 14th century only in Karlštejn Castle. The lower row of wall paintings (Passion cycle) is by **Master Oswald** of Prague (1373); the upper row with the Wenceslas legend is from the workshop of the **Master of the Litomice altar** (*c*1509). However it does display contemporary figures (Vladislav II and his wife Anna on the east wall). The decoration of the chapel is of a high order and anticipates the Renaissance.

Yet the most important work is the statue of the saint himself. It was probably done by **Heinrich Parler**, nephew of Peter Parler; the family emblem is found on the pedestal of the 2m/6.6ft statue. The duke appears in armour: in his left hand he holds his shield with the eagle, in his right hand he carries the lance. Contrasting with this is the flowing movement, and the absent, almost trance-like look of the subject, embodying the ideal image of the saint. Two angels are painted on the sides of the statue; according to legend, they accompanied him to his audience with King Heinrich the Fowler.

Coronation chamber

A staircase leads from the Chapel of St Wenceslas to the coronation chamber above the south doorway, where the Bohemian crown jewels are kept – crown, sceptre, imperial orb, royal mantle and stole. They are secured by seven locks and only very rarely displayed.

✷ ✷ Old Royal Palace (Královský palác)

Historical development

The ducal and royal palace is located on the east side of the Third Courtyard; traces of the historical development of the building are clearly visible. A first ducal edifice of the 9th century was replaced in the 11th century by a Romanesque palace, which was remodelled in 1135 in the course of alterations to the whole castle site. From the mid-13th century, during the reign of Otokar II, it was enlarged all round, and under Emperor Charles IV further alterations were made. At the end of the 15th century **Benedikt Ried** undertook the last major alterations for Vladislav Jagiello. Until the end of the 16th century the Old Royal Palace was the ruler's seat. When the actual residence moved west under the Habsburgs, the palace rooms were turned into chancellery offices or storerooms.

Parts of the Romanesque palace are preserved beneath Vladislav Hall on the ground floor and below; parts of the original castle fortifications are also visible. Above are the parts of the palace newly built by Přemysl Otokar II, Charles IV and Wenceslas IV. The centre of Vladislav Jagiello's new second floor, created by alteration and expansion, is Vladislav Hall – the *pièce de résistance* of secular castle buildings.

Passing through the central entrance beneath the balcony, and to the right of the eagle fountain by **Francesco della Torre** (1664), there is access via a vestibule to the Green Room. This was Charles IV's court of law, and from the 16th century seat of the high court and criminal court. The walls on the east side are decorated by Upper and Lower Lausitz coats-of-arms; several coats-of-arms recall 18th-century owners. In 1963 the copy of the Baroque ceiling fresco *Solomon's Judgement* was transferred from the Burgrave's office to the Green Room.
The Green Room connects to **Vladislav's Bedchamber** (also: **Small Audience Room**) and the Land Roll repository, the latter with fine late-Gothic polychrome-ribbed vaulting; the arms of Bohemia, Moravia, Silesia and Luxembourg are displayed, as is the royal monogram of Vladislav Jagiello, over the window. In the repository, the coats-of-arms of the high treasurers may be seen.

Green Room

Also known as the Hall of Homage, Vladislav Hall is 62m/203ft long, 16m/52ft wide and 13m/43ft high. It was built between 1493 and 1503 by **Benedikt Ried** from Piesting, and with its late-Gothic reticulated vaulting it is one of the most splendid parts of Prague Castle. The boldly composed ceiling, with ribs reaching far down into the room, has a delicacy and lightness from which the massive wall pilasters in no way detract. In spite of the Gothic vault, there is already a Renaissance flavour to its slightly superelevated proportions. The wooden floor probably dates from the late 18th century; three of the chandeliers date from the 16th century, the other two are copies.

Vladislav Hall

Royal Palace Plan

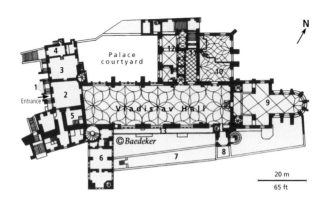

1 Eagle fountain
2 Antechamber
  (Small hall)
3 Green Room
4 Vladislav bedchamber
5 Romanesque tower
6 Bohemian
  chancellery
7 Theresian wing
8 Viewing terrace
9 All Saints Chapel
10 Diet
11 Riders' Staircase
12 New Appeal Court
13 Viewing gallery

The hall was used mostly for ceremonial purposes. Here, Bohemia's kings were elected, the Diet met, and tournaments were held. Since 1934 the president of the republic has been elected in this hall. Stairs lead up to a gallery from which the interior of All Saints Chapel can be viewed.

Ludvík Wing The Ludvík Wing adjoins Vladislav Hall. It was erected (1502–1509) by for the Jagiellonians. A door in the southwest corner gives access to the rooms of the **Bohemian Chancellery**, on the same level as Vladislav Hall. The larger room with a Gothic vault was once the office of the governors of Bohemia. The smaller meeting-room is linked to the large one by a Renaissance doorway of 1509, on which Ludvík's monogram can be seen.

In 1618 the imperial governors were thrown out of a Bohemian chancellery window.

It was from a window in this second room of the Bohemian Chancellery that in 1618 the imperial governors, Jaroslav Bořita z Martinic and Vilém Slavata of Chlum, together with their personal secretary, F. Fabricius, were thrown 15m/49ft down into the castle ditch below (where they escaped, however, with »mortal fear, their lives and a few scratches«). This **Second Prague Defenestration** was the signal for the start of the Bohemian revolt against the Habsburgs and precipitated the Thirty Years' War.

A spiral staircase leads to the former **chancellery of the imperial Hofrat**. Here the 27 leaders of the Estates' revolt against the Habsburgs were sentenced to death on 19 June 1621, to be executed on Old Town Square. This was the end of the Estates' revolt which had started with the defenestration of the governors one floor below. The door is ornamented with 17th-century inlay work; the interior is decorated in late-Renaissance style, with 17th/18th-century chancellery furnishings and tiled stove. The portrait of Spain's King Philip IV, to the left above the door, is a copy of a Velásquez painting.

ROYAL PALACE

✶ ✶ Until the 16th century, the city's rulers lived in the Royal Palace. One highlight is Vladislav Hall, 66m/217ft long, 16m/52ft wide and 13m/43ft high. Here, in olden times, Bohemian kings were elected, and state presidents are still sworn in the hall today. The late-Gothic reticulated vaulting is most impressive.

🕐 Open:
April–Oct daily 9am–6pm
Nov–March daily 9am–4pm

① West façade
After the alterations made to the castle under Maria Theresa, the west façade of the old Royal Palace was modified to harmonize with the buildings in the castle's third courtyard.

② Entrance
Entering the west wing with its late-Gothic and Renaissance extensions, the visitor passes the Baroque eagle well, to which Josip Plenik added a fountain.

③ Riders' Staircase
The riders' staircase was intended for knights on horseback taking part in tournaments in the hall.

Vladislav II rebuilt the palace from 1483; Benedikt Ried was commissioned to build the staircase and Vladislav Hall.

④ Diet
The Diet, too, was originally constructed from plans by Benedikt Ried. Bonifaz Wohlgemut renovated the late-Gothic reticulated vaulting in 1559–1563, after a devastating fire. Meetings were often stormy, especially prior to the Battle of the White Mountain. Some regional representatives gave preference to activities more agreeable than their duties. The lord of Roupov issued a warning during the reign of Friedrich of the Palatinate: »If you tarry a little longer, gentlemen, beware lest you squander your homeland over your meal«.

⑤ New Land Rolls Rooms
The Land Rolls were books in which the outcomes of debates were entered before the Diet. These entries had the character of law. Most of the rolls were destroyed when Prague Castle burnt down, and Ferdinand I used the opportunity to annul some of the old privileges of the Estates.

⑥ Vladislav Hall
In its time, Vladislav Hall was the largest secular vaulted building in central Europe. Its construction, 1492–1502, was undertaken by Benedikt Ried. The bold and elaborate late-Gothic stellar vaulting conducts the load down two storeys through massive supporting pillars.

⑦ Viewing platform
From the viewing platform it is possible to look out onto the Malá Strana rooftops and the whole Vltava valley. Below the terrace is the Theresian Wing, and behind is the Garden on the Ramparts.

The Second Prague Defenestration sparked off the Thirty Years' War. Later the two imperial governors were richly rewarded by the Habsburgs.

From the south side of Vladislav Hall there is access to a viewing platform, looking onto the castle's south gardens. Beneath is the Theresian Wing, beyond which lies the Garden on the Ramparts. The view to the west is blocked by the Ludvík Wing.

Viewing platform

From the east side of Vladislav Hall a short staircase leads to All Saints' Chapel, built by Peter Parler between 1370 and 1387. After a fire in 1541, Queen Elisabeth, daughter of Maximilian II, had the chapel altered, enlarged and connected to Vladislav Hall (1579–1580). Parler's reticulated vaulting, destroyed in the fire, was replaced by something simpler. The Renaissance doorway gives access to a gallery with view of the high altar (by Peter Prachner, c1750), adorned with an All Saints picture by **Wenzel Lorenz Reiner** of 1732. Unfortunately the angel triptych beneath the gallery, designed at the end of the 16th century by Hans of Aachen, cannot be seen. The carved tomb (1739) in the north section of the chapel, with relics of St Procopius, is by **Franz Ignaz Weiss**. The chapel originally served the erstwhile Theresian religious foundation for ladies of high rank (adjacent building to the east).

All Saints' Chapel

The first door in the north wall gives access to a spiral staircase which leads to the **New Land Rolls Room** on the first floor. The interior decoration dates from the 17th century. Walls and ceilings are painted with arms of the Land Roll officials, except that the arms of Bohuslav of Michalowitz have been whitewashed; he was executed because of his part in the Bohemian Estates' revolt. In the second room, the carved bookcase from the time of Rudolf II has reproductions of Land Rolls; the spines were coloured for classification purposes.

Before finally leaving Vladislav Hall by the Riders' Staircase doorway, it is worth passing through the rear door at the north end of the hall to enter the Diet, also built by Benedikt Ried (c1500). It was renovated (1559–1563) by **Bonifaz Wohlmut** after a devastating fire, replicating late-Gothic ribbed vaulting. Busts commemorate the master builder and Emperor Ferdinand I, patron of the building.

Diet

Built into the northwest corner is the parliamentary clerk's tribune, a Renaissance addition. Portraits of Habsburg rulers adorn the walls. The tiled stove by the entrance was made in 1836 in neo-Gothic style. Between the windows stands the neo-Gothic royal throne (19th century); the lion emblem above it dates from the 17th century. To the right of the throne sat the spiritual lords and highest officials of the realm, opposite the throne sat aristocrats and knights. The balustraded space was reserved for representatives of the royal towns. The supreme court and the Estates met here until 1847. Today the president of the republic signs his oath in this room after he has been elected. The Czech national council also meets here on solemn occasions.

Remains of Romanesque wall paintings in St George's Basilica show the Heavenly Jerusalem.

12th century; the crossed vaulting is supported by pillars with cubi-form capitals.

In the raised chancel, reached by symmetrical double Baroque stairs, are remains of Romanesque ceiling frescoes of the New Jerusalem, dating from the beginning of the 13th century. Late-Renaissance frescoes (16th century) on the apse ceiling depict the Coronation of the Virgin Mary. Adjacent to the chancel on the south side is the **Chapel of St Ludmila**, separated by marble balustrade and grille. Built in the 13th century, the national patron saint's chapel was altered in the 14th century to receive her relics. In the Renaissance vault – the 14th-century extension had to be re-vaulted after a fire – is the sepulchre of Ludmila (murdered in 921) made in around 1380 by **Peter Parler**. Her life is depicted on the west wall of the chapel – difficult to see – in a fresco (1858) by J. V. Hellich. Further paintings from the late 16th century portray Christ, the Virgin Mary, the evangelists, and Bohemian sovereigns.

Adjoining the south side of the basilica **František Maximilian Kaňka** built St John Nepomuk Chapel (1718–1722), now used as an exit from St George's Basilica. The saint is portrayed twice by **Wenzel Lorenz Reiner**: in the *Apotheosis of the Saint* of the cupola frescoes and in the altar picture. The statues of St Adalbert and St Norbert in the chapel niches date from about 1730.

St John Nepomuk Chapel

✻ Convent of St George (Klášter svatého Jiří)

Bohemia's oldest monastic building Next to St George's Basilica stands the Benedictine Convent of St George, founded in 973 by Duke Boleslav II and his sister Mlada, the first abbess. The pre-Romanesque, Ottonian building is the oldest monastic building in Bohemia, consisting originally of one small building without cloisters. Following damage caused by raging fires during the siege of Prague Castle in 1142, and again in 1541, the monastery was altered and enlarged several times, given a Baroque look (1657–1680), and closed in 1782. Today it is part of the National Gallery (Národní galerie; www.ngprague.cz) and houses, in addition to temporary exhibitions, the Bohemian Mannerism and Baroque collection.

Národní galerie/ collection The first floor display shows the development from Mannerism (late 16th century) through the Baroque and Rococo eras up to the end of the 18th century.

🕐 **Opening hours:**
Tue–Sun
10am–6pm
www.ngprague.cz

It begins with the artists of northern **Mannerism at the court of Rudolf II** (1576–1611): the Flemish painter Bartholomäus Spranger (1546–1611), Prague court artist Hans of Aachen (1552–1615), Swiss painter Josef Heintz Roelandt Savery (1564–1609) and Flemish sculptor Adriaen de Vries (1560–1627).

Especially notable **Baroque paintings** are those by Karel Škréta (1610–1674), Peter Johann Brandl (1669–1735) and portraitist Jan Kupecký (1667–1740), and also the works of Wenzel Lorenz Reiner (1689–1743) and Michael Leopold Willmann (1630–1706). There are notable sculptures by Tyrolean-born Matthias Bernhard Braun (1684–1738) and Ferdinand Maximilian Brokoff (1688–1731).
Rococo development is evident in pictures by Anton Kern (1709–1747) and the painter of scenes from rural life, Norbert Grund (1717–1767).

Equestrian statue of St George Further along the north passage is the original of the equestrian statue of St George, originally erected in the Third Courtyard of Prague Castle and now replaced there by a copy. The figure cast in bronze in 1373 by **Martin and George of Klausenburg** is regarded as the first free-standing sculpture – that is, detached from any architectural context – north of the Alps.

✻ Golden Lane (Zlatá ulička)

Golden Lane – also known as Alchemists' Lane – runs from the castle fortifications built by Vladislav Jagiello to the old Burgrave's house; once it went all the way to the Convent of St George. Battlements linked the White Tower to Daliborka Tower. The surviving north frontage consists of picturesque cottages, which are built into the battlement arches. Rudolf II assigned them to his 24 castle guards, who practised a skilled craft in their spare time. The name »Alchemists' Lane« refers to Rudolf II's alchemists, who are traditionally said to have lived here and tried to produce gold; however, there is evidence that their laboratories were in Mihulka Tower (Alchemists' room). Later on, craftsmen and poor people lived in the cottages. It was in number 22 that Franz Kafka (► Famous People) worked on his stories and essays in 1916/1917; among works written here are *A Country Doctor, Up in the Gallery, A Report for the Academy* and *A Message for the Emperor*. Today, little souvenir shops and brightly coloured houses line Golden Lane.

! **Baedeker TIP**

Childhood memories

The Toy Museum in the former Burgrave's house behind Golden Lane (Toy Museum Hraček, entrance from Jiská) is delightful, and not only for children. Crumpled old teddy bears await visitors large and small, along with 270 Barbie dolls, the earliest Märklin engines, aeroplanes, old airships and an abundance of metal toys. Daily 9.30am–5.30pm.

From the bastion, which offers a good view, there is access to the large Garden on the Ramparts. Two obelisks mark the spots where the imperial governors fell into what was then the moat on the occasion of the Second Prague Defenestration in 1618. Above the New Castle Steps lies the Paradise Garden, with Matthias Pavilion and a music pavilion.

Garden on the Ramparts

Rarely can Zlatá ulicka (Golden Lane) be seen in such contemplative mode: it is one of the most popular sights on the castle site.

The deep **Stag Moat** in the north of the castle precinct was once used to raise animals for the hunt. To the north of Stag Moat are the Royal Gardens; on the west side – in Lion's Court – Rudolf II kept lions, tigers and bears.

Prague City Museum

F 4

Location: Praha 8, Karlín, Na poříčí 52   **Tram:** 3, 5, 8, 24
Metro: Florenc   **Internet:** www.muzeumprahy.cz

⊙
Opening hours:
Tue–Sun
9am–6pm

Prague City Museum (Muzeum hlavního města Prahy) was completed in 1898 according to designs by Antonín Balšánek and Antonín Wiehl. The neo-Renaissance façade was ornamented by various sculptors. In the stairway hangs the disk of the months that **Josef Mánes** created for the town hall's Astronomical Clock in Staré Město (▶ Old Town Square). The picture circles on the inside show the signs of the zodiac; the twelve outer pictures show the astronomical course of the year. The City Museum, founded in 1884, offers a permanent exhibition concerning Prague's economic, architectural and cultural development. Alongside completely furnished rooms, historic costumes, ceramics and sculpture, the museum boasts a collection of Prague house-signs. The 20sq m/215sq ft model of the city (1826–1834) by lithographer Antonín Langweil is most impressive. It shows how little of the old city has changed in the past almost two centuries, and also gives a glimpse of the beautiful architecture of buildings that are not open to the public.

Rotunda of the Holy Cross
(Rotunda svatého Kříže)

E 5

Location: Praha 1, Staré Město, Karoliny   **Tram:** 6, 9, 17, 18, 22
Světlé/corner with Konviktská

Romanesque
jewel

The Rotunda of the Holy Cross, just a few steps from the Vltava waterfront, is one of three surviving Romanesque rotundas (round chapels) in Prague. It was built in about 1100.
Scheduled for demolition, it was saved by an objection lodged by the Czech Society of Artists, and renovation work was undertaken in the years 1863–1865 by architect **Vojtech Ignaz Ullmann** and painter **Bedřich Wachsmann**, who also designed the new altar. Remains of Gothic wall frescoes inside the chapel, which depict the Coronation of Our Lady, were supplemented by **Soběslav Pinkas** and František Sequens. The ironwork screen is by **Josef Mánes**, the paintings for the triumphal arch and apse by **Peter Maixner**.

Rudolfinum • Dům umělců

E 4

Location: Praha 1, Staré Město, Náměstí Jana Palacha
Bus: 207

Metro: Staroměstská
Tram: 17, 18

The Rudolfinum (also: House of Artists; Dům umělců) is the home of the Czech Philharmonic (Česká Filharmonie); in addition, exhibitions and concerts are put on here, especially during the internationally renowned »Prague Spring«.

The Rudolfinum was designed (1876–1884) by the architects of the ► National Theatre, **Josef Zítek** and **Josef Schulz**, and named after the Austrian crown prince Rudolf. Alongside the ► National Theatre and the ► National Museum it is one of Prague's most important neo-Renaissance buildings. Between 1919 and 1939 it was the seat of parliament, and there was also a picture gallery (now in ► Sternberg Palace).

The interior of the Dvořák Hall was modelled on Gabriel's theatre at Versailles. An allegory of music by A. Wagner adorns the main entrance (1885); the lion and sphinx statues are by B. Schnirch. The parapet features sculptures of famous artists and composers.

The Rudolfinum is approached by an impressive flight of wide steps.

St Longinus Rotunda

E 5

Location: Praha 1, Nové Město,   **Metro:** I.P. Pavlova Karlovo náměstí
Na Rybníčku   **Tram:** 4, 6, 10, 16, 22, 23

The St Longinus Rotunda (Rotunda svatého Longina) was originally built in Romanesque style as Rybníček village church. The village, now attested to only by the street named after it, was absorbed into Nové Město after 1257. Up to the 14th century the rotunda was dedicated to St Stephen, but the Gothic parish church took his name when it was built (see below). In the 17th century the rotunda was given an open-structure lantern to replace the previous small tower.
It is worth taking a look at the Baroque altar and the crucifixion scene with St Longinus. According to apocryphal documents associated with Pilate, Longinus was the Roman soldier, or captain, who pierced Christ's side with his lance. Longinus is said to have been active as bishop in Cappadocia following his conversion, and to have died a martyr's death.

Church of St Stephen
(Kostel svatého Štěpána)

From Na Rybníčku it is not far to Štěpánská, in which St Stephen's Church is located. Charles IV founded it in 1351 as the parish church for upper Nové Město; it was completed in 1394. The tower was not added until the beginning of the 15th century. In spite of restorations (1876 and 1936), the Gothic exterior has been preserved.
In addition to the Baroque interior decoration as a whole, it is worth notingthe following in particular: the Gothic pewter font by B. Kovář (1462); the Gothic picture of the Madonna (1472); the late-Gothic stone pulpit (15th century); and three paintings, *St Rosalia* (*c*1660; second pillar on the right), *St Wenceslas* (*c*1650; left side of the chancel) and *Baptism of Christ* (1649; end of the left aisle) by **Karel Škréta**, as well as the tomb of Baroque sculptor **Matthias Bernhard Braun** (1684–1738).

Smetana Museum

D 4

🕐
Opening hours:
Wed–Mon
10am–noon
12.30pm–5pm
www.nm.cz

An embankment leads past the Emperor Francis I monument to Old Town Water Tower (15th century). West of it is the Smetana Museum, which belongs to the ►National Museum; it was set up in 1936 in the former Prague waterworks, a neo-Renaissance building dating from 1883, and its sgrafitto décor is well worth seeing. The museum's exhibits include original manuscripts, letters, the famous composer's grand piano and numerous costumes from his operas. Concerts and

! *Baedeker* TIP

A fine view of Prague Castle
The embankment named after Bedřich Smetana (Smetanovo nábřeží) runs from the National Theatre to a small peninsula just before Charles Bridge; it offers a wonderful view of the bridge and Prague Castle.

lectures take place in the large hall. Outside the museum, on Novotného lávka, is the Smetana statue by J. Malejovský (1984).

Smíchov (city district)

B – D 6 – 7

Location: Praha 5
Tram: 4, 6, 7, 9, 12, 16

Metro: Anděl

The district of Smíchov lies west of the Vltava; in the 18th century it was discovered by the aristocracy, who built several summer palaces with lovely gardens here. Among them are ► Villa Bertramka, Villa Kinský with Kinský Gardens extending south of the Hunger Wall (► Petřín), and the Dientzenhofer Summer Palace.

Upgrading of a city district

In the 19th century the appearance of Smíchov was altered by the arrival of workers' dwellings and light industry. Yet the new industrial quarter had hardly arisen when it began its decline, becoming ever more dilapidated, because of emigration and factory closures. Only in the last ten years have efforts been made to upgrade the neglected district. Now it is undergoing a transformation into a very attractive shopping and entertainment area: easy to reach from Metro station Anděl, **Prague's largest shopping-centre** »Obchodní centrum Novy Smichov« has more than 130 brand shops, an enormous supermarket, restaurants, cafés, bars and multiplex cinema, on the site of a former coach factory. No less gigantic is **»Angel City«** (Anděl City), a complex of offices, apartments, shops, restaurants, bowling and cinema with several screens. On the site of the former House of the Golden Angel (U zlatého anděla), star architect **Jean Nouvel** created the Golden Angel (Zlatý

The most recent shopping centre, Zlatý Anděl

Anděl) office and shop building with more than 13,000 sq m/140,000 sq ft of office space and 7000 sq m/75,000 sq ft of shop-floor space. Nouvel adorned the striking glass façade on the main street with a blown-up image of actor Bruno Ganz from the Wim Wenders film *Wings of Desire*; as in the film, Ganz gazes down at the crowds of passers-by. The »Angel« also gave the shopping-centre its name. Alongside are quotations from poets whose names are closely connected with the city of Prague – notably Franz Kafka, Rainer Maria Rilke and Gustav Meyrink – inscribed in red against a background of grey and white clouds.

Dientzenhofer Summer Palace   **Kilian Ignaz Dientzenhofer** built this Baroque summer palace (Portheimka) at number 12 Štefánikova in 1725 for his own family. The magnificent *Bacchus Festival* fresco (1729) on the ceiling of the central hall is by **Wenzel Lorenz Reiner**.
In 1758 the summer palace became the property of Count Francis Buquoy, and in the 19th century it was purchased by Prague industrialist Porges von Portheim. Part of the palace was demolished in 1884 in order to make room for the new Church of St Wenceslas. Today, Galerie D is located in the former palace (► Museums and Exhibitions).

★ Sternberg Palace (Šternberský palác)

C 4

Location: Praha 1,
Hradčanské náměstí 15
Tram: 12, 22, 23

Metro: Hradčanská, Malostranská
Internet: www.ngprague.cz

🕐
Opening hours:
Tue–Sun
10am–6pm

From ► Hradčany Square a passage in the left portal of the Archbishop's Palace leads to a steep lane down to Sternberg Palace, where the National Gallery's collection of European art (Sbírka starého evropského umění Národní galerie) is housed.
The palace was designed in high Baroque style by **Domenico Martinelli** and completed by **Giovanni Battista Alliprandi** (1698– 1707). It is a four-winged building with a cylindrical projection, an inner courtyard enclosed by stuccoed walls, and ceiling paintings by Pompeus Aldovrandini.
The collection shows works mainly by early Italian, Flemish and German painters. The palace was reopened, and the collection reorganized, after restoration work had been completed on a ceiling painting on the ground floor and other items.

Ground floor   The ground floor of Sternberg Palace has mostly 15th–18th-century **German and Austrian paintings**. The acknowledged highlight is the picture painted by **Albrecht Dürer** in 1506 for German merchants in Venice, the *Feast of the Rosary*: the Blessed Virgin with Child,

The »Rosary Feast« by Albrecht Dürer is one of the most beautiful exhibits in Prague's National Gallery.

crowned by angels, gives her blessing to Emperor Maximilian (kneeling on the right-hand side of the picture). Dürer immortalized himself in the painting, too (standing at the edge of the picture on the right with a sheet of paper in his hand). Further personalities of the age are likewise portrayed, such as Pope Julius II, but some are difficult to identify. It was Dürer's ability to combine Italian qualities such as generous composition and radiant colouring with close attention to detail that made the picture important; Emperor Rudolf purchased it and had it brought to Prague.

There are also some works by **Lucas Cranach the Elder** (1472–1553) in Sternberg Palace, including the small *Portrait of an Old Man*, an example of the satirico-erotic genre in which unequal love is ridiculed. German and Austrian painting of the 17th and 18th centuries is represented, for instance, by the still-life painter **Georg Flegel** (1566–1638), in the utter realism of his *Cabinet Painting with Flowers, Fruit and Goblets*. **Jakob Marell** (1614–1681), a pupil of Flegel, even goes so far as to integrate his own self-portrait as a reflection in his *Vase with Flowers*. **Johann Michael Rottmayr's** virtuoso use of colour in his depiction of the *Death of Seneca* (pre-1695) creates a contrast between the serene resignation of Seneca in the face of death and the animation of the other figures.

The first floor is mainly given over to painters of the 14th-century **First floor** Florentine School. These include Giotto's pupil **Bernardo Daddi** (active 1327–*c*1348), who has bequeathed to posterity, among other things, a small portable altar for private meditation. **Pietro Lorenzetti** (end of 13th century–*c*1348) was one of the leading Siena masters of the first half of the Trecento. Two panels portraying an unknown *Martyr Saint* and *St Anthony* are by him. There are also two notable terracotta sculptures by **Andrea della Robbia** (1435–1525). These are followed by Flemish masters of the 15th and16th centuries. The triptych by **Geertgen tot Sint Jans**, *Adoration of the Magi* (c1490–1495), is one of the most important examples of Flemish painting. Jan Gossaert, called Mabuse, displays clear traces of Italian influence in *St Luke Drawing the Virgin* (c1513). Gossaert had studied ancient sculpture and Renaissance architecture in Italy.

Second floor On the second floor are works by Italian, Spanish, French, English, Flemish and Dutch artists of the 16th to 18th centuries. The French are represented, for instance, by **Simon Vouet** with his picture *Death of Lucretia* (c1624/1625), whose light and dark effects show a marked orientation towards Caravaggio's use of chiaroscuro. Italian painting is represented, for instance, by **Tintoretto's** *St Jerome* (c1500). Tintoretto gives the Father of the Church an individualized face, and shows him in cardinal's garb. The Flemish are represented by such important artists as **Jacob Jordaens** and 17th-century landscape masters **Joos de Momper** (mountain scene with Temptation of Christ) and **David Tenniers the Younger**. Of special note are the numerous works by **Peter Paul Rubens**, which include the *Portrait of Commander-in-Chief Ambrosius Spinola* (c1627), who had himself immortalized in full armour. Further portraits, notably those by Rembrandt and Franz Hals, attest to the mastery of the Dutch and Flemish. **Pieter Bruegel the Elder's** *Haymaking* shows the harmony between man and the land in July; the picture belongs to the five surviving pictures of the months dating from 1565, of which others are in Vienna and New York.

✔ DON'T MISS

- Albrecht Dürer's *Feast of the Rosary*: highlight of the National Gallery (ground floor)
- Jan »Mabuse« Grossaert's *St Luke Drawing the Virgin*: monumental altar picture (first floor)
- Pieter Bruegel's *Haymaking*: one of five surviving pictures of the months (second floor)
- Lion in inner courtyard: Bohemia's heraldic animal in impressive form
- Ceiling frescoes and wall paintings, by no means inferior to the masterpieces in the collection

★ Strahov Monastery (Strahovský klášter)

C 4

Location: Praha 1, Hradčany, Strahovské nádvoří 132

Tram: 22, 23

The second-oldest monastery in Prague was built by Duke Vladislav II at the request of Jindřich Zdík, bishop of Olmütz, for the Premonstratensian order. Its name, Strahov, derives from the location of the monastery on a hill above Malá Strana, at the entrance to Prague Castle (strahovati = guard). After a great fire in 1258, which destroyed the first library, the monastery was renovated in Gothic style. In 1360 Charles IV brought the monastery – till then outside the city gates – within the city walls. In the 15th century the Gothic renovations were interrupted by the bloody Hussite Wars. The monastery flourished most under abbots Jan Lohel, Kašpar of Questenberk and Kryšpín Fuk, who worked hard on the generous remodelling in Renaissance style.

At the end of the Thirty Years' War the monastery was ransacked by Swedish soldiers. After the Peace of Westphalia a new library – the Theological Hall – was set up in 1671 with a core of newly acquired books. Between 1682 and 1689 the whole area was given a Baroque appearance, overseen by architect **Jean Baptiste Mathey**. Extensive landscaping, gardens and fruit trees framed the whole complex in a fitting manner.

Through the Austrian Wars of Succession the monastery once more suffered severe damage, in 1741; the repairs took more than four decades. They were completed with the Classical Philosophical Hall,

> ## ! *Baedeker* TIP
>
> ### Hellishly good
>
> Peklo, Czech for »hell«, is the name of a wine cellar in the catacombs of Strahov Monastery. The stylish vaulted cellar dates back all the way to 1140 and offers tempting grill and fish dishes, both at lunchtime and in the evening. Strahovské nádvoří 1, daily noon–midnight, tel. 220 516 652.

On a hill above Malá Strana lies Prague's second-oldest monastery.

Books galore beneath an enormous ceiling fresco

the most important Prague building of Emperor Joseph II's era. Remains of the original Romanesque foundations were exposed during careful restoration work undertaken between 1950 and 1954.

Monastery complex

Entry to the monastery courtyard is either direct, through passage and steps at number 8, or, more rewardingly, by passing this entrance and going up a short ramp at the west end of the square and through a Baroque gate (1742), crowned in the middle by a statue of St Norbert, founder of the Premonstratensian order. The statue, dating from 1719, is by **Johann Anton Quittainer**.

In the courtyard, immediately to the left, is the former Chapel of St Roch (Kaple svatého Rocha). Rudolf II had the chapel built (1603–1617) in gratitude for the city's being spared the plague in 1599. Today there is a gallery here, also used for concerts.

Church of the Assumption of Our Lady

Straight ahead, beyond the St Norbert Column, is the 17th-century Church of the Assumption of Our Lady(Kostel Nanebevzetí Panny Marie), with a richly fitted Baroque interior of the mid-18th century (restored in the 1970s). The stucco cartouches by **Michael Ignaz Palliardi** contain Marian pictures by **Josef Kramolín** and **Ignaz Raab**; the main altar, of 1768, is by Jan Lauermann with a relief of saints by Ignaz Franz Platzer the Elder. In the Pappenheim Chapel in the right side aisle is the tomb of imperial cavalry general Gottfried Heinrich Pappenheim (1594–1632, killed at the Battle of Lützen). Adjacent to the church stand the monastery buildings, in part Romanesque, with a library and a cloister.

Monastery Library

The historic monastery library now belongs once again to the Pre-monstratensian order. Among the precious holdings of this unique library – approximately 280,000 volumes dating from the 9th to the 18th centuries – are about 2500 incunabula, 5000 manuscripts and numerous historic maps.

🕐
Opening hours:
daily 9am–noon
1pm–5pm

The extent of the collection, readily made available to secular scholars, was one of the contributory factors to Emperor Joseph II's (and others') decision at the end of the 18th century to preserve the monastic community.

Particularly worthy of note are the richly stuccoed Theological Hall, painted (1723–1727) by Strahov monk Siard Nosecký, with early-Baroque barrel vault by **Giovanni Domenico Orsi de Orsini**, and the Philosophical Hall, located in a Classical extension (west wing; 1782–1784) by **Michael Ignaz Palliardi**.

**✸✸
Theological Hall**

In the decoration of the Theological Hall, monk Siard Nosecký was inspired by abbot Hieronymus Hirnheim's *De typo generis humani* (1670–1679), and by biblical quotations. The 25 frescoes symbolize the struggle for wisdom in relation to the love of scholarship and literature. The southern part of the vault shows *The Assumption of Mary*; there then follows a celebration of the building of the library. Next appears Christ teaching in the temple, then the creation of the earth, and finally a depiction of the limits of human reason confronted with the complexity of the world, shown by five questioners gathered round a globe.

There is a self-portrait of the artist in a window embrasure on the right. Along the length of the hall, terrestrial and celestial globes alternate; three come from the workshop of the famous Flemish cartographer Willem Blaeus.

The dimensions of the Philosophical Hall – 32m/105ft long, 10m/33ft wide and 14m/46ft high – were calculated to accommodate the richly carved bookcases (Jan Lachhofer) from Louka Monastery in Southern Moravia. Arching over the hall is a mighty ceiling fresco, in which **Franz Anton Maulbertsch** (1724–1796), from Langenargen on Lake Constance, depicts scenes from the intellectual history of mankind in the allegorical style of the Vienna Academy. In the middle of the hall an old case houses the six-volume botanical work *Les Liliacées* and the four-volume treatise *Le Musée Francais*, both gifts of the French Empress Marie Louise (1812). The marble bust of Emperor Francis I was created by Franz Xaver Lederer in about 1800. Neither hall is open to visitors, but both can be observed from the doorway.

**✸✸
Philosophical
Hall**

Among the library's most valuable manuscripts is the Strahov Evangeliary (9th/10th century), an Ottonian Renaissance artefact from the circle of the Trier School. The Latin text was written in golden

Library holdings

uncials on 218 parchment folios; later the manuscript was embellished with four elaborate gospel illustrations. This manuscript, the St Mark Torsi and the famous **Codex Vyšehradiensis** belong to the earliest surviving manuscripts in Central Europe. Further highly notable items are the *Historia Anglorum* , the account of Friedrich Barbarossa's Italian campaign, the partially preserved Dalimil Chronicle, the Doxan Bible, the late-Gothic Schelmenberg Bible (Pontifical of Albrecht of Sternberg from the time of Charles IV), and writings by Tomaš of Štítné and Jan Hus. Dating from the 15th century are the Strahov Herbarium, a Latin lexicon and the medical books of Magister Ambrož. The 16th and 17th centuries are represented by works of the Utraquists, the *Unitas fratrum*, and Catholic literature. Travel narratives, atlases, alchemical works, astronomical treatises by Tycho Brahe, Johannes Kepler and Nicolaus Copernicus, oriental manuscripts and other bibliographical curiosities continue the long list of valuable holdings.

Strahov Picture Gallery The Strahov Picture Gallery (Strahovská obrazárna) on the first floor of the cloisters contains one of the most important monastic collections, from the Gothic era to the 19th century. The exhibits include Gothic art from Bohemia and Moravia, with such pieces as the Strahov Madonna from the workshop of the Master of Hohenfurth and the Strahov Retable by the Master of the Litoměřice Altar, of which, however, only the panels with the Annunciation, Nativity and Flight into Egypt have survived.

Among the painters at the court of Rudolf II were Joseph Heintz the Elder and Bartholomäus Spranger, whose works are just as well worth seeing as the Baroque and Rococo works, or those of the first half of the 19th century.

Stromovka

D–F 2

Location: Praha 7, Holešovice   **Tram:** 5, 12, 17

North of Letná Gardens (▶Letná Gardens), the splendid Stromovka park extends to the Vltava.

In the southwestern part is a neo-Gothic hunting lodge, built by King Vladislav Jagiello at the end of the 15th century. In the early 19th century it was remodelled in line with the informal landscaping of the garden.

Exhibition Grounds (Výstaviště)

Opening hours:
Tue–Sat

In the southeastern part of the park, exhibition grounds were laid out for the Jubilee exhibition of 1891 and ethnographic exhibition of 1895, based on plans by **Antonín Wiehl**; since 1918 the Prague trade

Impressive: the old Industry Palace with its fountains

fairs have been held here. At the beginning of the 1950s the grounds were extended to become a recreational park.

The iron construction of the **Industry Palace** (Sjezdový palác) built in about 1900 from designs by **Bedřich Münzberger** and **Josef Fanta** is very impressive. Until the opening of the ▶ Vyšehrad Palace of Culture, congresses and conferences took place in the Industry Palace.

The façade of Prague pavilion showsfigures from Bohemian history; it was also constructed in the late 19th/early 20th century, by G. Zoula, with allegorical sculptures by F. Hergesell. Today the pavilion houses the ▶ National Museum's **Lapidarium** (collection of stone works), with notable 11th–19th-century architectural and sculptural exhibits. The originals of many sculptures in and around Prague that have been replaced by copies over the years – in order to protect them from inclement weather – can be viewed here, including the Charles Bridge statues by Braun and Brokoff. Open: Tue–Fri noon–6pm, Sat, Sun 10am–6pm.

The round **pavilion** with the diorama »Battle of Lipany« was designed by J. Koula in 1908. Inside is a painting by L. Marolds (1898) of the Hussite battle of 30 May 1434. The **planetarium** was built (1960–1962) from a design by J. Fragner on circular foundations. At around the same time, the former engineering exhibition pavilion (1907) was converted into a **sports hall** with seating for 18,500 spectators. Around 1990 the **Křižíkova fountain** was built, which is illuminated very impressively in the evening, as were an ampitheatre and several pavilions.

Troja Chateau (Letohrádek Troja · Trojský zámek)

D 1

Location: Praha 7, Trója   **Bus:** 112

🕒 Opening hours:
April–Oct
Tue–Sun
10am–5pm
Nov–March
Sat, Sun
10am–5pm

North of ▶Stromovka Park – in the outlying district of Troja – is the Baroque Troja Chateau (Letohrádek Trója), built in the years 1679–1685 by **Jean Baptiste Mathey**. The magnificent steps up to the entrance were added later; their decorative figures (a gigantomachia, or battle of the giants) are by two pairs of brothers, Johann Georg and Paul Herrmann from Dresden, and **Johann Josef and Ferdinand Maximilian Brokoff**. Figures and steps form one entity, yet no figure is required to sacrifice its individuality. On the inner side the figures gradually rise up, mirroring the movement from bottom to top, until they finally stand upright. On the outer balustrade are busts, allegories of the times of day, continents and elements.

Baroque delight on the outskirts of Prague

Notable features of the interior are the Imperial Hall with wall and ceiling frescoes (1691–1697) by Flemish artist Abraham Godin, and the mythological frescoes by the Italians Giovanni and Giovanni Francesco Marchetti in the side rooms. Early Baroque vases and 17th-century busts adorn the terrace. Today, the restored chateau houses an exhibition of 19th-century Czech painting from the City of Prague Gallery (www.citygalleryprague.cz).

Directly to the west of Troja Chateau is Prague's **Zoological Garden** (Zoologická zahrada, Praha 7, U Trojskeho zamku 3/120, www.zoopraha.cz). It was set up in 1931 in an area of 45ha/111ac of natural countryside, with meadows, groves, gorges and cliffs; differences in altitude are overcome by a chair-lift (Lanovka).

🕒 Opening hours:
March
daily 9am–5pm
April, May, Sept, Oct
until 6pm
June–Aug until 7pm
Nov–Feb until 4pm

Today more than 3800 animals are kept in an area of 60ha/148ac – more than 540 different species, including mammals, fish and lower life-forms – leading a cheerless life, far from their natural habitats. In 2002 almost half the area suffered flood damage, but in the meantime most of the enclosures and buildings have been repaired. The zoo has had a notable success in breeding original Przewalski wild horses – predecessors of the domestic horse – now extinct in the wild. In the terrarium visitors can observe tortoises, cobras, rattlesnakes and a rare sauria species.

★ Týn Courtyard

(Týnský dvůr · Týn ·in German, Ungelt)

E 4

Location: Praha 1, Staré Město, Týnský dvůr (Ungelt)

Metro: Staroměstská, Můstek
Tram: 5, 14, 26

The medieval marketplace of Týn courtyard, extensively renovated in the 1920s, received its German name from the toll (Ungeld) that once had to be paid here. The creation of a princely farmstead dates back to the 11th century. Under the ruler's protection, for which dues were payable, foreign merchants stored, sold and levied tolls on their goods until 1773.

The most important building in the courtyard is the Renaissance **Granovský Palace** with an open first-floor loggia (1560), which served as lodgings for visiting merchants. The loggia wall paintings depict biblical and mythological scenes. The doorway bears the date, 1560, and the coat-of-arms of the Granovský family. The adjoining 14th–19th-century burgher houses are also worth seeing.

✳ Church of St James
(Kostel svatého Jakuba)

East of Týn courtyard, on the corner of Malá Štupartská and Jakub-ská, stands the Church of St James – founded in 1232 as church of the former Minorite monastery (on the north side). In 1366 the church burnt down, and was then rebuilt in Gothic style; the current Baroque architecture was created between 1689 and 1739, the work of master builder Jan Šimon Pánek, who succeeded in creating a consummate model of Baroque remodelling of Gothic architecture. The stucco front with SS James, Francis and Anthony of Padua is by Ottavio Mosto.

The **interior** is of particular note, being divided by very delicately moulded pilasters, with 21 altars. With the exception of St Vitus Cathedral (►Prague Castle), St James's is the longest church in Prague and, on account of its rich ornamentation, one of the most beautiful. **Wenzel Lorenz Reiner** painted the *Martyrdom of St James* for the high altar, while Franz Guido Voget created the ceiling frescoes (*Life of Mary, Glorification of the Trinity*). The Baroque tomb of Count Vratislav of Mitrovic was designed by **Johann Bernhard Fischer von Erlach** and executed by **Ferdinand Maximilian Brokoff** between 1714 and 1716. The arrangement of the figures recalls the Pietà: the count reclines on the sarcophagus, supported by the shoulders of a female figure. Since the church acoustics are very good, concerts are often given here. Adjacent to the north side of the church are the cloisters of the Minorite monastery, itself remodelled in Gothic and later in Baroque style. Today it houses an art school.

Tyrš House (Tyršův dům)

Location: Praha 1, Malá Straná, Újezd 40

Tram: 12, 22

⊙ Opening hours:
Thu, Sat, Sun
9am–noon
1pm–4pm

Tyrš Houseis the home of the Museum of Physical Education and Sport (Muzeum tělesné výchovy a sportu), with extensive collections that give an overall view of the development of Czech sport. A permanent exhibition is devoted to the »Sokol« gymnastics competitions (sokol = falcon) and »Spartakiáda«.

After the Habsburg victory at the Battle of the ► White Mountain (1620), Pavel Michna of Vacínov, who had acquired wealth by means of possessions confiscated from the Bohemian aristocracy, bought the small Renaissance palace in around 1580. His son had it converted in late-Renaissance style, and enlarged into a big palace by the addition of an east wing. From 1767 the palace was used as an arsenal. After 1918 **Michna Palace** (Michnův palác) was bought by the Czech nationalist physical education movement, Sokol, and named Tyrš House after the founder of the Sokol movement, Miroslav Tyrš. Further along Újezd to the north is the ►Church of our Lady Victorious, then Vrtba Palace, and almost opposite is the lower station of the ►Petřínfunicular railway.

Veletržní Palace (Veletržní palác)

Location: Praha 7, Holešovice, Dukelských Hrdinů 47

Tram: 5, 12, 17
Internet: www.ngprague.cz

This enormous palace, with eight storeys and 40,000 cubic metres / 1.4 million cubic feet of usable space, was built as long ago as 1924–1928 by architects **Oldřich Tyl** and **Josef Fuchs**. The building was conceived as part of a trade fair complex, and was initially to be followed by further buildings. Although it was the only one to be realized, the Functionalist building is a supreme achievement of the era. Le Corbusier, in 1928, spoke admiringly of Veletržní Palace, with its multi-level exhibition spaces grouped around an enormous glass-roofed industrial hall. Especially impressive is the »Small Hall« – not so very small, with seven floors, an open gallery, and a further glass roof. From the beginning of the 1950s Veletržní Palace was used for administrative purposes. After it was gutted by fire in the 1970s, the authorities decided that it should be reconstructed and used to house the collection of modern art.

Národní galerie   Since the most recent reorganization of the **collections of the National Gallery**, the museum has exhibited the art of the 19th and

20th centuries. It is a wide-ranging display, drawing not only on painting, but also on architecture, film and design to give a picture of the intellectual and cultural creativity of the period. Much of the display is devoted to Czech painting and sculpture, represented in works by Mucha, Šíma, Kupka, Filla, Štýrský, Kolíbal, Gutfreund, Makovsky, Wichterlova and others.

Yet **French art**, too, is uniquely honoured: the Veletržní Palace collection is one of the most extensive in the world. In part it was acquired by the Czechoslovakian state as early as 1923, purchased after a Mánes Artists' Society exhibition. Key works are 19 pictures by Picasso as well as numerous Impressionist works, including pictures by Renoir, Gauguin, van Gogh, Pissarro, Monet, Cézanne, Rousseau, Matisse and Sisley. The National Gallery also owns several Rodin sculptures. The museum is further enriched by outstanding sculptures and paintings by Kokoschka, Klimt, Schiele, Klee, de Chirico, Miró, Munch and others.

On the second floor of Veletržní Palace is the **Lidice collection**, with works by a total of 52 German artists. In 1967 the Berlin gallery owner René Block organized an exhibition »Hommage à Lidice« for a projected museum in the town. In July 1968 Block brought works donated by renowned artists Joseph Beuys, Dieter Roth, Wolf Vostell and others to Prague, where they were shown in a gallery.

After the upheavals caused by the arrival of Warsaw Pact troops they were for three decades thought to have disappeared. In the spring of 1997 they were rediscovered, and supplemented by the work of 31 artists of the younger generation, thanks once again to Block's initiative. Both components of the collection are now on show here, since the projected museum in Lidice cannot yet be realized owing to financial constraints.

✔ **DON'T MISS**

- Mikoláš Aleš: neo-Romanticism of the »National Theatre generation«, late 19th century (4th floor)
- František Kupka: *Prometheus*, representative of the abstract art movement (3rd floor)
- Jan Zrzavý: *Cleopatra II*, Prague's Picasso (3rd floor)
- Pablo Picasso: *Violin, Glass, Pipe and Inkpot* (1912), first painting in the style of Cubism (3rd floor)
- Josef Svoboda, scenographer and stage designer, Oscar for *Amadeus* (2nd floor)
- František Drtikol, avant-garde photography of the 1920s (2nd floor)
- Gustav Klimt: *Virgin* in gold (1st floor)
- »Trpaslík«: Prague's tallest dwarf, almost 3m/ 10ft, in the internet café (ground floor)

🕐 Opening hours:
Tue–Sun
10am–6pm

The »small hall« shows all seven floors at once and gives an impression of Veletržní Palace's size.

Villa Amerika (with Dvořák Museum)

Location: Praha 2, Nové Město,
Ke Karlovu 20
Bus: 148

Metro: I. P. Pavlova
Tram: 4, 6, 16, 22

🕐 Opening hours:
April–Sept Tue–Sun
10am–1.30pm
2pm–5.30pm,
Oct–March from
9.30am

Villa Amerika (Letohrádek Amerika), also known as **Chateau Michna** (Michnův letohrádek) after its original owner, Jan Václav Michna of Vacínov, today houses the Dvořák Museum.
Kilian Ignaz Dientzenhofer built the Baroque chateau (1717–1720) as a summer residence for Count Michna. The elaborate architecture and structuring of the front make the villa one of Prague's finest secular buildings of the Baroque era. The original Baroque wrought-iron gate at the entrance has been replaced by a copy. Inside, the frescoes are by Johann Ferdinand Schor (1720); the workshop of Anton Braun provided the sculptural ornamentation in the garden (c1730).
The Dvořák Museum has musical scores and documents relating to the important composer Antonín Dvořák (►Famous People), notably his correspondence with Hans von Bülow and Johannes Brahms.

St Catherine
The former church of St Catherine's Monastery (Bývalý kostel svaté Kateřiny) is not far from Villa Amerika. It is located on Kateřinská; the entrance is on Viničná, but currently the church is not open to the public. When the church was remodelled (1737–1741) **František Maximilian Kaňka** incorporated the Gothic tower into the new Baroque part of the building. Because of its slender form the octagonal tower is sometimes referred to as the »Prague minaret«. The interior is adorned with frescoes by **Wenzel Lorenz Reiner** (*Life of St Catherine*) and stucco work by Bernardo Spinetti. The regional psychiatric hospital is located in the former monastery complex.

Villa Bertramka (with Mozart Museum, Bertramka)

Location: Praha 5, Smíchov,
Mozartova 2/169

Metro: Anděl
Tram: 4, 7, 9

www.
bertramka.com

The story of this residence began in the 17th century, when Malá Strana master-brewer Jan František Pimskorn had the villa built. At the beginning of the 18th century it passed into the ownership of František Bertram of Bertram, after whom it has been named ever since. During the years 1784–1795 it belonged to opera singer Josefa Dušková, wife of the composer and music pedagogue František Xaver Dušek.

The Baroque Villa Amerika was built as a →
summer pleasure palace for Count Michna.

Wolfgang Amadeus Mozart lodged in the musicians' household during his frequent visits to Prague in these years. In the mid-19th century the Popelkas – father and son – made it into a Mozart memorial house; sculptor Tomáš Seidan created a bust of the composer for the garden.

Mozart in Prague

Wolfgang Amadeus Mozart (1756–1791) first visited Prague in 1787, after the resounding success there of his opera *The Marriage of Figaro*, and this was followed by further visits to the Golden City. Mozart dedicated the concert scene *Bella mia fiamma, addio* (KV 528), and other pieces, to the lady of the house, Josefa Dušková. His famous opera *Don Giovanni* was premiered in the ▶Estates Theatre on 29 October 1787.

Four years later, commissioned by impresario Guardasoni, Mozart composed the opera *La clemenza di Tito* for the Czech Estates on the occasion of the coronation of Leopold II as King of Bohemia. On his last visit to Prague, shortly before his death in 1791, Mozart attended the premiere.

Mozart Museum
Opening hours:
April–Oct
daily 9am–6pm
Nov–March
until 5pm

The Mozart exhibits in Villa Bertramka include original scores, the rooms where the composer slept and worked, correspondence, for instance with G. Jacquin, historic posters – and 13 Mozartian hairs! Classical concerts also take place here. Every year in September extravagant fashion and stylish accessories are presented at the »Late Summer« fashion show held at the villa. The ▶Smetana, Dvořák (▶Villa Amerika) and Mozart Museums form an independent music department of the National Museum.

★ Vyšehrad

E 6/7

Location: Praha 1, Vyšehrad
Bus: 148

Metro: Vyšehrad
Tram: 3, 7, 18, 24

www.praha-
vysehrad.cz

Legend has it that Princess Libuše lived at Vyšehrad rock (Vyšehrad = stronghold). The earliest Přemyslid rulers are also said to have resided here (▶City history). In Adalbert Stifter's late work *Witiko*, a historical novel set in the early period of Bohemian history, Vyšehrad is one scene of the action. Duke Soběslav lies on his deathbed and young Witiko is in Prague to gather information at his behest, the great having gathered in Vyšehrad to determine the succession:
»There on a rock beside the Vltava, before her waters reach Prague, stood the fortress Vyšehrad. It was built while the original forest still covered all these hills beside the Vltava, long before the hero Zaboy lived, or the singer Lumir. And then came Krok, and had his golden seat on the sacred hill. Thereafter it was Libuše, his favourite child amongst all the sisters, and she married the ploughman Přemysil,

SS Peter and Paul high up on Vyšehrad hill: the royal residence was once here, rather than in Hradčany.

and she had the first wooden stake cut for the castle of Prague. And from her came numerous progeny, and they ruled over the peoples. One of them received Christian baptism, because Christ was born and brought holy faith into the world. He was called Duke Bořivoj and his grandson was St Wenceslas, and his wife St Ludmila.«

Vyšehrad was probably founded in the 10th century as second **History** Prague stronghold. There is no historical evidence of a fortified site until the time of **King Vratislav** (1061–1092), who moved his residence here from ▶ Prague Castle. At that time Prague Castle was a bishop's see. Vratislav had a stone fortress and several churches built on the rock above the Vltava (SS Peter and Paul, St Lawrence), and founded the collegiate chapter, which for a long time was an important centre of learning. It was here that the **Codex Vyšehradiensis** was written, which is now preserved in the manuscript department of the ▶ Klementinum. The only surviving building from this era is the round chapel of St Martin. Soběslav I continued building, but after his death (1140) Vyšehrad rapidly became less important.

The Bohemian rulers moved their permanent residence back to Prague Castle. Under **Charles IV**, who had extensive renovation work done, a new flowering began. Between 1348 and 1350 a Gothic ring of fortifications, joined to the city walls, was built around the complex.

Vyšehrad Map

1 St Martin's Rotunda
2 Chapter church of SS Peter and Paul
3 Memorial cemetery
4 Slavín
5 St Lawrence Chapel
6 Vyšehrad grounds
7 St Wenceslas
8 Chotek gate
9 Chapel of Our Lady
10 Leopold gate
11 Tabor gate

Traditionally the Bohemian kings' **coronation procession** started from Vyšehrad, and led then via the ▶ Powder Gateacross ▶ Old Town Square and ▶Charles Bridge up to St Vitus Cathedral at ▶Prague Castle.

During the Hussite Wars, in the year 1420, almost all of Vyšehrad's buildings were destroyed. During the second half of the 15th century, craftsmen founded the »Free Town on Mount Vyšehrad«. In the late 17th century Vyšehrad was extended in its present form as Baroque fortress, and the citizens' houses were demolished. The fortress was closed as such in 1866, Vyšehrad became one of Prague's districts and the cemetery was extended; in 1911 Vyšehrad was razed to the ground. Only the fortress walls remained.

Especially during the Romantic era in the 19th century, Vyšehrad with all its legends was a favourite theme for fine artists, composers and writers. Well-known works include Smetana's opera *Libuše*, Mendelssohn's *Libussa's Prophecy* and Franz Grillparzer's play *Libussa*.

The best way to get to Vyšehrad is via Vratislavova, entering the complex from the north through the Cihelná brána gateway (1848); from there, the path to the right leads to a copy of the equestrian statue of St Wenceslas by Johann Georg Bendel (1678).

St Martin's Rotunda From the gateway, »V pevnosti« leads to the left, past the Chapel of Our Lady, to the oldest architectural monument in Prague, the Romanesque round chapel of St Martin (Rotunda svatého Martina), which dates back to the time of King Vratislav. After Vyšehrad was made into a fortress, the chapel was used as gunpowder store; it was renovated in 1878.

From the chapel, »K rotundě« leads to the chapter deanery, behind which are the foundations of the Romanesque basilica of St Lawrence.

Chapter church The towers of the chapter church of SS Peter and Paul (Kostel svatého Petra a Pavla), added only in 1902 from designs by Josef Mocker and F. Mikš, are today the emblem of Vyšehrad. The church itself dates from the second half of the 11th century. In the reign of Charles IV it was altered to become a basilica with nave and two aisles, and in the 16th century it was modified again in Renaissance style.At the beginning of the 18th century **František Maximilian Kaňka** and **C. Canevale** oversaw the conversion to Baroque, and the church was given its neo-Gothic style in the years 1885–1887. Notable items in the interior are an 11th-century Romanesque stone coffin (»St Longinus' tomb«), and a panel painting with the so-called »Rain Madonna«, believed to protect against drought, of 1355; this Marian picture is thought to have come from Emperor Rudolf II's collection. The main altar by Josef Mocker is adorned by figures of four saints (SS Peter and Paul, SS Cyril and Methodius), created by F. Hrubeš at the end of the 19th century. The wall frescoes with stylized plant décor were designed by U. Urbanová and František Urban, 1902–1903

Baedeker TIP

Go back in time ...

to the era of the Přemyslid rulers – quite feasible, if you stroll along the fortifications and open your eyes to the Vltava valley. Beneath the ramparts masonry can be seen, sometimes designated »Libuše's bath« – the remains of the medieval palace on this spot. According to legend, Libuše dallied here with her lovers, and pushed them through a crack in the rock into the Vltava if they failed to please.

Opening hours:
Oct–April
9.30am–6pm
Nov–March
daily until 5pm

The church of SS Peter and Paul is bordered on the north by the memorial cemetery (Vyšehradský hřbitov). When the fortress as such was given up in 1866, the medieval churchyard was extended to become a national memorial for representatives of art and culture. Composers Bedřich Smetana and Antonín Dvořák, writers Božena Němcová, Karel Čapek and Jan Neruda, and painter Mikoláš Aleš are among those buried in the cemetery and cemetery arcades. The »Slavín« monument, a work by **Antonín Wiehl** and **Josef Maudr**, is the resting-place of sculptors Josef Václav Myslbek, Bohumil Kafka and Ladislav Šaloun, painter Alfons Mucha and violinist Jan Kubelík, among others.

★★
Memorial cemetery

South of the chapter church a Baroque gate opens onto the grounds of Vyšehrad. Four groups of statues (1881–1897) by **Josef Václav Myslbek** present figures from Czech legend: Přemysl and Libuše, Lumír and Song, Slavoj and Záboj, Ctirad and Šárka. Made to be viewed from below, the sculptures originally stood on the pylons of Palacky Bridge. Some damage was done to them in 1945, and after reconstruction and restoration they were placed in this new location, where, however, much of their original impact is lost.

Vyšehrad grounds

At the southeast end of Vyšehrad is the **Leopold gate** (Leopoldova brána), and beyond it the early-Baroque projecting **Tábor gate** (Táborská brána), part of the earlier fortifications. Between them lies the remains of the Peak Gate (Špička), which now houses an information office, shop and tourist facilities.

Beneath Vyšehrad, at number 30 Neklanova, is one of the most famous examples of Cubist architecture. The **apartment house** by **Josef Chochol**, one of Prague's best-known Cubist architects, was built in the years 1911–1913.

The house stands in an angle where two streets converge and sticks out like a wedge. The façade flows in vertical and horizontal lines, especially through the jagged accentuations which project from the flat surface. The movement reaches its peak at the top, emphasized by the cornice that juts out boldly (see Baedeker Special p.140).

★ Wallenstein Palace (Valdštejnský palác)

D 4

Location: Praha 1, Malá Strana, Valdš-   **Metro:** Malostranská
tejnskě náměstí   **Tram:** 12, 22, 23

Laid out on a large scale, the most magnificent of Prague's aristocratic residences was built in the years 1624–1630 for Albrecht of Wallenstein (one and the same as depicted in Schiller's trilogy), one of the wealthiest noblemen of the time, imperial generalissimo and later Duke of Friedland (murdered in 1634). Wallenstein had 25 houses, three gardens and a city gate demolished in order to build the city's first Baroque palace opposite ►Prague Castle. The designs were by **Andrea Spezza** and **Giovanni Pieroni, while** supervision of the building project was entrusted to **Giovanni Battista Marini**. A ceiling fresco in the central Knights' Hall shows Albrecht of Wallenstein as the god Mars on his triumphal chariot (B. Bianco, 1630). In the other rooms are an equestrian portrait of Wallenstein (F. Leux, 1631) and 19th-century paintings with motifs from antiquity by Peter Maixner. The palace chapel contains Prague's earliest Baroque altar, created by E. Heidelberger. Today, Wallenstein Palace is the seat of the Czech senate; it is open to visitors only at weekends (Sat, Sun 10am–4pm). In his *Wallenstein*, Golo Mann describes the scale and splendour of the Wallenstein residence:

»The front is Bohemian Italian, modelled on Palazzo Farnese ... In order to grasp the true dimensions of Wallenstein Palace it is necessary to inspect the inner courtyards and park. From the square, only the façade is visible ... The rest, the entirety, was no ordinary lordly seat. It was an autarchy, a mini-empire amidst the bustle of the city, enclosed by outbuildings and a fortress-like park wall. Once Wallen-

! *Baedeker* TIP

Heavenly violins

The belligerent general loved music, too. The 17th-century Sala terrene, modelled on buildings in Florence, protects the chamber orchestra and functions as an amplifier. In the evenings Prague Castle is floodlit, adding to the magical setting. The garden has seating. Start: 7pm. Tickets: tel. 257 010 401.

Wallenstein Palace, built in Italian Baroque style

stein's coach had entered the yard to the left of the front, he had everything he required; a chapel for his prayers; a riding-course at the lower end of the park; a bathing grotto with crystals, shells and stalactites, of paramount importance; and paths between statues and fountains.«

Wallenstein Garden (Valdštejnská zahrada)

The Wallenstein Garden was designed in Italian Baroque style with grottoes, a pool and an aviary. Access is from Letenská. The paths and fountain are embellished by copies of bronze statues by the Flemish sculptor Adriaen de Vries, who was working in Prague at the time. The originals were carried off by the Swedes during the Thirty Years' War; they are at Drottningholm Castle near Stockholm. From the garden there is a good view of ►Prague Castle with St Vitus Cathedral. On the west side is the Sala terrena designed by Giovanni Pieroni and adorned with frescoes by Baccio del Bianco. In summer, theatrical performances and concerts take place here.

Opening hours:
April–Oct
daily 10am–6pm

Valdštejnská

On Valdštejnská running north from Wallenstein Palace Baroque Prague is still fully in evidence. On the left-hand side rises **Pálffy Palace** (no. 14), now the conservatoire; two doors before that (no. 12) is the entrance to the ►Palace Gardens beneath Prague Castle.

A few steps away (no. 10) is **Kolovrat Palace** (18th century, now part of the ministry of culture); next to it is Fürstenberg Palace, built between 1743 and 1747 (no. 8; now the Polish embassy). Diagonally opposite, on the right-hand side of Valdštejnská, is the former **Wallenstein riding-school** (Jízdárna Valdštejnského palác), in which the National Gallery puts on temporary exhibitions.

✶ Wenceslas Square (Václavské náměstí)

E/F 4/5

Location: Praha 1, Nové Město, Václavské náměstí

Metro: Můstek, Muzeum
Tram: 3, 9, 14, 24

Centre of modern Prague

When Nové Město was founded, Charles IV had the square developed as a horse market; in 1848 it was given its present name. However the 750m/820yd-long and 60m/66yd-wide Wenceslas Square is more like a boulevard.

It is the vibrant centre of modern Prague, surrounded by hotels rich in tradition such as the Art Nouveau »Evropa«, by stores and shopping passages, restaurants and cafés, cinemas and cabaret venues. With the streets ►Na příkopé, Na Můstku, 28. října and Národní it forms the »Golden Cross«, within which the city's business and social life have developed most vigorously.

Many key events in recent political history have taken place on Wenceslas Square (1969, self-immolation of Jan Palachand Jan Zajíc; 1988 and especially 1989, demonstrations against the regime; ►city history).

! *Baedeker* TIP

Hotel Evropa

There are a number of hotels and restaurants in Prague that can look back on long and rich traditions, and Hotel Evropa is certainly one of them: pay a visit to the Art Nouveau café for a whiff of nostalgia. It's difficult to resist the stylish atmosphere, so the less-than-impeccable service doesn't seem to matter (Václavské náměstí 29, tel. 224 215 387, www.evropahotel.cz).

✶ Wenceslas Monument (Pomník svatého Václava)

At the southeast end of Wenceslas Square, in front of the ►National Museum, stands the Wenceslas Monument created in the years 1912 and 1913 by **Josef Václav Myslbek**. Wenceslas, who ruled from 921 as Duke of Bohemia, was murdered in 935 by his brother Boleslav I. Reports of miracles caused him to become patron saint of Bohemia – in his honour, 28 September is celebrated as a national holiday in the Czech Republic. Although Wenceslas' murder probably resulted from the power struggle between Saxons and Bavarians in Bohemia, he is nonetheless revered as a martyr. His name was so popular among the Czechs that the writer Johann Fischart (1546–1590) commented after one of his journeys: »Bohemians are called Wenceslas, Poles are called Stanislav.«

The equestrian statue of the duke is surrounded by the figures of four further patron saints of the country. On the right in the front is St Ludmila (»loved by the people«), grandmother of St Wenceslas and wife of the first duke of Bohemia to receive Christian baptism. When she was murdered by pagan opponents she became Bohemia's first female martyr.

On the left in the front is St Procopius, at the back are St Agnes (Anežka) and St Adalbert (Vojtěch) of Prague.

St Wenceslas on the square that bears his name – in the background, the National Museum

There is another Wenceslas statue on ►Knights of the Cross Square (Vintner Column with sculpture of St Wenceslas), yet another in ►Vyšehrad (equestrian statue).

Former parliament Next to the National Museum is the former seat of the Czechoslovak parliament, which needed temporary quarters after 1945. The design (1966) by Karel Prager imposed a two-storey steel structure on the former stock exchange building – a combination of different architectural styles which does not look particularly successful today. Since 1995 the premises have been occupied by Radio Liberty/Radio Free Europe. There are subterranean links to the Prague **State Opera** (Státní opera), which was built by Viennese architects Ferdinand Fellner and Hermann Helmer in neo-Rococo style. In 1888 the German Theatre Society building opened with Wagner's *Meistersinger*.

Mucha Museum

Opening hours:
daily 10am–6pm
www.mucha.cz

In **Kaunický Palace** at number 7 Panská, a street running parallel to Wenceslas Square, is the small, yet notable Mucha Museum. The name of this Art Nouveau artist (1880–1939) is inseparably linked with the city, even though Alfons Mucha was born in southern Moravia and came to Prague only after living and working in Vienna, Munich, Paris and America.

The exhibition begins with »Panneaux Décoratifs«, with which Mucha made his name. These are posters made in Paris at the turn of the century, affordable because they were produced in large quantities, and they include Mucha's designs for Sarah Bernhardt which made him a high-profile representative of Parisian Art Nouveau. The exhibition also displays Mucha's handbook for decorative artists, in which he recorded his designs, first *Documents Décoratifs*, and then, three years later, *Figures Décoratives* (use of the human body as decorative element). After his return to Bohemia Mucha worked on a Slav epic; the paintings for this project were created in tandem with further illustrations and designs in his unmistakeable style. Alongside the few oil paintings the exhibits include photos of models, sketches, notes and pastel drawings.

White Mountain (with Star Castle, Bílá Hora)

Location: Praha 6, Břevnov, Bílá Hora   **Bus:** 108, 167, 174, 179, 180, 191, 214
Tram: 1, 2, 8, 18, 22

It was on the bare limestone heights (318m/1043ft above sea level) that rise up on the western edge of the city and are now partially built over that the Battle of the White Mountain took place on 8 November 1620. The battle had decisive consequences for the destiny of the Bohemian lands under the Habsburgs. Within a single hour the army of the Bohemian Protestant Estates, an army of mercenaries led by Count Matthias von Thun, was defeated by the Catholic League led by Maximilian of Bavaria. The Palatine Elector Friedrich V – the »Winter King« 1619–1620 – had recently been elected king of Bohemia by the Estates according to a new constitution (which made Bohemia into an elective monarchy), and now had to flee; this meant that the country lost its independence, until 1918. A chapel was later erected on the battle site, which K. Luna converted in the 18th century into a Church of our Lady Victorious. A little way to the north, a monument recalls the Battle of the White Mountain.

Star Summer Palace (Letohrádek Hvězda)

In the former Star Zoo (Obora Hvězda) on the slopes of the hill stands Star Summer Palace. King Ferdinand I had established a hunting-park in Malejov forest in 1530, and later royal festivities and shooting matches took place here as well. In 1797 the game enclosure was turned into an informal park with wide promenades; it took its name from the hunting-lodge that had been erected here, known as Star Lodge.

The castle lies north of the main avenue. The unusual, externally modest Renaissance building with hexagonal ground plan was commissioned by Archduke Ferdinand of Tyrol as a hunting-lodge and constructed by Italian master builders (1555–1558); it served as residence for his wife-to-be, Philippine Welser from Augsburg, who came from a patrician family in that city. Later the castle was used to store gunpowder. Inside are delightful Italian stucco decorations by Giovanni Campione and Andrea Avostali from the years 1556–1563, which show 334 scenes from Greek mythology (Aeneas and Anchises, Bacchantes, sea divinities) and Roman history (Mucius Scaevola, Horatius Cocles, Marcus Curtius). The glazed Renaissance tiles in the former dining-room on the second floor are also worth seeing.

Since the restoration of the castle, it has housed an exhibition of Czech history recalling the Battle of the White Mountain (lower floor, ground floor). There are also displays curated by the Museum of Czech Literature, which change every year. Sometimes concerts and lectures on literature are arranged.

Opening hours:
April–Oct Tue–Sun
10am–5pm
May–Sept Tue–Sun
daily 10am–6pm

Museum of Czech Literature

Žižkov (city district)

G – J 4 – 5

The district of Žižkov, east of the city centre, has developed from workers' quarters to a location popular with Prague's middle classes. In the Czech Republic, as elsewhere, life is shifting more and more from the metropolitan centre to the outskirts – for instance, to Žižkov. Prices for food and accommodation in the centre are no longer affordable for Czechs. Žižkov is well known for its bars, where the atmosphere is better than in the centre. In the meantime tourists have also discovered this district at the foot of Vítkov(St Vitus) Hill, especially the area between Husitská and Seifertova. It was on Vítkov Hill that the Hussites under Jan Žižka vanquished the numerically superior troops under King Sigismund in 1420.

A bronze monument has been erected on Vítkov Hill in memory of the Hussite leader. Alongside it is **Prague's TV tower**, visible from afar, with the Old Jewish Cemetery at its foot, just as well worth seeing as the New Jewish Cemetery. Prague writer Franz Kafka (▶ Famous People) is buried here.

Original Prague

The Vítkov National Monument (Národní památník na hoře Vítkově) is best approached via the streets Wilsonova, Husitská třída and U Památníku (At the monument), and finally by climbing the steps. The memorial was erected in the years 1929–1932, but not

Vítkov monument

completed until after 1948. The monumental building is impressive even at a distance. The tall granite-faced stone marks the tomb of the Unknown Soldier. In addition, until 1990 this served as memorial burial-place for top Communist Party officials. After the Velvet Revolution the mausoleum was closed. A new use has yet to be found.

On the terrace is the **equestrian statue** of the victorious Hussite general Jan Žižka of Trocnov. The monumental sculpture is the largest equestrian bronze in the world, 9m/30ft high, with a weight of 16.5 tons. It was created in 1930 by Bohumil Kafka, but not cast until 1950.

TV tower   Today the 216m/709ft-high TV tower is a distinctive feature of Prague's skyline. Situated about 800m/875yd south of Vítkov Hill, it was built in the years 1987–1990, and soars up in bizarre architectural forms. At a height of 95m/312ft is a panorama restaurant (daily 11am–11pm, www.tower.cz). Since 2000 stylized sculptures of crawling children have adorned the base of the tower – the work of Czech sculptor David Černý.

Church of the Sacred Heart   The Church of the Sacred Heart was built between 1929 and 1932 on Jiřího z Poděbrad (George of Poděbrady) Square, near the Metro station of the same name. It is considered the major work of **Josip Plečniks**(1872–1957), who gave ▶ Prague Castle its new look at the request of the first state president, Tomáš G. Masaryk. For the sacral building of the Church of the Sacred Heart, Plečnik sought inspiration in eclectic manner from simple, early Christian architecture combined with modern forms of expression. The main space of the hall church, 13m/43ft high, appears outside as a cube, with the lower two-thirds clinkered and the top third, in which the windows are set, rendered in white. The most striking feature is the 42m/138ft stelene tower, which is dominated by a clock in the window embrasure (diameter 7.6m/25ft). Inside, a concrete ramp leads to the top of the »clock-tower« The view through the glass clockface is of the southern castle gardens, also redesigned by Plečnik.

On Fibichova, directly at the foot of the TV tower, is the Jewish Cemetery, recently opened to the public. It was established in 1680 because of an outbreak of the plague, and was used again during an epidemic in the second half of the 18th century. It was taken into full use from 1787, when the Josefov cemetery had become too small; but only until 1890, at which point another new cemetery was established.

Jewish Cemetery

🕐

Opening hours:
Tue and Thu
9am–1pm

INDEX

a

Aachen, Hans of **229, 234**
airport **68**
Alchemists' Lane **234, 235**
Aleš, Mikoláš **44, 198**
Alliprandi, Giovanni Battista **42, 127, 177, 240**
Anežský klášter **140**
antiques **98**
Archbishop's Palace **149**
Arcibiskupský palác **149**
Arras, Matthias of **36, 165, 220**
arrival **66**
Asam, Cosmas Damian **127**
Asam, Peter, the Elder. **210**
Ass at the Cradle **202**
Astronomical Clock **205**

b

Bresnov Monastery **126**
Ball-Game Court **125**
Balšanek, Antonín **44, 236**
Bartoněk, Vojtěch **213**
Basilica of St George **232**
Bassi, Carlo **192**
Battle of the White Mountain **28, 262**
Battle of Vitkov Mountain **27**
Bayer, Paul Ignaz **127, 135**
Bazilika svatého Jiří **232**
Bechterel, Caspar **224**
before the journey **66**
Belvedere **124**
Bendl, Johann Georg **40, 147, 170, 171, 220**
Beneš, Edvard **31**
Bertramka **252**
Bethlehem Chapel **125**
Betlémská kaple **125**
Black Horse, the **193**
Bludiště **213**
Blue Pike **164**
Blue Star, the **193**
boat trips **106**
Bossi, Campione de **175**
Botanical Garden **145**
Botanická zahrada **145**
Brahe, Tycho **28, 49, 209**
Brandl, Peter Johann **199, 234**

Braun, Anton **127, 210**
Braun, Matthias **139**
Braun, Matthias Bernhard **43, 125, 131, 147, 169, 184, 234, 238**
Bretfeld Palace **202**
Brokoff, Ferdinand Maximilian **43, 127, 131, 138, 148, 177, 199, 232, 234, 249**
Brokoff, Ferdinand Maximilian **149**
Brokoff, Johann **131, 145, 150**
Brokoff, Johann Josef and Ferdinand Maximilian **248**
Brussels Expo 1958 **171**
Bílek, František **161**
Buquoyský Palace **130, 147**
Bývalý kostel svaté Kateřiny **252**

c

cabaret **104**
cafés **83**
camping **58**
Canevale, Marc Antonio **199**
Capuchin monastery **182**
Caratti, Francesco **148, 168, 170, 182**
Caretto-Millesimo Palace **130**
Carlone, Carlo **184**
Castle Gallery **217**
Celetná **127**
Ceremonial hall **160**
Ceremonial House of the City of Prague **185**
Chapel of St Wenceslas **225**
Chapel of the Holy Cross (Prague Castle) **218**
Charles Bridge **131**
Charles IV **49**
Charles IV monument **171**
Charles Square **134**
Charles University **137**
Charter 77 **32**
Chateau Michna **252**
Chochol, Josef **44, 258**
Chotek Park **125**
Chotkovy sady **125**
Chrám svatého Mikuláše **174**
Chrám svatého Víta **220**
Church of Our Lady Before Týn **208**

Church of Our Lady Below the Chain **147**
Church of Our Lady of the Snows **162**
Church of Our Lady Victorious **138**
Church of Our Lady, Emmaus Monastery **145**
Church of St Francis Seraphinus **170**
Church of St Giles **126**
Church of St Ignatius **135**
Church of St James **249**
Church of St Lawrence **212**
Church of St Margaret, Břevnov Monastery **127**
Church of St Nicholas, Staré Město **210**
Church of St Stephen **238**
Church of the Assumption of Our Lady (Strahov monastery) **244**
Church of the Assumption of the Virgin Mary and Charlemagne **139**
Church of the Holy Cross **192**
Church of the Holy Saviour **169**
Church of the Holy Saviour (Josefov) **162**
Church of the Knights of the Cross **170**
Church of the Sacred Heart **264**
City Gallery Prague **140**
City of Prague Gallery **248**
Clam-Gallas Palace **184**
Clam-Gallasův palác **184**
classical music **101**
Clubs **70**
Cock House **205**
Codex Vyšehradiensis **35, 246**
concerts **101**
Convent of St Agnes **140**
Convent of St George **234**
Counter-Reformation **28**
Cranach, Lucas the Elder **241**
currency **93**
customs regulations **68**
Czech Technical University **135**
Czechoslovakian Socialist Republic (ČSSR) **31**
Černín Palace **182**
Černý, David **171**

Čzernín, Humprecht Count
of **40**
Čzernínský palác **182**

Daddi, Bernardo **241**
daily newspapers **93**
Dancing House **45, 143**
della Robbia, Andrea **241**
della Torre, Francesco **217**
Dientzenhofer Baroque **41**
Dientzenhofer Summer
Palace **240**
Dientzenhofer, Christoph **41,
49, 126127, 181**
Dientzenhofer, Kilian Ignaz **41,
49, 126, 127, 136, 140,
145, 174, 175, 209, 210,
252**
diplomatic representation **86**
Dubček, Alexander **31, 33**
Dvořák Museum **252**
Dvořák, Antonín **50**
Dvořák, Karel **131**
Dům umělců **237**
Dürer, Albrecht **240**

economy **19**
electricity **69**
Emauzy **144**
embassies **86**
emergency services **69**
Emmaus Monastery **144**
Engelmüller, Ferdinand **178**
Equestrian statue of Jan **264**
Estates Theatre **145**
European art collection **240**
European Union **18**
Events **72**
exchange regulations **93**
execution in Old Town
Square **29**
exhibition grounds **246**
Èerny, David **45**

Fanta, Josef **247**
Faust **134**
Faust House **134**
Ferdinand I **124, 168**

Ferdinand II **126**
Festivals **72**
first Prague defenestration **27,
135, 163**
Fischer von Erlach, Johann
Bernhard **41, 184, 249**
Fischer von Erlach, Joseph
Emanuel **224**
Fischer, Georg **43, 186**
Flegel, Georg **241**
food and drink **74**
Franciscan garden **163**
Františkánská zahrada **163**
Franz Kafka Museum **96**
Fuchs, Josef **44, 250**
funicular **212**
Führich, Joseph von **44**

Galerie D in Dientzenhofer
Pavillon **94**
Galerie hlavního města
Prahy **140**
Gali, Agostino **151**
galleries **94**
Garden on the
Ramparts **235**
Gehry, Frank O. **45, 143**
Geiger, Ferdinand **172**
German House **192**
Ginger & Fred **143**
Gočár, Josef **44**
Golden Cross **187, 260**
Golden Gate **221**
Golden Lane **234**
Golden Serpent **164**
Golden Unicorn **207**
Golden Well **164**
Goltz-Kínský Palace **209**
Gossaert, Jan **242**
Grafická sbírka Národní
galerie **209**
Grand Priory Palace **146**
Grand Priory Square **146**
Granovský Palace **249**
Grund, Norbert **43, 234**
Gutfreund, Otto **44**

Hanavský Pavilion **171**
Havel, Václav **51**
Hašek, Jaroslav **50**

health insurance **69**
Heintsch, Johann Georg **135,
182**
Hellich, Josef **209**
help for disabled travellers **108**
Hergertova Cihelna **94**
Herz, Juda Goldschmied de **153**
Hibernian House **186**
Hiernle, Karl Josef **127**
High Synagogue **162**
history **22**
House at the Black
Madonna **130**
House Koruna **192**
House of Artists **237**
House of the Blue Star **207**
House of the Golden
Chalice **199**
House of the Golden
Horseshoe **202**
House of the Golden Lion **202**
House of the Golden Ring **140**
House of the Two Suns **199**
Hradčanské náměstí **148**
Hradčany Square **148**
Hradčany Town Hall **178**
Hrad Karlštejn **165**
Hradní galerie **217**
Hrzán Palace **127, 178**
Hunger Wall **214**
Hus, Jan **26, 125**
Hussite Wars **27**
Hynais, Vojtěch **198**

identity cards **68**
information **85**
International style **37**
internet **87**
internet cafés **87**
Italian Chapel **168**

Jagiello, Vladislav **246**
Jan Hus **202**
Jan Hus preacher's house **126**
Janák, Pavel **44**
Jaroš, Tomáš **124**
Jazz **102**
Jäckel, Matthias Wenceslas **170**
Jäckel, Matthias Wenzel **42,
181**

Jesenská, Milena **52**
Jewish Cemetery, Žižkov **265**
Jewish Museum **152**
Jewish Town Hall **161**
Jewish town, former **151**
John Nepomuk **131**
Jordaens, Jacob **242**
Josefov **151**
Judith Bridge **134**
Jungmann Square **162**
Jungmann, Josef **162**
Jungmannovo náměstí **162**
Jungmannův pomník **162**
Jízdárna Valdštejnského
    palác **260**

Kříž **205**
Kaňka, František
    Maximilian **42, 137, 139,
    147, 168, 170, 182, 233,
    252, 257**
Kafka, Bohumil **44, 264**
Kafka, Franz **53**
Kaiserstein Palace **172**
Kampa **163**
Kampa Museum **94**
Kaple svatého Kříže,
    (Hradčany) **218**
Kapucínský klášter **182**
Karel Lidický **204**
Karlova **164**
Karlštejn Castle **165**
Karlův most **131**
Karolinum **137**
Kaunický Palace **262**
Kepler, Johannes **28**
Kern, Anton **234**
Kinský Garden **212**
Kinský Square **214**
Klaus Synagogue **160**
Klausenburg, Georg and Martin
    of **219**
Klausenburg, Martin and
    Georg **36**
Klausenburg, Martin and
    George of **234**
Klausova synagóga **160**
Klášter na Slovanech **144**
Klementinum **167**
Klouček, Celda **192**
Knights of the
    Cross Square **169**

Kohl, Hieronymus **40, 175,
    217**
Kohl, Johann Friedrich **174**
Kolovrat Garden **212**
Kolovrat Palace **260**
Kostel Nanebevzetí Panny
    Marie (Strahovský
    klášter) **244**
Kostel Nanebevzetí Panny
    Marie a Karla Velikého **139**
Kostel Panny Marie pod
    Řőetězem **147**
Kostel Panny Marie před
    Týnem **208**
Kostel Panny Marie Sněžné **162**
Kostel Panny Marie Vít **138**
Kostel sv Františka
    Serafínského **170**
Kostel svaté Markéty (Břevnov
    Monastery) **127**
Kostel svaté Voršily **199**
Kostel svatého Havla **138**
Kostel svatého Ignáce **135**
Kostel svatého Jakuba **249**
Kostel svatého Jana
    Nepomuckého na Skalce **145**
Kostel svatého Jiljí **126**
Kostel svatého Klimenta **169**
Kostel svatého Kříže **192**
Kostel svatého Mikuláše **210**
Kostel svatého Petra a
    Pavla **256**
Kostel svatého Salvátora **169**
Kostel svatého Salvátora
    (Josefov) **162**
Kostel svatého Tomáše **175**
Kostel svatého Václava na
    Zderaze **136**
Kostel svatého Vavřince **212**
Kostel svatého Štěpána **238**
Ková **170**
Kovář, Karel **145**
Košice programme **31**
Kracker, Johann Lukas **175**
Královský letohrádek **124**
Královský palác **226**
Kramolín, Josef **244**
Křížovnické náměstí **169**
Křížíkova fountain **247**

language **87**
Lapidarium **247**

Large Pálffy Garden **211**
Laterna Magica **198**
Lauermann, Jan **244**
Ledeburg Garden **211**
Ledeburská zahrada **211**
Lesser Quarter Square **172**
Letenské sady **171**
Letná Gardens **171**
Letná heights **171**
Letohrádek Amerika **252**
Letohrádek Hvězda **262**
Libuše **23, 254**
Lichtenstein Palace **173**
Liebscher, Adolf **198**
Liebscher, Karl and Adolf **213**
Lipany Pavilion **247**
Liika, Johann Christoph **171**
literature **91**
Lobkovický palác **177**
Lobkowicz Palace **177**
Loos, Adolf **44**
Lorenzetti, Pietro **241**
Loreta **179**
Loreta Square **179**
Loretánská ulička **178**
Loretánské náměstí **179**
Loretogasse **179**
Lurago, Anselmo **174, 182,
    192, 210, 218**
Lurago, Carl **170**
Lurago, Carlo **135, 147**

Maisel Synagogue **152**
Maixner, Peter **236**
Malá Strana Bridge Towers **134**
Malá Strana Town Hall **173**
Malostranská radnice **173**
Malostranské náměstí **172**
Mánes Exhibition Hall **183**
Mánes Gallery **183**
Mánes, Josef **44, 236**
Marell, Jakob **241**
Mariánské náměstí **183**
Mariánské Square **183**
Martinelli, Domenico **240**
Martinický Palace **150**
Masaryk, Tomáš Garrigue **30**
Master Matthias Rejsek of
    Prostějov **209**
Master of Hohenfurth **141**
Master of the Litoměřice
    altar **38, 143, 226**

Master of the Rajhrad
   Altarpiece **142**
Master of Třebo **142**
Master Oswald **226**
Master Theoderic **167**
Master Theoderich **141**
Mathey, Jean Baptiste **40, 149,
   150, 170, 243, 248**
Matthias Gate **216**
Matyášova brána **216**
Maulbertsch, Franz Anton **245**
Max, Emanuel **208**
Max, Emanuel and Josef **131**
Mayer, Johann Ulrich **172**
media **93**
medical assistance **85**
Memorial cemetery **257**
Menhart House **130**
metro **107**
metronome **171**
Michna Palace **250**
Michnův letohrádek **252**
Michnův palác **250**
Military History Museum **151**
Military Museum **96**
Milunič, Vlado **45**
Ministry of Foreign Affairs **182**
Minute House **206**
Mirror Maze **213**
Mistr Rajhradského oltáře **142**
Mistr Vyšebrodského oltáře **141**
Mladota Palace **135**
Mocker, Josef **256**
Modena, Tomaso da **166**
Momper, Joos de **242**
Monastery of the Slavs **144**
money **93**
Morzin Palace **199**
Morzinský palác **199**
Mozart Museum **252**
Mozart, Wolfgang
   Amadeus **254**
Mucha Museum **262**
Mucha, Alfons **54, 185, 262**
Munich Agreement **30**
Municipal House **185**
Museum of Czech
   Literature **263**
Museum of
   Decorative Arts **186**
Museum of Physical Education
   and Sport **250**
museums **94**
music **101**

Muzeum hlavního města
   Prahy **236**
Muzeum tělesné výchovy a
   sportu **250**
Myslbek, Josef Václav **44, 136,
   185, 198, 257, 261**
Müller, Ignaz **177**
Müntzer, Thomas **125**
Münzberger, Bedřich **247**

n

Na Kamenci **207**
Na přikopě **187**
Náměstí Kinských **214**
Náměstí sovětských tankistů
   214
Náprstek Museum **95**
Národní divadlo **195**
Národní galerie **141, 209, 234,
   250**
Národní technické muzeum **195**
National Gallery **193, 240,
   250**
National Gallery's graphic art
   collection **209**
National Museum **193**
National Technical
   Museum **195**
National Theatre **195**
Nepomuk, St John of **224**
Neruda, Jan **54**
Nerudova **199**
New Town Hall **135, 184**
newspapers **93**
newspapers in English **93**
Nostický Palace **147**
Nouvel, Jean **45**
Nová radnice **184**
Nová scéna **198**
Novák, Karel **185**
Novoměstská radnice **135**
Novotný, Otakar **183**

o

Obecní dům **185**
Old Jewish Cemetery **154**
Old Provost's Lodging **220**
Old Royal Palace **226**
Old Town Bridge Tower **133**
Old Town Hall **204**
Old Town Square **202**
Old-New School **160**

Old-New Synagogue **160**
On the Moat **187**
Orloj **205**
Orsi de Orsini, Domenico **40**
Orsi de Orsini, Giovanni
   Domenico **245**
Osel u kolébky **202**

p

Pacassi, Nikolaus **216**
Pachtovský Palace **130**
Palác Goltz-Kinských **209**
Palác Jiřiho z
   Poděbrady **214**
Palác maltézského
   velkopřevora **146**
Palace Gardens beneath
   Prague Castle **211**
Palace of the Czech State
   Bank **193**
Palach, Jan **31, 260**
Palácové zahrady **211**
Palais Colloredo-
   Mansfeld **164**
Palais Pötting **164**
Pálffy Palace **259**
Palliardi, Ignaz **213**
Palliardi, Michael Ignaz **136,
   177, 212, 244, 245**
Parler Gothic **36**
Parler House **149**
Parler, Heinrich **226**
Parler, Peter **25, 36, 54, 133,
   178, 208, 220, 225**
Parler, Wenzel and
   Johann **220**
Pedagogical Museum
   Komenského **96**
pets **68**
Petřín **212**
Petřín lookout tower **212**
Pfeiffer, Antonín **192**
pharmacies **85**
phone cards **97**
Pinkas Synagogue **153**
Pinkas, Soběslav **236**
Pinkasova synagóga **153**
plague column **172**
planetarium **247**
Platzer the Elder, Ignaz **210**
Platzer, Franz Ignaz the
   Elder **199, 244**
Platzer, Ignaz Franz **182**

Platzer, Ignaz Franz the
   Elder **175, 216**
Platzer, Ignaz the Elder **43**
Platzer, Ignaz, the Elder **192**
Plečnik, Josip **44, 216, 219,
   264**
Poděbrady Palace **214**
Podebrady, George of **27**
Police Museum **96**
political parties **18**
Polivka, Osvald **44**
Pomník svatého
   Václava **260**
Portheimka **240**
post **97**
Post Museum **96**
Powder Gate **185**
Prachner, Peter **229**
Prachner, Richard **43, 126**
Prachner, Václav **184**
Prague Castle **215**
Prague City Gallery **209**
Prague City Museum **236**
Prague Infant Jesus **138**
Prague Jewellery
   Collection **94**
Prague Spring **31, 102**
Prague trade fairs **247**
Prague »Malerzeche« **36**
Prague's Eiffel Tower **212**
Prague's Venice **163**
Prašná brána **185**
Pražské Benátky **163**
Pražský hrad **215**
Prince Boleslav II **126**
private accommodation **65**
Puppet Museum **96**

Quittainer, Jan Antonín **170**
Quittainer, Johann Anton **43,
   135, 177, 244**

Raab, Ignaz **135, 244**
Rabbi Löw **155, 185**
Rauchmüller, Matthias **131**
Reiner, Wenzel Lorenz **126,
   139, 163, 171, 175, 182,
   229, 233, 240, 249, 252**
Representační dům hlavního
   města Prahy **185**

Republic of Czechoslovakia
   (ČSR) **30**
restaurants **78**
Ried, Benedikt **38, 226, 228,
   229, 232**
Rilke, Rainer Maria **55**
Roder, Pankraz **162**
Rothlev House **137**
Rottmayr, Johann Michael **241**
Rotunda of the Holy Cross **236**
Rotunda svatého Kříže **236**
Rotunda svatého Longina **238**
Rotunda svatého Martina **256**
Royal Garden **217**
Royal Oratory **224**
Rubens, Peter Paul **242**
Rudolf Gallery **217**
Rudolfinum (Dům umělců) **237**

S

St Adalbert **126**
St Catherine **252**
St Clement's Church **169**
St Cyril and Methodius **136**
St Gall **138**
St John Nepomuk **170**
St John of Nepomuk on the
   Rock **145**
St Kajetan **202**
St Longinus Rotunda **238**
St Margaret's Church **126**
St Mark Torsi **246**
St Martin's Rotunda **256**
St Nicholas **174**
St Thomas **175**
St Ursula **199**
St Vitus **263**
St Vitus Cathedral **36, 220**
St Vitus Rotunda **35**
St Wenceslas **24, 261**
St Wenceslas on Na
   Zderaze **136**
Santini-Aichl, Giovanni **42,
   147, 178, 199, 202**
satirical theatre **104**
Savery, Josef Heintz
   Roelandt **234**
Sbírka starého evropského
   umění Národní galerie **240**
Schoenborn Palace **178**
Schulz, Josef **44, 186, 194,
   195, 237**
Schwarzenberg Palace **150**

Schwarzenberský palác **150**
Schönbornský palác **178**
Scotti, Bartolomeo **147**
second Prague
   defenestration **28**
Sequens, František **236**
shopping **98**
Singing Fountain **124**
Sint Jans, Geertgen tot **242**
Sixt House **127**
Sjezdový palác **247**
Skréta, Karel **147**
Slav Island **183**
Slavín **257**
Slovanský dům **192**
Slovanský ostrov **183**
Small Pálffy Garden **211**
Smetana Museum **238**
Smetana, Bedřich **55, 207**
Smíchov **239**
Soft style **37**
Soviet Tank Square **214**
Spanish Synagogue **152**
Spartadiádní Stadion **214**
Spartakiáda Stadium **214**
Spiess, Hans **224**
Spinetti, Bernardo **127, 210,
   252**
spirits **78**
sport **100**
sports hall **247**
Spranger, Bartholomäus **234**
SS Peter and Paul **256**
Stag Moat **236**
Star Summer Palace **262**
Staré proboitství **220**
Staroměstská radnice **204**
Staroměstské náměstí **202**
Staronová synagóga **160**
Starý židovský hřbitov **154**
State Opera **261**
Státní opera **261**
Stavovské divadlo **145**
Stella, Paolo della **39, 124**
Sternberg Palace **240**
Stifter, Adalbert **254**
Stone Bell, The **209**
Strahov Evangeliary **245**
Strahov Monastery **242**
Strahov Picture Gallery **246**
Strahovska obrazárna **246**
Strahovský klášter **242**
Stromovka **246**
Stříbra, Jakoubek ze **126**

Sucharda, Stanislav **185, 192**
Svatého Cyrila
   a Metoděje **136**
Sylva-Taroucca Palace **192**
Šaloun, Ladislav **45, 185, 204**
Škréta , Karel **135**
Škréta, Karel **40, 138, 177,
   208, 234**
Španělská synagóga **152**
Štefánik Observatory **214**
Šternberský palác **240**
Štorchův dům **207**
Štursa, Jan **44**
Šítkovská věž **183**
Švabinský, Max **45, 185, 221**
Švec, Otokar **171**

t

Tančicí dům **143**
Tenniers, David the
   Younger **242**
Teyfl, Andreas **150**
The Black Rose **192**
The Golden Grape **173**
The Mint **130**
The Stone Mermaid **164**
The Three Ostriches **134**
The Vulture **130**
Thirty Years' War **28**
Thun, Marie Josefa von **147**
Thun-Hohenstein Palace **202**
tickets in advance **101**
time **105**
Tintoretto **242**
tipping **78**
tomb of Tycho Brahe **209**
Torre, Francesco della **227**
Toskánský Palace **150**
tour organizers **105**
tours and guides **105**
traffic regulations **106**
travel documents **68**
travelling by car **106**
travelling by taxi **106**
Troja Chateau **248**
Trojský zámek **248**
TV tower **264**
Tyl Theatre **145**
Tyl, Oldřich **44, 250**
Tyrol, Hans of **221**
Tyri, Miroslav **250**
Tyriův dům **250**
Tyrš House **250**

Týn **249**
Týn Church **208**
Týn courtyard **249**
Týn School **208**
Týnská škola **208**
Týnský dvůr **249**

U bílé labutě **202**
U černé Matky boží **130**
U černé růže **192**
U dvou sluncu **199**
U hybernů **186**
U kamenného
   zvonu **209**
U kohouta **205**
U minuty **206**
U modré hvězdy **207**
U Petzoldů **172**
U Schönfloku **130**
U zlaté číše **199**
U zlaté podkovy **202**
U zlatého hroznu **173**
U zlatého Iva **202**
U zlatého jednorožce **207**
U zlatého prstenu **140**
Uměleckoprůmslové
   muzeum **186**
Ungelt **249**

Václavské náměstí **260**
Valditejnská **259**
Valditejnská zahrada **259**
Valdštejnský palác **258**
Valkoun House **199**
Valkounský dům **199**
Veletržní palác **250**
Veletržní Palace **250**
Velvet Revolution **32**
Vernier, Jean B. **192**
vignette **106**
Villa Amerika **252**
Villa Bertramka **252**
Vlado Miluni **143**
Vouet, Simon **242**
Vries, Adriaen de **234, 259**
Vrtba Garden **139**
Vrtba Palace **139**
Vrtbovská zahrada **139**
Vrtbovský palác **139**
Vítkov **263**

Vítkov National
   Monument **263**
Vyiehrad **254**
Vysoká synagóga **162**
Vyšehradský h **257**
Výstaviště **246**

Wallenstein Garden **259**
Wallenstein Palace **258**
Wallenstein
   riding-school **260**
Wallenstein, Albrecht of **40,
   258**
Wax Museum **96**
Weiss, Franz Ignaz **229**
Wenceslas IV **137**
Wenceslas
   Monument **260**
Wenceslas Square **260**
Wenzel Lorenz
   Reiner **234**
Werfel, Franz **55**
when to go **109**
White Mountain **262**
Wiehl, Antonín **236, 246, 257**
Willmann, Michael **40**
Willmann, Michael
   Leopold **234**
wine **75**
Wirch, Johann Joseph **43, 149**
Wohlmut, Bonifaz **39, 125,
   140, 221, 229**
Würth, Johann
   Joseph **224**

youth hostels **65**

Zajíc, Jan **260**
Zlatá brána **221**
Zlatá ulička **234**
Zoological Garden **248**
Zoologická zahrada **248**
Zítek, Josef **44, 195, 237**
Želivský, Jan **27, 135, 163,
   204**
Žižka, Jan **27, 263**
Žižkov **263**
Žofín **183**

PHOTO CREDITS

LIST OF MAPS AND ILLUSTRATIONS

Prague in Europe **20**
Prague Districts **20**
Hotels and Restaurants in Prague **60/61**
Prague Metro **107**
Climate **109**
Tours through Prague **112/113**
Tour 1 **115**
Tour 2 **117**
Tour 3 **119**
Sculptures on Charles Bridge **132**
Josefov **155**
Karlštejn Castle **165**

Lesser Quarter Square **172**
National Museum **194**
National Theatre (3D) **197**
Týb Church **208**
Prague Castle **218/219**
St Vitus Cathedral (3D) **223**
Royal Palace (plan) **227**
Royal Palace (3D) **231**
Vyšehrad **256**
Prague Highlights **back cover inside**

PUBLISHER'S INFORMATION

Illustrations etc: 181 illustrations, 22 maps and diagrams, one large city plan
Text: Dr. Madeleine Reincke;
with contributions by Barbara Branscheid, Jutta Buness, Rainer Eisenschmid, Sabine Herre, Dr. František Kafka, Dr. Otakar Mohyla, Thomas Veszelits and Andrea Wurth
Editing: Baedeker editorial team (Rob Taylor)
Translation: Charity Scott-Stokes
Cartography: Franz Huber, Munich; MAIRDUMONT/Falk Verlag, Ostfildern (city plan)
3D illustrations: jangled nerves, Stuttgart
Design: independent Medien-Design, Munich; Kathrin Schemel

Editor-in-chief: Rainer Eisenschmid, Baedeker Ostfildern

1st edition 2008

Copyright: Karl Baedeker Verlag, Ostfildern
Publication rights: MAIRDUMONT GmbH & Co; Ostfildern

DEAR READER,

We would like to thank you for choosing this Baedeker travel guide. It will be a reliable companion on your travels and will not disappoint you.
This book describes the major sights, of course, but it also recommends the best pubs, as well as hotels in the luxury and budget categories, and includes tips about where to eat or go shopping and much more, helping to make your trip an enjoyable experience. Our authors ensure the quality of this information by making regular journeys to Prague and putting all their know-how into this book.

Nevertheless, experience shows us that it is impossible to rule out errors and changes made after the book goes to press, for which Baedeker accepts no liability. Please send us your criticisms, corrections and suggestions for improvement: we appreciate your contribution. Contact us by post or e-mail, or phone us:

▶ **Verlag Karl Baedeker GmbH**
  Editorial department
  Postfach 3162
  73751 Ostfildern
  Germany
  Tel. 49-711-4502-262, fax -343
  www.baedeker.com
  E-Mail: baedeker@mairdumont.com

Baedeker Travel Guides in English at a glance:

▶ Andalusia
▶ Barcelona
▶ Berlin
▶ Budapest
▶ Dubai · Emirates
▶ Egypt
▶ Ireland
▶ Italy
▶ London
▶ Mexico

▶ New York
▶ Paris
▶ Portugal
▶ Prague
▶ Rome
▶ Thailand
▶ Tuscany
▶ Venice
▶ Vienna